Bridge Endplays for Everyone*

*Yes, Even You!

David Bird

MASTER POINT PRESS • TORONTO

Master Point Press
331 Douglas Ave.
Toronto, Ontario, Canada
M5M 1H2
(416) 781-0351
Website: http://www.masterpointpress.com
Email: info@masterpointpress.com

Library and Archives Canada Cataloguing in Publication

Bird, David, 1946-
    Bridge endplays for everyone : yes, even you! / written by David Bird.

 ISBN 978-1-897106-36-5

1. Contract bridge–Dummy play. I. Title.

GV1282.435.B539 2008   795.41'53   C2007-907140-6

Editor   Ray Lee
Interior format and copy editing Suzanne Hocking
Cover and interior design   Olena S. Sullivan/New Mediatrix

Printed in Canada

1 2 3 4 5 6 7   12 11 10 09 08

Table of contents

Chapter 1   Basics of Elimination Play   5

Chapter 2   Variations of Elimination Play   25

Chapter 3   Loser-on-Loser Elimination Play   47

Chapter 4   Exiting in the Trump Suit   65

Chapter 5   Partial Elimination Play   83

Chapter 6   Advanced Elimination Play   99

Chapter 7   The Throw-In   121

Chapter 8   The Strip Squeeze   143

Chapter 9   Avoidance Play to Set Up an Endplay   163

Chapter 10   Endplays to Gain an Entry   181

Chapter 11   The Trump Coup   201

Chapter 12   Trump Elopement   221

Chapter 13   The Trump Endplay   241

Chapter 14   Endplay Exotica   259

My thanks are due to friend and fellow writer Tim Bourke, who constructed many of the best deals in this book.

Basics of Elimination Play

One of the most frequently occurring endplay techniques is known as 'elimination play'. Suppose you are in a contract of 4♠. You have a side suit where it would assist you if the defenders made the first play:

	◇ Q 8 2	
◇ K 10 3		◇ A 9 7 4
	◇ J 6 5	

As the cards lie, you cannot make a diamond trick if you play the suit yourself. However, if East or West has to lead the suit first, the situation is different. One of them will have to play high in third seat and you will then make the queen or jack on the third round.

The idea of elimination play is to put a defender on lead at a time when he will have to make the first play in your problem suit (diamonds, here) or give you a ruff-and-sluff. Let's put those diamonds into the context of a complete deal:

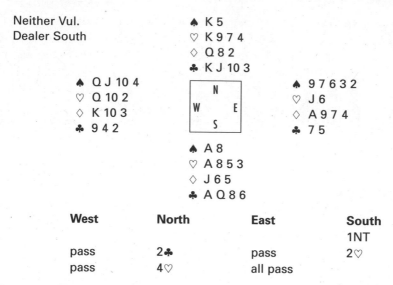

Neither Vul.
Dealer South

♠ K 5
♡ K 9 7 4
♢ Q 8 2
♣ K J 10 3

♠ Q J 10 4
♡ Q 10 2
♢ K 10 3
♣ 9 4 2

♠ 9 7 6 3 2
♡ J 6
♢ A 9 7 4
♣ 7 5

♠ A 8
♡ A 8 5 3
♢ J 6 5
♣ A Q 8 6

West	North	East	South
			1NT
pass	2♣	pass	2♡
pass	4♡	all pass	

West leads the ♠Q against your heart game. How will you play the contract?

The black suits are solid. You have one loser in the trump suit, provided it breaks 3-2 (as you must hope). Diamonds is your 'problem suit' and you would dearly like the defenders to make the first lead there. This wish is about to be granted!

You win the spade lead and play the ace and king of trumps, both defenders following. The idea now is to put a defender on lead with a third round of trumps. It is no good doing this immediately because then the defender would have a safe exit in either black suit. Before exiting with a trump, you must 'eliminate' the two black suits.

The first step is to cash your remaining spade honor. This is the first way to eliminate a suit — by leaving yourself with no cards in either hand, the defenders will not be able to play a spade without giving you a ruff-and-sluff.

Next you cash three rounds of clubs. This is the second way of eliminating a suit. By removing all of the defenders' cards, you again prevent them from exiting safely in the suit. This position remains:

♠ —
♡ 9 7
♢ Q 8 2
♣ J

♠ J 10
♡ Q
♢ K 10 3
♣ —

♠ 9 7
♡ —
♢ A 9 7 4
♣ —

♠ —
♡ 8 5
♢ J 6 5
♣ 8

You play a trump, putting West on lead and at the same time eliminating the trump suit by removing the defenders' last card there. What is the result of all of this hard work? West must either play on your problem suit (diamonds), saving you a trick there, or he must lead a spade and give you a ruff-and-sluff. In the latter case, you will be able to ruff in one hand and throw a diamond from the other, again restricting your diamond losers to two.

Look back at what happened. You eliminated the black suits and threw a defender on lead with the third round of trumps. He then had to give you a trick with his return.

It is an important condition of every elimination play that both the dummy and declarer's hand contain at least one trump when the defender has been put on lead. That is exactly why West, on the present deal, could not exit safely in spades. It would give you a ruff-and-sluff.

Three different ways of eliminating a suit

There are three main ways of eliminating a suit, two of which we saw in the previous section. Look at these three side-suit holdings:

(a) ♠ A 7
[   ]
♠ K 6

(b) ♣ K J 8 2
[   ]
♣ A Q 9 4

(c) ◇ K 10 3
[   ]
◇ A 6

With the spade side-suit shown in (a), you cash the ace and king, thereby removing your own holdings. The defenders will not be able to play a spade without giving you a ruff-and-sluff.

When you have the club side-suit shown in (b), you play sufficient rounds to remove the clubs in both of the defenders' hands. They cannot then play a club because they have no cards left in the suit.

The diamond holding in (c) offers a third possibility. You eliminate the suit by cashing the ace and king and ruffing the third round. As with (a), the defenders will not be able to play on that side suit without giving you a ruff-and-sluff.

Eliminate-exiting in a suit

Suppose you are playing in a major-suit contract and have a side suit of ♣A-6 opposite ♣9-5. After drawing trumps and eliminating one of the side suits, you will have the chance to play ace and another club. The second round of clubs will simultaneously eliminate the club suit and put one of the defenders on lead. We will refer to this as 'eliminate-exiting' in clubs. Think of this as a fourth way of eliminating a suit, along with the three methods we saw in the previous section.

Here is a deal where you would use this technique:

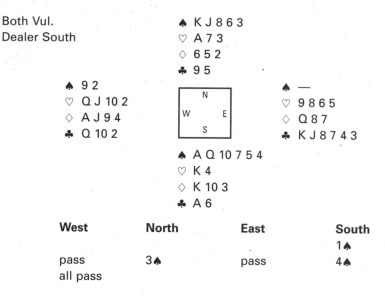

Both Vul.
Dealer South

North
♠ K J 8 6 3
♡ A 7 3
◇ 6 5 2
♣ 9 5

West
♠ 9 2
♡ Q J 10 2
◇ A J 9 4
♣ Q 10 2

East
♠ —
♡ 9 8 6 5
◇ Q 8 7
♣ K J 8 7 4 3

South
♠ A Q 10 7 5 4
♡ K 4
◇ K 10 3
♣ A 6

West	North	East	South
			1♠
pass	3♠	pass	4♠
all pass			

West leads the ♡Q against your spade game. What is your plan?

You win the heart lead with the king and draw trumps in two rounds. You then eliminate hearts by cashing the king and ace and ruffing the third round. These cards remain:

North
♠ J 8 6
♡ —
◇ 6 5 2
♣ 9 5

West
♠ —
♡ J
◇ A J 9 4
♣ Q 10 2

East
♠ —
♡ 9
◇ Q 8 7
♣ K J 8 7

South
♠ Q 10 7
♡ —
◇ K 10 3
♣ A 6

You now eliminate-exit in clubs. In other words, you play ace and another club, eliminating the club suit and exiting at the same time. It makes no difference on this deal which defender wins the second round of clubs. If West wins, he will have to play a diamond and give you a trick with the ◇K (or concede a ruff-and-sluff). Suppose instead that it is East who wins the second club. If he exits with the ◇8 or ◇7, you will cover with the ◇10, endplaying West. If East chooses instead to exit with the ◇Q, this will be covered with the king and ace. West will then have to give a trick to your ◇10.

Look at these three side-suit holdings and see if you think they are suitable for eliminate-exiting:

(a) ♣ A 7 5
　　 □
　　♣ K 9 3

(b) ◇ A 8 2
　　 □
　　◇ 10 7 6

(c) ♡ A 10 4
　　 □
　　♡ 9 7

With holding (a), you can cash the ace and king of clubs and eliminate-exit on the third round of the suit. No problem. With (b), you can play ace and another diamond. The effect is exactly the same. The defenders are welcome to cash a second trick in diamonds; with their next play, they will have to assist you.

The heart holding in (c) is no good. Playing ace and another heart will not help you because the defenders can safely play a third round of the suit without giving you a ruff-and-sluff.

Exiting in the problem suit itself

Another very common form of elimination play is to eliminate two side suits and then exit on the first round of the problem suit itself. Suppose your problem suit is ◇6-5-3 in dummy opposite ◇A-Q-10 in your hand. If you can draw trumps and eliminate the other two side suits, you will be able to play a diamond to the ten. Even if your left-hand opponent wins with the jack, he will be endplayed. He will have to lead back into the ◇A-Q or give you a ruff-and-sluff.

Here is an example of this technique:

Both Vul.
Dealer North

```
                    ♠ A 6 3 2
                    ♡ A 8 7 2
                    ◇ 7.3 2
                    ♣ A K
     ♠ 5 4                            ♠ 8
     ♡ K Q J 9          N             ♡ 10 6 5 3
     ◇ K J 6 4     W         E        ◇ 10 8
     ♣ 9 7 2           S             ♣ Q 10 8 6 4 3
                    ♠ K Q J 10 9 7
                    ♡ 4
                    ◇ A Q 9 5
                    ♣ J 5
```

West	North	East	South
	1NT	pass	3♠
pass	4♣	pass	4NT
pass	5♣	pass	6♠
all pass			

How will you play the spade slam when West leads the ♡K?

Diamonds is the problem suit. If you can eliminate hearts and clubs, you will be able to play a diamond to the nine, endplaying West no matter how the diamond suit lies.

How will the play go? After ruffing three hearts in your hand, you will need to return to dummy so you can lead a diamond to the nine. After the opening lead, only three entries to dummy remain, so you must take your first heart ruff immediately. The king and ace of trumps pull the defenders' cards in the suit and another heart is ruffed. A club to the king allows dummy's last heart to be ruffed and you return to dummy with the ♣A. These cards remain:

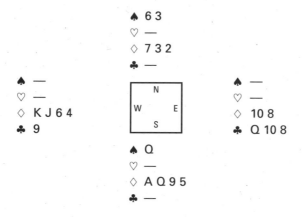

With hearts and clubs eliminated, you lead a diamond and insert the ◇9. West wins with the ◇J and is endplayed. He must return a diamond into the ◇A-Q or give you a ruff-and-sluff. It would have made no difference if East had risen with the ◇10 on the first round. This would have been covered by the queen and king and then your remaining ◇A-9 would have been an effective tenace against West's jack.

Elimination play to save a guess

Sometimes you can make a contract by straightforward play, but only if you guess correctly in your 'problem suit'. By forcing the defenders to play this suit, you can avoid the risk of guessing wrongly. Here is a straightforward example:

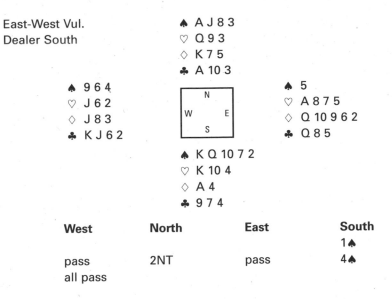

East-West Vul.
Dealer South

♠ A J 8 3
♡ Q 9 3
◇ K 7 5
♣ A 10 3

♠ 9 6 4
♡ J 6 2
◇ J 8 3
♣ K J 6 2

♠ 5
♡ A 8 7 5
◇ Q 10 9 6 2
♣ Q 8 5

♠ K Q 10 7 2
♡ K 10 4
◇ A 4
♣ 9 7 4

West	North	East	South
			1♠
pass	2NT	pass	4♠
all pass			

North bids a Jacoby 2NT to show a good spade fit and you sign off in 4♠. How will you play this contract when West leads a trump, East following?

You have two losers in the club suit. Hearts is your 'problem suit' because if you play it yourself, you will have to guess who holds the ♡J in order to lose only one trick there. You would very much like the defenders to make the first play in hearts. This can easily be arranged.

You win the trump lead and draw trumps in two further rounds. You then play the ace and king of diamonds, followed by a diamond ruff. By removing all of the diamonds from your own hand and the dummy, you have eliminated the diamond suit. The defenders will not be able to play a diamond without conceding a ruff-and-sluff.

You cash the ♣A and exit with a club. The defenders can delay their fate by cashing another club winner. This eliminates the clubs, leaving these cards out:

```
              ♠ J
              ♡ Q 9 3
              ◇ —
              ♣ —
♠ —                        ♠ —
♡ J 6 2      N             ♡ A 8 7
◇ —        W   E           ◇ Q
♣ K          S             ♣ —
              ♠ K
              ♡ K 10 4
              ◇ —
              ♣ —
```

It makes no difference which defender is on lead after the second club has been cashed. He cannot play a minor-suit card without giving you a ruff-and-sluff and will therefore have to lead a heart. This will allow you to score the two heart tricks that you need without having to guess who holds the ♡J. Mission accomplished!

Increasing your prospects in the problem suit

Forcing a defender to make the first play in a suit doesn't always guarantee you an extra trick. Sometimes it merely increases your chances. Look at the diamond position on this deal:

Neither Vul.
Dealer North

```
                    ♠ A 10 8 5
                    ♡ A 9 2
                    ◇ A 9 6 3
                    ♣ 7 4
    ♠ K 9 3                          ♠ Q J 7 4 2
    ♡ 8 4            N               ♡ 6
    ◇ Q 8 5      W       E           ◇ 10 7 4
    ♣ Q J 10 5 2      S              ♣ K 9 8 3
                    ♠ 6
                    ♡ K Q J 10 7 5 3
                    ◇ K J 2
                    ♣ A 6
```

West	North	East	South
	1NT	pass	3♡
pass	3♠	pass	4NT
pass	5♣	pass	6♡
all pass			

South's 3♡ shows a single-suited slam try and North's 3♠ agrees hearts, indicating a control in spades. Over South's Roman Keycard Blackwood, North shows three (or zero) keycards. How would you play the heart slam when West leads the ♣Q?

If trumps break 2-1, you can set up an elimination end position. You win the club lead, cross to the ♠A and ruff a spade high. You return to dummy with the ♡9, confirming that trumps are 2-1, and ruff another spade high. A trump to the ace draws the outstanding trump and you ruff dummy's last spade.

The time is now right to exit with your remaining club. The defender who wins the trick will have to make the first play in the diamond suit or give you a ruff-and-sluff (allowing you to ruff in the dummy and throw a diamond from your hand).

If West wins the club trick, the contract is assured, since a diamond lead would run into your king-jack tenace. If instead East wins the second round of clubs, exiting with a low diamond, you will have two chances. You can play the ◇2 from your hand, forcing West to play the ◇Q when, as here, he does not hold the ◇10. If West does produce the ◇10, you can win with dummy's ace and take your second chance, a finesse of the ◇J. Two chances for the price of one!

The stars come out to play:

the basic elimination play ──────────────── ☆

In the final of the 1985 Bermuda Bowl in São Paulo, the USA faced Austria and Chip Martel reached a contract of 5◇ on this deal.

Both Vul.
Dealer South

```
                    ♠ K 6 5 4
                    ♡ A
                    ◇ J 8 6 5
                    ♣ K J 10 5
   ♠ Q J 10 8                        ♠ A 9 7 2
   ♡ J 8 5 3          N              ♡ Q 10 6 4 2
   ◇ K 9          W       E          ◇ Q
   ♣ Q 7 4            S              ♣ 9 6 2
                    ♠ 3
                    ♡ K 9 7
                    ◇ A 10 7 4 3 2
                    ♣ A 8 3
```

West	North	East	South
Terraneo	Stansby	Fucik	Martel
			1◇
pass	1♠	pass	2◇
pass	3♣	pass	3♡
pass	5◇	all pass	

How would you play the diamond game when West leads the ♠Q?

Martel played low from dummy, allowing the queen to win. The Austrian West, Franz Terraneo, then persevered with the ♠J. Martel ruffed the second spade and laid down the ◇A. Why do you think he spurned the safety play in trumps (leading low from the dummy and finessing the ◇10)? He could see that if the trumps divided 2-1, there was an excellent chance of an elimination play that would save him a guess in the club suit.

When both defenders followed to the first round of trumps, Martel crossed to the ♡A and ruffed another spade. He then cashed the ♡K, throwing the ♠K from dummy, and ruffed his last heart. With both major suits eliminated, he exited in trumps. West won with the trump king and either had to lead a club, saving declarer a guess in the suit, or give a ruff-and-sluff.

The next deal arose in the Blue Ribbon Pairs at the 1993 Fall Nationals in Orlando. Bob Hamman succeeded with his elimination play after a chance was missed by the defenders.

Both Vul.
Dealer South

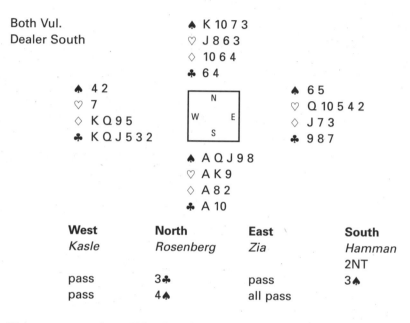

West	North	East	South
Kasle	Rosenberg	Zia	Hamman
			2NT
pass	3♣	pass	3♠
pass	4♠	all pass	

Hamman won the ♣K lead and drew trumps in two rounds with the ace and queen. There were nine top tricks, so a third trick from the heart suit would give him his game. He began with the ace and king of hearts, but the suit did not oblige, West showing out on the second round. How would you have continued?

Hamman eliminate-exited with the ♣10 and Gaylor Kasle won in the West seat. Since a third round of clubs would concede a ruff-and-sluff, Kasle then had to open the diamond suit. He chose to play the ◇5, which went to East's jack, ducked by the declarer. Zia, sitting East, could not afford to cash the ♡Q because this would establish dummy's ♡J for a diamond discard. He therefore had to return a diamond. Hamman won with the ace and played a third round of diamonds, which West had to win. It was the end of the road for the defense. West had to concede a ruff-and-sluff and Hamman was able to ditch his ♡9. The game had been made.

Did you spot where the defense went wrong? West needed to lead the ◇K instead of a low diamond, continuing with the ◇Q if the king was allowed to win. East could then have won the third round of diamonds and cashed the ♡Q for the setting trick.

In 2000, the team known as 'The Zia All-Stars' won the Lederer Memorial Trophy for the third consecutive time. They would go on to make it five victories in a row. Andrew Robson was one of several successful declarers in six spades on this deal:

North-South Vul.
Dealer North

```
                    ♠ K Q 7 3
                    ♡ A K
                    ◇ 10 9 4
                    ♣ A K 6 5
   ♠ J 6                              ♠ 10 2
   ♡ Q J 5 2          N               ♡ 10 9 8 7 6 4 3
   ◇ K Q 5        W       E           ◇ 7 6 2
   ♣ 10 9 8 2         S               ♣ Q
                    ♠ A 9 8 5 4
                    ♡ —
                    ◇ A J 8 3
                    ♣ J 7 4 3
```

West	North	East	South
Liggins	Zia	Fawcett	Robson
	1♣	pass	1♠
pass	4♠	pass	6♠
all pass			

West led the ♣10, won with the ace, and the queen fell from East. How would you play the spade slam after this start?

Robson drew trumps in two rounds and cashed the ace-king of hearts, throwing a diamond and a club from his hand. He continued with the jack and king of clubs and ruffed a club in the South hand, eliminating that suit. He returned to dummy with a third round of trumps, leaving these cards still to be played:

```
                    ♠ 7
                    ♡ —
                    ◇ 10 9 4
                    ♣ —
   ♠ —                               ♠ —
   ♡ Q            N                   ♡ 10
   ◇ K Q 5     W     E                ◇ 7 6 2
   ♣ —            S                   ♣ —
                    ♠ 9
                    ♡ —
                    ◇ A J 8
                    ♣ —
```

Looking good for declarer, isn't it? This is an example of the type of elimination play where you exit in the problem suit itself. Robson ran the ◇10 to the ◇Q and West had to return a diamond into the tenace or concede a ruff-and-sluff.

We will end this section with a contract that was cleverly played by Israel's Ophar Herbst in the semifinals of the 2003 European Open Championships in Menton.

Both Vul.
Dealer South

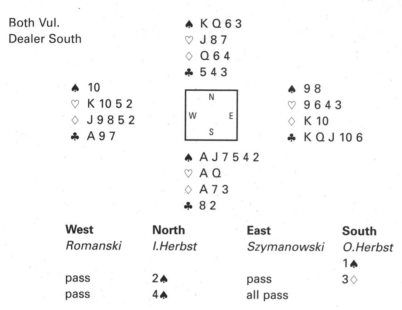

| ♠ K Q 6 3 |
| ♡ J 8 7 |
| ◇ Q 6 4 |
| ♣ 5 4 3 |

♠ 10
♡ K 10 5 2
◇ J 9 8 5 2
♣ A 9 7

♠ 9 8
♡ 9 6 4 3
◇ K 10
♣ K Q J 10 6

♠ A J 7 5 4 2
♡ A Q
◇ A 7 3
♣ 8 2

West	North	East	South
Romanski	I.Herbst	Szymanowski	O.Herbst
			1♠
pass	2♠	pass	3◇
pass	4♠	all pass	

Both Herbst brothers took an optimistic view and a poor contract was reached. How would you play to give it a chance when the ten of trumps is led?

Ophar Herbst won the trump lead in his hand and immediately led the ♡Q! West won with the ♡K and could see no reason to switch to clubs. When he exited passively with another heart, declarer won with the ace and crossed to dummy with a trump to ditch a club loser on the ♡J. All would be well if the ◇K was onside. Herbst saw an extra chance — that East might hold a doubleton ◇K. He played a club from dummy, East winning and playing another club. Herbst ruffed in the South hand, crossed to dummy with a third round of trumps and ruffed the last club, eliminating that suit. He then cashed the ◇A, leaving these cards still out:

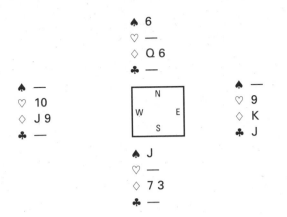

A diamond to dummy's queen lost to the king, but East had indeed been dealt a doubleton diamond. He had to return a heart or a club, giving declarer a ruff-and-sluff, and the adventurous game was made.

NOW TRY THESE...

A.

    ♠ J 5 4 2
    ♡ A 9 2
    ◇ Q 5
    ♣ Q 6 5 2

♡ Q led

```
    N
W       E
    S
```

    ♠ A K Q 10 7 3
    ♡ 5
    ◇ A K
    ♣ A J 9 4

West	North	East	South
			2♣
pass	2NT	pass	3♠
pass	4♡	pass	4NT
pass	5◇	pass	5NT
pass	6♠	all pass	

How will you play the spade slam when West leads the ♡Q?

B.

    ♠ A K 10 9 8 6
    ♡ A
    ◇ A K J 2
    ♣ A 5

♡ K led

```
    N
W       E
    S
```

    ♠ J 5 4 2
    ♡ 6 4 3
    ◇ 8 6 5 4
    ♣ K 9

West	North	East	South
2♡	dbl	pass	2♠
pass	6♠	all pass	

How will you play the spade slam when West leads the ♡K? (The trump suit will break 2-1.)

C.

♠ 3 2
♡ K Q 9 8 6 5
◇ Q J 9
♣ J 8

♠Q led

```
      N
  W       E
      S
```

♠ A 7
♡ A J 4 3
◇ A 6 5
♣ A K 5 3

West	North	East	South
			2NT
pass	3◇	pass	4♡
pass	5♡	pass	6♡
all pass			

How will you play the heart slam when West leads the ♠Q?

D.

♠ 10 7 6 5 3 2
♡ Q
◇ J 8 6 2
♣ A 8

♡K led

```
      N
  W       E
      S
```

♠ A Q 9 8 4
♡ 10 2
◇ K Q 3
♣ Q 5 4

West	North	East	South
			1♠
dbl	4♠	pass	pass
dbl	all pass		

How will you play the doubled spade game when West leads the ♡K and continues with the ♡A?

Answers 🖉

A.

```
            ♠ J 5 4 2
            ♡ A 9 2
            ◇ Q 5
            ♣ Q 6 5 2

♠ —                        ♠ 9 8 6
♡ Q J 10 6       N         ♡ K 8 7 4 3
◇ J 9 4 3 2  W     E       ◇ 10 8 7 6
♣ K 10 8 3       S         ♣ 7

            ♠ A K Q 10 7 3
            ♡ 5
            ◇ A K
            ♣ A J 9 4
```

West	North	East	South
			2♣
pass	2NT	pass	3♠
pass	4♡	pass	4NT
pass	5◇	pass	5NT
pass	6♠	all pass	

West leads the ♡Q against your spade slam. What is your plan?

Clubs is the 'problem suit'. To set up an elimination ending, you need to ruff two hearts in your hand. Entries to dummy are scarce, so you ruff a heart with the ♠A at Trick 2. You draw trumps in three rounds, ending in the dummy, and ruff dummy's last heart, retaining the ♠3. You cash the ◇A-K and these cards remain:

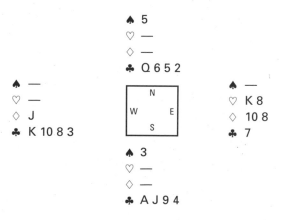

```
            ♠ 5
            ♡ —
            ◇ —
            ♣ Q 6 5 2

♠ —                        ♠ —
♡ —           N            ♡ K 8
◇ J        W     E         ◇ 10 8
♣ K 10 8 3       S         ♣ 7

            ♠ 3
            ♡ —
            ◇ —
            ♣ A J 9 4
```

You lead the ♣J from hand. If West wins, he will have to lead into your club tenace or give a ruff-and-sluff. If instead your ♣J wins, you will lead low to the ♣Q next.

If East held ♣K-10-8-x, he would be similarly inconvenienced.

B.

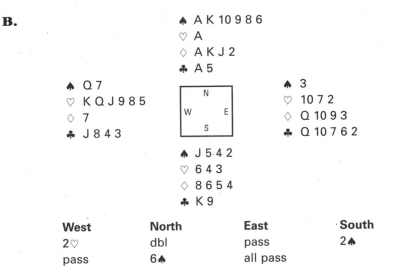

```
              ♠ A K 10 9 8 6
              ♡ A
              ◇ A K J 2
              ♣ A 5
♠ Q 7                              ♠ 3
♡ K Q J 9 8 5        N             ♡ 10 7 2
◇ 7             W         E        ◇ Q 10 9 3
♣ J 8 4 3            S             ♣ Q 10 7 6 2
              ♠ J 5 4 2
              ♡ 6 4 3
              ◇ 8 6 5 4
              ♣ K 9
```

West	North	East	South
2♡	dbl	pass	2♠
pass	6♠	all pass	

West leads the ♡K against your spade slam and you win with dummy's ace. Both defenders follow to the ace of trumps and you draw the last trump with the king. The slam is in danger only when East holds four or five diamonds to the queen. In that case, you may be able to endplay East on the second round of diamonds, provided you have eliminated both hearts and clubs.

You cash the ace and king of clubs and ruff a heart in the dummy. After re-entering your hand with the ♠J, you ruff your last heart, eliminating that suit. The time is now right to play on diamonds. You cash the ◇A, leaving this position:

```
              ♠ 10
              ♡ —
              ◇ K J 2
              ♣ —
♠ —                               ♠ —
♡ Q J              N              ♡ —
◇ —           W         E         ◇ Q 10 9
♣ J 8              S              ♣ Q
              ♠ 5
              ♡ —
              ◇ 8 6 5
              ♣ —
```

Next, you lead the ◇2 from dummy. The contract is guaranteed at this point. When the cards lie as in the diagram, East has to win the second round of diamonds and is endplayed. If instead West began with ◇Q-10-9-7, he would have to play a third round of diamonds, allowing you to finesse the ◇J, or give you a ruff-and-sluff.

C.

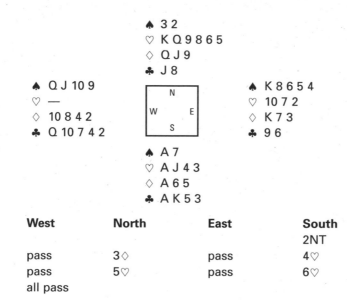

```
              ♠ 3 2
              ♡ K Q 9 8 6 5
              ◇ Q J 9
              ♣ J 8
♠ Q J 10 9                      ♠ K 8 6 5 4
♡ —            N                ♡ 10 7 2
◇ 10 8 4 2   W   E              ◇ K 7 3
♣ Q 10 7 4 2   S                ♣ 9 6
              ♠ A 7
              ♡ A J 4 3
              ◇ A 6 5
              ♣ A K 5 3
```

West	North	East	South
			2NT
pass	3◇	pass	4♡
pass	5♡	pass	6♡
all pass			

How will you play the heart slam when West leads the ♠Q?

On a non-spade lead, the best chance is to lead towards the ♣J. If West holds the ♣Q, you will make the contract easily.

Once a spade has been led, prospects take a dive. With a spade loser exposed, you cannot make use of the ♣J. Your best remaining chance is an elimination play. You win the spade lead and play the ace of trumps, West showing out. You cash the ace and king of clubs and ruff a club with the king. You then lead the nine of trumps, intending to run the card. Whether or not East covers with the ten, you will draw trumps and ruff your last club. These cards remain:

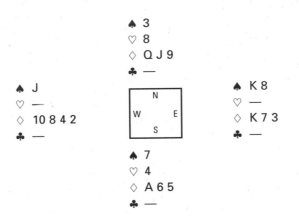

```
              ♠ 3
              ♡ 8
              ◇ Q J 9
              ♣ —
♠ J                          ♠ K 8
♡ —              N           ♡ —
◇ 10 8 4 2   W     E         ◇ K 7 3
♣ —              S           ♣ —
              ♠ 7
              ♡ 4
              ◇ A 6 5
              ♣ —
```

When West wins your spade exit and plays a diamond, you try your luck with dummy's ◇9. Since West holds the ◇10 and East holds the ◇K, the slam is yours. If East allows the ◇9 to win, you will run the ◇Q on the second round.

D.

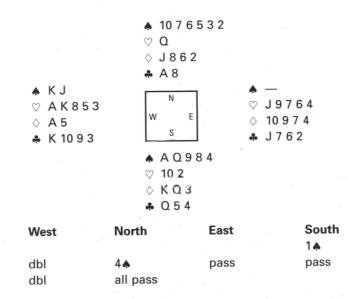

```
                ♠ 10 7 6 5 3 2
                ♡ Q
                ◇ J 8 6 2
                ♣ A 8
♠ K J                              ♠ —
♡ A K 8 5 3          N             ♡ J 9 7 6 4
◇ A 5           W         E        ◇ 10 9 7 4
♣ K 10 9 3           S             ♣ J 7 6 2
                ♠ A Q 9 8 4
                ♡ 10 2
                ◇ K Q 3
                ♣ Q 5 4
```

West	North	East	South
			1♠
dbl	4♠	pass	pass
dbl	all pass		

East-West would have done well playing the contract their way. That is their problem. How will you play the doubled spade game when West leads the ♡K and continues with the ♡A?

If West has a trump trick, you will need to endplay him to avoid a loser in every suit. After ruffing the second round of hearts, you should play a diamond to the king. West wins with the ace and has to exit with a diamond to avoid giving you a tenth trick immediately. You win with the ◇Q and cash the ace of trumps, East showing out. When you play a third round of diamonds towards dummy, West is in no hurry to endplay himself. He declines to ruff, throwing a heart, and dummy's ◇J wins the trick. These cards remain:

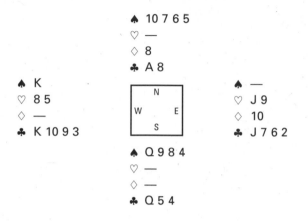

You exit with a trump and West is endplayed, forced to lead from the ♣K or to give you a ruff-and-sluff. (If you had cashed the ♠A at Trick 3, West would have been able to win the ◇3 with the ◇A, cash the ♠K and avoid the endplay.)

Variations of Elimination Play

In the previous chapter, we saw the basic mechanics of elimination play. In this chapter, we will explore the many situations where you can benefit from this productive technique.

Taking a finesse when there is no entry

Sometimes when you have a finessing position, the missing honor card is onside but you have no entry to dummy to take the finesse. By using elimination play, you may be able to force the defenders to assist you. Look at this deal:

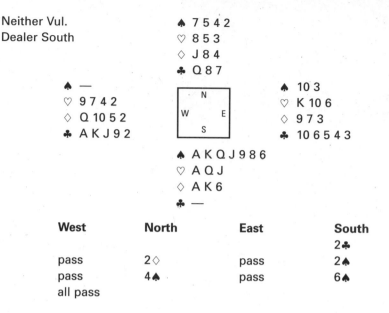

Neither Vul.
Dealer South

	♠ 7 5 4 2
	♡ 8 5 3
	◇ J 8 4
	♣ Q 8 7

♠ —	N	♠ 10 3
♡ 9 7 4 2	W E	♡ K 10 6
◇ Q 10 5 2	S	◇ 9 7 3
♣ A K J 9 2		♣ 10 6 5 4 3

	♠ A K Q J 9 8 6
	♡ A Q J
	◇ A K 6
	♣ —

West	North	East	South
			2♣
pass	2◇	pass	2♠
pass	4♠	pass	6♠
all pass			

How will you play the contract when West leads the ♣K?

Unless the ◇Q falls in two rounds, you will need to pick up the heart suit. Even if East holds the ♡K, as you must hope, you will probably have to finesse twice in the suit. The ♠7 is the only entry to dummy, unfortunately, so what can be done?

You ruff the club lead with the ♠8 (retaining your ♠6) and draw trumps in two rounds. You then play ace, king and another diamond. By good fortune, it is West who has to win the trick. He has no safe return. If he plays another club, high or low, you will enjoy a heart discard on dummy's ♣Q; a simple heart finesse will then give you the contract. West cannot afford to play another diamond, if he still has one, because this would concede a ruff-and-sluff. His only remaining alternative is to play a heart. Suppose he plays the ♡7 (a high spot card to warn partner that he holds no honor in the suit). You win East's ♡10 with the ♡J and cross to dummy's ♠7 to finesse the ♡Q. The slam is yours.

Elimination play with two problem suits

Sometimes you leave your victim with two suits that he can play without giving a ruff-and-sluff. Whichever one he chooses, he will surrender the extra trick that you need.

Neither Vul.
Dealer South

```
                        ♠ 5 2
                        ♡ A J 8 6 5
                        ◇ K 5 2
                        ♣ K 4 3
    ♠ K 10 3                             ♠ J 8 7 6 4
    ♡ 10             ┌─────────┐         ♡ 9 2
    ◇ Q 9 6 4       │    N    │         ◇ 10 8 7
    ♣ Q J 10 7 6    │ W     E │         ♣ 9 8 2
                    │    S    │
                    └─────────┘
                        ♠ A Q 9
                        ♡ K Q 7 4 3
                        ◇ A J 3
                        ♣ A 5
```

West	North	East	South
			2NT
pass	3◇	pass	4♡
pass	6♡	all pass	

How will you play the heart slam when West leads the ♣Q?

You win with the ♣A and draw trumps with the king and queen. Next you eliminate clubs by crossing to the ♣K and ruffing a club. A diamond to the king returns the lead to dummy and you continue with a spade to the nine. West wins with the ♠10, but he must then give you a trick. A spade return will allow you to score the queen and ace, throwing a diamond from dummy. Similarly, a diamond return would be into your tenace, giving you an extra trick. If instead West chooses to play a fourth round of clubs, you will discard a diamond from one hand and ruff in the other.

This is the first deal we have seen with two 'problem suits' (here spades and diamonds). The defender could not return either of these without giving you a trick. Nor, of course, could he safely play the one suit (clubs) that you had eliminated.

Forcing a ruff-and-sluff

In most elimination plays, the thrown-in defender has a choice of assisting you in a side suit or giving a ruff-and-sluff. When the key defender holds a long suit — perhaps he has announced this with a preempt — you can sometimes put him on lead in that suit, having previously removed all of his cards in the other suits. He will then be forced to give you a ruff-and-sluff, as on this deal:

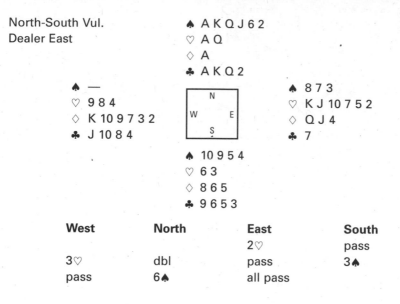

North-South Vul.
Dealer East

```
              ♠ A K Q J 6 2
              ♡ A Q
              ◇ A
              ♣ A K Q 2
♠ —                          ♠ 8 7 3
♡ 9 8 4            N          ♡ K J 10 7 5 2
◇ K 10 9 7 3 2   W   E        ◇ Q J 4
♣ J 10 8 4         S          ♣ 7
              ♠ 10 9 5 4
              ♡ 6 3
              ◇ 8 6 5
              ♣ 9 6 5 3
```

West	North	East	South
		2♡	pass
3♡	dbl	pass	3♠
pass	6♠	all pass	

North has bid somewhat lazily, since there might have been a grand slam available. That is no excuse for you to play lazily! How will you tackle the contract when West leads the ♡9?

You win with dummy's ♡A and draw a round of trumps with the ace, West showing out. If your next move is to draw another round of trumps, you will go down. Instead, you must make a plan to overcome the only threat to the contract: a 4-1 break in clubs. You must aim to eliminate the diamond suit. If clubs do break badly, you will then have a chance to put East on lead with the ♡Q.

So, after just one round of trumps, you cash the ◇A. You then cross to the ♠10 and ruff a diamond high. A trump to the nine allows you to ruff your last diamond. That's better! When you cash two rounds of clubs, the 4-1 break comes to light. This will cause no problem after your careful preparation. You exit with the ♡Q to East's ♡K and he has to return a heart, giving you a ruff-and-sluff. You discard a losing club from one hand or the other, ruffing in the opposite hand, and the slam is yours.

Exiting where a defender holds a doubleton honor

A defender with a doubleton honor can often be endplayed on the second round of that suit. Sometimes he cannot afford to unblock the honor. Even when he could safely have unblocked it, you may catch him napping. On the first of the deals below, the defenders were powerless.

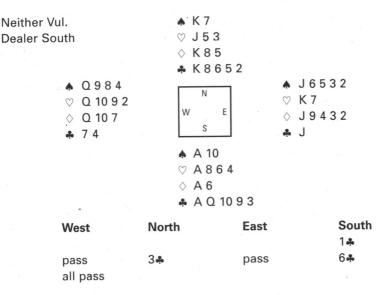

Neither Vul.
Dealer South

♠ K 7
♡ J 5 3
◇ K 8 5
♣ K 8 6 5 2

♠ Q 9 8 4
♡ Q 10 9 2
◇ Q 10 7
♣ 7 4

N
W E
S

♠ J 6 5 3 2
♡ K 7
◇ J 9 4 3 2
♣ J

♠ A 10
♡ A 8 6 4
◇ A 6
♣ A Q 10 9 3

West	North	East	South
			1♣
pass	3♣	pass	6♣
all pass			

How will you play 6♣ when West leads a low trump?

Hearts is the problem suit. Suppose you draw trumps and eliminate the spades and diamonds. What are your main chances of restricting your heart losers to one?

One chance is to find West with the king and queen of hearts. You could then lead low towards dummy's jack. West would have to win with one honor and lead away from the other, allowing the jack to score.

Another chance is to find East with a doubleton king or queen. You would then play ace and another heart. East could not afford to unblock his honor under the ace or you could establish the ♡J by leading towards it. If instead he retained a bare honor, he would be endplayed on the second round, forced to give you a ruff-and-sluff.

Playing ace and another heart also succeeds when West started with ♡K-x or ♡Q-x and fails to unblock his honor under the ace. So, all in all, this is a better shot than leading low towards the jack. Indeed, if West did hold ♡K-Q-x(-x), he might have led the suit rather than a nebulous trump.

Some defenders are careless when they hold a doubleton honor in a side suit and elimination play will give you many a contract that could have been beaten. That is what happened on this deal:

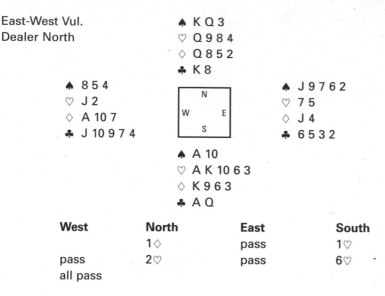

East-West Vul.
Dealer North

		♠ K Q 3	
		♡ Q 9 8 4	
		◇ Q 8 5 2	
		♣ K 8	

♠ 8 5 4   ♠ J 9 7 6 2
♡ J 2   ♡ 7 5
◇ A 10 7   ◇ J 4
♣ J 10 9 7 4   ♣ 6 5 3 2

♠ A 10
♡ A K 10 6 3
◇ K 9 6 3
♣ A Q

West	North	East	South
	1◇	pass	1♡
pass	2♡	pass	6♡
all pass			

After a commendably brief auction, West leads the ♣J against your heart slam. How will you play the contract?

You win the club lead and draw trumps in two rounds. You then eliminate the black suits, throwing a diamond on dummy's third spade. This still leaves you with two potential diamond losers. What position will you need in diamonds, the problem suit, to make the slam?

Your main hope is to find a chosen defender with ◇A-x. He will have to play low when you lead through his ace. When you duck the second round to the bare ace, the suit will be yours. Let's say that you decide to play West for a doubleton ◇A. You will reach this position with the lead in the South hand:

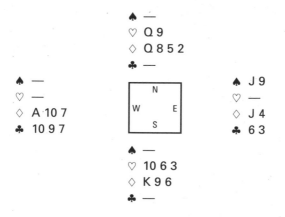

You lead a diamond to the queen. West does not, in fact, hold the ◇A-x, as you were hoping. However, a second chance has emerged. East now has to unblock the jack to beat the contract! If instead he follows with the ◇4, as many defenders would, you can see what will happen on the next round of diamonds. You lead dummy's ◊2, the ◊J appearing from East. You play the ◊9 from your hand and there is nothing that West can do. If East is left on lead, he will have to give a ruff-and-sluff. If instead West overtakes with the ◊A, he will set up your ◊K.

Of course, it is foolish of East to retain the ◊J. It cannot possibly assist the defense to retain this card and may well give the slam away. I'm sure that you or I would never make such a mistake. Well, fairly sure…

Guessing correctly in the end position

Sometimes the best you can achieve by forcing the defenders to open a new suit is the chance to make a winning guess. Look at the spade suit on this deal:

```
Both Vul.              ♠ Q 6
Dealer South           ♡ J 9 8 6 5 2
                       ◊ A 4
                       ♣ Q J 6
        ♠ J 9 5 2              ♠ K 8 7 3
        ♡ 10          N        ♡ 4
        ◊ Q J 10 7  W   E      ◊ K 9 6 5 2
        ♣ 10 8 4 2    S        ♣ 9 7 3
                       ♠ A 10 4
                       ♡ A K Q 7 3
                       ◊ 8 3
                       ♣ A K 5
```

West	North	East	South
			1♡
pass	4♡	pass	6♡
all pass			

Taking a gamble on the diamond position, South leaps to 6♡. How would you play this contract when West leads the ◊Q?

You win with dummy's ace and draw trumps in one round. The only chance is to eliminate the club suit and then eliminate-exit in diamonds. When you do this, West wins with the ◊10. A diamond continuation would give you a ruff-and-sluff and the contract. Realizing this, with the aid of a count signal from his partner, West exits with a low spade. You now have a guess to make. Should you play dummy's ♠Q, hoping that West holds the ♠K? Or should you run the spade exit to your hand, hoping that West holds the ♠J and that East will be forced to play the ♠K? If you have not already considered this problem, take a moment to do so now.

You should play low from dummy, playing West for the ♠J. Why is that? Because if West held the ♠K, East would surely have won the second round of diamonds and played a spade through your ace! Since you can be confident that East has the ♠K, the only chance is to play West for the ♠J.

Let's look at another deal where the defenders are forced to open your problem suit, and you must then guess how the cards lie.

Neither Vul.
Dealer South

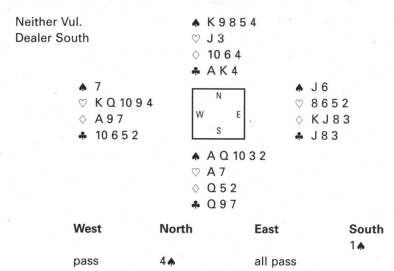

```
              ♠ K 9 8 5 4
              ♡ J 3
              ◇ 10 6 4
              ♣ A K 4
♠ 7                              ♠ J 6
♡ K Q 10 9 4                     ♡ 8 6 5 2
◇ A 9 7                          ◇ K J 8 3
♣ 10 6 5 2                       ♣ J 8 3
              ♠ A Q 10 3 2
              ♡ A 7
              ◇ Q 5 2
              ♣ Q 9 7
```

West	North	East	South
			1♠
pass	4♠	all pass	

How will you play the contract when West leads the ♡K?

You win the heart lead and draw trumps in two rounds. After eliminating the clubs, you eliminate-exit in hearts, putting West on lead. These cards remain:

```
              ♠ 9 8 5
              ♡ —
              ◇ 10 6 4
              ♣ —
♠ —                              ♠ —
♡ 10 9                           ♡ 8 5
◇ A 9 7                          ◇ K J 8 3
♣ 10                             ♣ —
              ♠ Q 10 3
              ♡ —
              ◇ Q 5 2
              ♣ —
```

A heart or a club exit will give you a ruff-and-sluff. Realizing this, West will play the ◇7 to East's ◇K. Back comes a low diamond. How should you play?

If East began with the ace and king of diamonds, West holding the jack, you must rise with the ◇Q to make the contract. If instead East holds the ◇J, you must play low from the South hand. Which is the better prospect?

This is an example of Restricted Choice. Playing low on the second round of diamonds will gain when East's diamonds are headed by the ace-jack or king-jack. The alternative of rising with the queen is only half as good, gaining when East began with the ace-king of diamonds. On the present deal, justice is done. You play low on the second diamond and West has to play the ◇A. Your ◇Q will then score the game-going trick.

The position is similar when the defenders have to open this problem suit:

```
                ♣ 10 8 3

♣ K 9 4     [            ]     ♣ Q 7 6 2

                ♣ A J 5
```

You eliminate-exit in another suit and the defenders are forced to play on clubs (or give a ruff-and-sluff). If West is on lead, you are certain to score the two club tricks that you need. Suppose, however, that East wins your exit and leads the ♣2. You play low from your hand and West wins with one honor or the other (the ♣K here). Which card will you play from dummy when West returns the ♣4?

Once again it is an example of Restricted Choice. If you play the ♣8 from dummy on the second round, you will succeed whenever West holds ♣K 9 x(-x) or ♣Q-9-x(-x). The alternative play of the ♣10 from dummy gains only against ♣K-Q-x(-x). By following the recommended line of play, you will have odds of 2-to-1 in your favor. Vociferous non-believers in Restricted Choice, of whom there are a surprising number, must endure odds of 2-to-1 against.

Exiting in the right suit first

Sometimes you have two potential exit suits and plan to lose a trick in each of them. It will often be critical which suit you play first. Test yourself on this spade game:

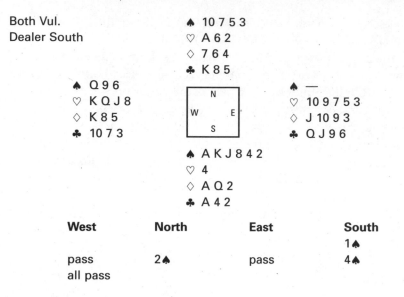

Both Vul.
Dealer South

```
              ♠ 10 7 5 3
              ♡ A 6 2
              ◇ 7 6 4
              ♣ K 8 5
♠ Q 9 6                        ♠ —
♡ K Q J 8        N             ♡ 10 9 7 5 3
◇ K 8 5       W     E          ◇ J 10 9 3
♣ 10 7 3         S             ♣ Q J 9 6
              ♠ A K J 8 4 2
              ♡ 4
              ◇ A Q 2
              ♣ A 4 2
```

West	North	East	South
			1♠
pass	2♠	pass	4♠
all pass			

West leads the ♡K against your spade game. The dummy is very suitable and prospects are excellent. How will you play the contract?

On deals like this, when everything looks rosy, you must ask yourself: 'What can possibly go wrong?' The answer here is that West may hold all three missing trumps and the ◇K. What can be done in that case?

Perhaps you can arrange an endplay on West. With limited entries to dummy, you must start to eliminate the hearts immediately. You ruff a heart and play the ♠A, finding that West does indeed hold a trump trick. What next?

You cross to the ♣K and ruff dummy's last heart. You now have two suits — spades and clubs — in which you can exit on the third round. Which suit should you play first? Suppose you play king and another spade first, putting West on lead. He can exit safely in clubs. When you subsequently eliminate-exit in clubs, East will win and send the ◇J through your tenace, beating the contract.

What happens if instead you play ace and another club, exiting on the third round? East will win and switch to the ◇J. This will not cause a problem now. You will win with the ◇A and cash the ♠K, leaving this position:

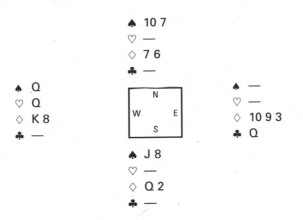

```
                    ♠ 10 7
                    ♡ —
                    ◇ 7 6
                    ♣ —
    ♠ Q                              ♠ —
    ♡ Q         ┌─────────┐          ♡ —
    ◇ K 8       │    N    │          ◇ 10 9 3
    ♣ —         │ W     E │          ♣ Q
                │    S    │
                └─────────┘
                    ♠ J 8
                    ♡ —
                    ◇ Q 2
                    ♣ —
```

You throw West in with his top trump and he has no safe exit. He must give you a trick with your ◇Q or concede a ruff-and-sluff.

West was your intended victim for the throw-in, with a trump, so it was right to play on clubs first.

Handling a 4-4 problem suit

When a potential unwanted loser lies in a suit where you have four cards opposite four, it may be beneficial to cash one top card in the suit before relinquishing the lead. When the suit breaks 4-1, this will remove the singleton from one defender's hand. Clubs is your problem suit on this slam deal:

North-South Vul.
Dealer West

```
                    ♠ K J 10 9 3
                    ♡ A K 3
                    ◇ 4
                    ♣ A K 3 2
    ♠ 8 6                            ♠ 4 2
    ♡ J 9 4       ┌─────────┐        ♡ Q 10 6 2
    ◇ K Q J 10 7 5 3 │  N  │        ◇ 9 8 2
    ♣ 9           │ W     E │        ♣ J 10 7 6
                  │    S    │
                  └─────────┘
                    ♠ A Q 7 5
                    ♡ 8 7 5
                    ◇ A 6
                    ♣ Q 8 5 4
```

West	North	East	South
3◇	dbl	pass	4♠
pass	4NT	pass	5♠
pass	6♠	all pass	

West leads the ◇K against your small slam in spades. How will you play the contract?

You win the diamond lead, draw trumps in two rounds and ruff your remaining diamond, eliminating the suit. What now? If you play ace, king and another heart, eliminate-exiting immediately, you will go down. West can win the third round of hearts and exit safely with the ♣9 (or East can win and play a low club). You need to cash dummy's ♣A before playing three rounds of hearts. When West holds a singleton nine, ten or jack in the club suit, you will survive a 4-1 club break. If West wins the third round of hearts, he will have to give you a ruff-and-sluff. If instead East wins the third heart, he can avoid giving you a ruff-and-sluff only by playing a club from his remaining ♣J-10-7. If he leads the jack or ten, you will win with the ♣K and finesse the ♣8 on the third round. If instead he exits with the ♣7, you will cover with your ♣8, winning the trick.

It is not always right to cash one round when your problem suit contains four cards opposite four. You must judge each case on its merits. Look at the club suit here:

East-West Vul.
Dealer South

```
                    ♠ 10 8 5 4
                    ♡ K 9 2
                    ◇ A 10
                    ♣ K 7 6 4
      ♠ 9 6 2                          ♠ —
      ♡ J 8 5          N               ♡ Q 10 7 6 4 3
      ◇ K Q J      W       E           ◇ 9 8 6 4 3 2
      ♣ Q J 8 2        S               ♣ 10
                    ♠ A K Q J 7 3
                    ♡ A
                    ◇ 7 5
                    ♣ A 9 5 3
```

West	North	East	South
			1♠
pass	3♠	pass	4♣
pass	4◇	pass	4♡
pass	5♣	pass	6♠
all pass			

You impress everyone present with a sequence of four cuebids. West leads the ◇K against your eventual small slam in spades. How will you play?

You win the diamond lead and play a trump to the ace, East showing out. After cashing the ♡A, you return to dummy by finessing the ♠8. You ditch your diamond loser on the ♡K and ruff a diamond high. You then cross to the ♠10 to ruff dummy's remaining heart. Both red suits have been eliminated and these cards remain:

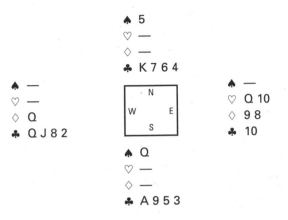

```
              ♠ 5
              ♡ —
              ◊ —
              ♣ K 7 6 4
♠ —                            ♠ —
♡ —          ┌─────────┐       ♡ Q 10
◊ Q          │   N     │       ◊ 9 8
♣ Q J 8 2    │ W     E │       ♣ 10
             │   S     │
             └─────────┘
              ♠ Q
              ♡ —
              ◊ —
              ♣ A 9 5 3
```

If your next move is to cash either the ♣A or the ♣K, you will go down. West's ♣Q-J-8 will then be worth two tricks. Instead, you must duck the first round of clubs, taking advantage of the fact that a singleton queen, jack, ten or eight will cause a blockage for the defenders.

What can they do here? If East wins the ducked first round of clubs with the ten, he will have to give you a ruff-and-sluff. If instead West snaffles his partner's ♣10 with the ♣Q or ♣J, he will have to lead away from his remaining honor. By running this to the ♣A-9, you will score the three club tricks that you need.

The stars come out to play:

variations of elimination play ☆

This first deal is from the final of the 1997 Bermuda Bowl in Tunisia's Hammamet. (It so happens that I met my wife, Thelma, there some 33 years ago.) France faces USA 2 and Bobby Wolff is in the hot seat.

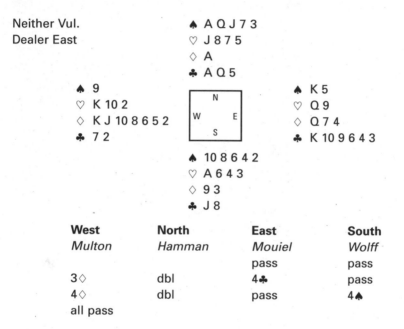

Neither Vul.
Dealer East

♠ A Q J 7 3
♡ J 8 7 5
◇ A
♣ A Q 5

♠ 9
♡ K 10 2
◇ K J 10 8 6 5 2
♣ 7 2

♠ K 5
♡ Q 9
◇ Q 7 4
♣ K 10 9 6 4 3

♠ 10 8 6 4 2
♡ A 6 4 3
◇ 9 3
♣ J 8

West	North	East	South
Multon	*Hamman*	*Mouiel*	*Wolff*
		pass	pass
3◇	dbl	4♣	pass
4◇	dbl	pass	4♠
all pass			

East's bid of 4♣ is worthy of our attention. It shows a raise to 4◇ and suggests a club lead, should South end up playing the contract. Many a contract can be beaten by using this bidding device. Wolff ended in 4♠ and West duly led the ♣7. How would you have played the contract?

    Wolff rose with dummy's ♣A and laid down the ♠A. It was unlikely that West held the ♠K, so he was not inclined to take a trump finesse. In any case, there was no convenient entry to his hand. The defenders followed with low cards and Wolff continued with a low club to East's king. Mouiel cashed the ♠K and exited with a third round of clubs. Wolff discarded a heart on this trick and returned to his hand with a trump to ruff his remaining diamond, eliminating the suit. These cards remained:

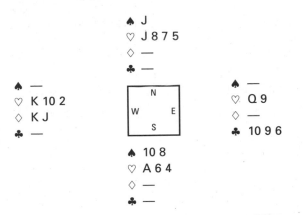

```
                    ♠ J
                    ♡ J 8 7 5
                    ◇ —
                    ♣ —
  ♠ —                              ♠ —
  ♡ K 10 2          ┌─────────┐     ♡ Q 9
  ◇ K J             │    N    │     ◇ —
  ♣ —               │ W     E │     ♣ 10 9 6
                    │    S    │
                    └─────────┘
                    ♠ 10 8
                    ♡ A 6 4
                    ◇ —
                    ♣ —
```

When Wolff cashed the ♡A, East had no counter. He chose to follow with the
♡9, but then had to win the second round of hearts with the queen. The
ensuing ruff-and-sluff allowed declarer to throw the last heart from his hand
and the game was made. If East unblocks the ♡Q (or West rises with the ♡K
to swallow his partner's ♡Q), declarer will score the game-going trick with
dummy's ♡J.

Teams from Belgium and the Netherlands met in the 1996 Forbo
International teams, contested in The Hague. Hans Gelders of Belgium sat
South on this deal:

```
North-South Vul.          ♠ K 4 2
Dealer North              ♡ 9 8 4 3
                          ◇ 5 2
                          ♣ A K 9 4
     ♠ 10 6 5          ┌─────────┐     ♠ A Q 7 3
     ♡ 7 5             │    N    │     ♡ K 6
     ◇ A Q J 9 4       │ W     E │     ◇ 10 8 7 3
     ♣ 7 6 3           │    S    │     ♣ 8 5 2
                       └─────────┘
                          ♠ J 9 8
                          ♡ A Q J 10 2
                          ◇ K 6
                          ♣ Q J 10
```

West	North	East	South
			Gelders
	pass	pass	1♡
pass	2NT	pass	4♡
all pass			

North's 2NT showed an invitational heart raise. How would you play the heart
game when West leads the ♣6?

Gelders won with the ♣A and ran the ♡9 successfully. Another round of trumps disclosed the 2-2 break. The contract can be guaranteed from this point. Do you see how?

At the other table, the Dutch declarer failed to spot the best line. He cashed three more club winners, throwing a spade from his hand. With the opponents' high cards ill-disposed, he could not then avoid four losers in the pointed suits.

Gelders also played the remaining three club winners, but he threw the ◇6 from his hand. He then played a diamond to the king and ace. West returned the ◇Q, ruffed by declarer, who could then run the ♠J or the ♠9 into the East hand. Even if East could win the trick cheaply, he would have to continue spades, establishing dummy's ♠K, or give declarer a ruff-and-sluff. It would not do West any good to cover the first round of spades, of course, since declarer could then establish a spade trick by force.

NOW TRY THESE...

A.

    ♠ K 10 4 2
    ♡ A 8
    ◇ K J 8 2
    ♣ 9 4 3

♡ Q led

```
      N
  W       E
      S
```

    ♠ A Q J 7 6 5
    ♡ 4
    ◇ A 9 3
    ♣ A K J

West	North	East	South
			1♠
pass	3♠	pass	4NT
pass	5♡	pass	6♠
all pass			

West leads the ♡Q against your small slam. How will you play it?

B.

    ♠ A Q J 3
    ♡ 7 5 2
    ◇ 6 2
    ♣ 7 6 4 3

◇ K led

```
      N
  W       E
      S
```

    ♠ K 10 7 5 4
    ♡ K Q 6
    ◇ A 3
    ♣ A K 9

West	North	East	South
			1♠
2♠	3♠	pass	4♠
all pass			

West's 2♠ was a Michaels cuebid, showing at least 5-5 shape in hearts and one of the minors. How will you play the spade game when West leads the ◇K?

C.

    ♠ Q 8
    ♡ 10 8 7 5
    ◇ K Q 7
    ♣ K Q 9 7

◇ J led

```
      N
  W       E
      S
```

    ♠ A 5 3
    ♡ A K Q J 4
    ◇ A 5 2
    ♣ J 5

West	North	East	South
			1♡
1♠	2♠	pass	3◇
pass	4♡	pass	6♡
all pass			

How will you tackle the heart slam when West leads the ◇J?

D.

    ♠ A K 8 3
    ♡ K 9 7 6 4
    ◇ A Q
    ♣ K J

♠Q led

```
      N
  W       E
      S
```

    ♠ 6 5 4
    ♡ A Q J 10 2
    ◇ 10 5
    ♣ A 9 2

West	North	East	South
			1♡
pass	2NT	pass	4♡
pass	4NT	pass	5♠
pass	6♡	all pass	

North responds with a Jacoby 2NT, showing a strong raise in hearts. You indi-
cate a minimum hand with no singleton or void, but he persists to a small slam
nevertheless. How will you play this contract when West leads the ♠Q?

Answers ✏

A.

```
                 ♠ K 10 4 2
                 ♡ A 8
                 ◇ K J 8 2
                 ♣ 9 4 3
  ♠ 9 3                          ♠ 8
  ♡ Q J 10 7 2      N           ♡ K 9 6 5 3
  ◇ 6 4          W     E        ◇ Q 10 7 5
  ♣ Q 7 6 2         S           ♣ 10 8 5
                 ♠ A Q J 7 6 5
                 ♡ 4
                 ◇ A 9 3
                 ♣ A K J
```

West	North	East	South
			1♠
pass	3♠	pass	4NT
pass	5♡	pass	6♠
all pass			

West leads the ♡Q, won with dummy's ace. How will you play the slam?

The contract is 100% with the help of elimination play. You ruff a heart high at Trick 2, eliminating that suit, and draw trumps with the ace and king. Next, you play a diamond to the nine, finessing towards the defender who will be endplayed if the finesse loses.

Suppose West holds the ◇10 and wins the trick. However the cards lie, he cannot return a diamond or a club without giving you a twelfth trick. (A third round of hearts would give you a ruff-and-sluff, of course.) As the cards lie in the diagram, a finesse of the ◇9 will succeed, ending your problems. If East were to split his diamond honors, you would win and gain an easy extra trick in the diamond suit.

B.

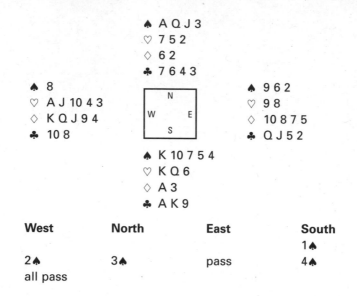

♠ A Q J 3
♡ 7 5 2
◇ 6 2
♣ 7 6 4 3

♠ 8
♡ A J 10 4 3
◇ K Q J 9 4
♣ 10 8

♠ 9 6 2
♡ 9 8
◇ 10 8 7 5
♣ Q J 5 2

♠ K 10 7 5 4
♡ K Q 6
◇ A 3
♣ A K 9

West	North	East	South
			1♠
2♠	3♠	pass	4♠
all pass			

West's 2♠ is a Michaels cuebid, showing hearts and one of the minors. How will you play the spade game when West leads the ◇K?

You might as well duck the opening lead to break communications between the defenders. You win the diamond continuation and draw trumps in three rounds. Your aim now is to strip West of his clubs and endplay him in hearts. Just in case East holds the ♡A, you play the ♡K before cashing your two top clubs. Suppose first that West wins and returns the ♡J. You will win with the ♡Q, cash the two top clubs and eliminate-exit with your last heart. West will then have to win and give you a ruff-and-sluff, allowing you to ditch your club loser.

What if West allows the ♡K to win? You will play the ♣A-K, leaving:

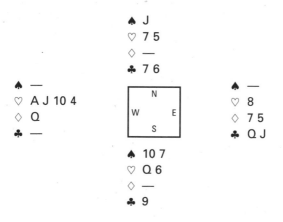

♠ J
♡ 7 5
◇ —
♣ 7 6

♠ —
♡ A J 10 4
◇ Q
♣ —

♠ —
♡ 8
◇ 7 5
♣ Q J

♠ 10 7
♡ Q 6
◇ —
♣ 9

You play the ♡Q to ensure that it is West who wins. He can cash a third heart, but he will then have to play one of the red suits, giving you a ruff-and-sluff.

c.

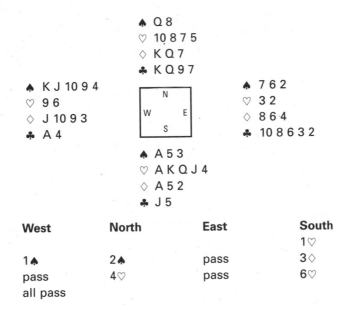

	♠ Q 8		
	♡ 10 8 7 5		
	◇ K Q 7		
	♣ K Q 9 7		

♠ K J 10 9 4
♡ 9 6
◇ J 10 9 3
♣ A 4

♠ 7 6 2
♡ 3 2
◇ 8 6 4
♣ 10 8 6 3 2

♠ A 5 3
♡ A K Q J 4
◇ A 5 2
♣ J 5

West	North	East	South
			1♡
1♠	2♠	pass	3◇
pass	4♡	pass	6♡
all pass			

West leads the ◇J against your small slam in hearts. How will you play the contract?

You have a certain club loser and must try to avoid a spade loser somehow. The main chance will be to find West with the ♣10. In that case, you will be able to score three club tricks and discard the two low spades in your hand. Can you see an extra chance?

You can also make the contract when West holds a doubleton ♣A. You win the diamond lead in dummy, draw trumps in two rounds with the ace and king and then lead the ♣5 towards dummy. If West rises with the ♣A, you will have the three club tricks you need for two spade discards. Let's say that West plays low instead and you win with dummy's ♣K. You play your remaining diamond winners, ending in the South hand, and lead the ♣J. West wins with the bare ♣A and is endplayed. A fourth round of diamonds will give you a ruff-and-sluff. His only alternative is to lead a spade into your split tenace.

As you see, West playing low on the first round from his ♣A-x would have cost the contract if you held two low clubs. It is better defense for West to rise with the ace, hoping that his partner holds the ♣J.

D.

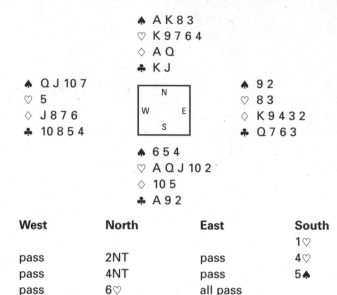

	♠ A K 8 3	
	♡ K 9 7 6 4	
	◇ A Q	
	♣ K J	
♠ Q J 10 7		♠ 9 2
♡ 5		♡ 8 3
◇ J 8 7 6		◇ K 9 4 3 2
♣ 10 8 5 4		♣ Q 7 6 3
	♠ 6 5 4	
	♡ A Q J 10 2	
	◇ 10 5	
	♣ A 9 2	

West	North	East	South
			1♡
pass	2NT	pass	4♡
pass	4NT	pass	5♠
pass	6♡	all pass	

How will you play the heart slam when West leads the ♠Q?

You have finessing possibilities in both of the minor suits, but such mundane mechanisms can wait. Perhaps you can endplay East with a doubleton ♠9 (or ♠10)! You win the opening lead with dummy's ♠A, draw trumps in two rounds and lead a second round of spades towards dummy. Let's say that West follows with the ♠7. You cover with the ♠8 and East wins with the ♠9. As the cards lie, he has no spade to return. If he returns either minor suit, he will give you an extra trick and spare you any further loser.

It will not help West to rise with the jack or ten of spades on the second round, of course. You would win with the ♠K, noting with interest the fall of East's ♠9. Subsequently, you could lead towards the ♠8 to set up a discard for your potential diamond loser.

Suppose the opening lead had been from ♠Q-J-7 and East held ♠10-9-2. East would not have been endplayed, but after his spade return you would have a diamond discard on dummy's thirteenth spade.

CHAPTER 3

Loser-on-Loser Elimination Play

Sometimes an elimination play will succeed only if you can throw a particular defender on lead. For example, suppose you have an ace-queen tenace in your hand. It will not help you to throw in your right-hand opponent because he can lead through the tenace; you would need the king to be onside anyway. Throw in the left-hand opponent, forcing a lead into your ace-queen, and it is a different story. In this chapter, we will look at one of the main ways in which you can direct your throw-in to a particular defender — the loser-on-loser elimination play.

Only one defender can beat the throw-in card by rank

We will begin with a straightforward example where your chosen victim has to win the throw-in trick because only he holds a card high enough to beat the throw-in card.

North-South Vul.
Dealer South

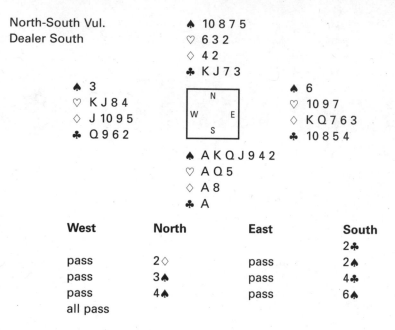

```
                        ♠ 10 8 7 5
                        ♡ 6 3 2
                        ◇ 4 2
                        ♣ K J 7 3
    ♠ 3                                    ♠ 6
    ♡ K J 8 4           N                  ♡ 10 9 7
    ◇ J 10 9 5       W     E               ◇ K Q 7 6 3
    ♣ Q 9 6 2           S                  ♣ 10 8 5 4
                        ♠ A K Q J 9 4 2
                        ♡ A Q 5
                        ◇ A 8
                        ♣ A
```

West	North	East	South
			2♣
pass	2◇	pass	2♠
pass	3♠	pass	4♣
pass	4♠	pass	6♠
all pass			

North's raise to 3♠ (rather than the weaker move of 4♠) suggested a useful card in his hand. When he could not cuebid a red-suit king at the four-level, South concluded that he must hold the ♣K. This would be good for a diamond discard and the slam would then depend on a heart finesse at worst. How would you play the spade slam when West leads the ◇J?

You win with the ace of diamonds, cash the club ace and cross to the eight of trumps, both defenders following. You can then cash the king of clubs, throwing your diamond loser, and ruff dummy's last diamond with a trump honor. Next you cross to the seven of trumps and ruff a club high. The queen does not appear, but you will have the chance to throw in West should he hold the ♣Q. You overtake the nine of trumps with the ten, reaching dummy once more, and these cards remain:

```
                        ♠ 5
                        ♡ 6 3 2
                        ◇ —
                        ♣ J
    ♠ —                                    ♠ —
    ♡ K J 8             N                  ♡ 10 9 7
    ◇ 10             W     E               ◇ K
    ♣ Q                  S                 ♣ 10
                        ♠ A K
                        ♡ A Q 5
                        ◇ —
                        ♣ —
```

When you lead the ♣J, East follows with the ♣10 and you discard a heart from your hand — a loser-on-loser play. West wins with the club queen and is end-played. A heart return will be into your ace-queen tenace, while a diamond return will give you a ruff-and-sluff. If East had produced the club queen, you would ruff and exit with a low heart, forcing the opponents to give you a chance to finesse the heart queen.

Suppose the ♣J and ♣10 had been swapped. To beat the contract, West would have to ditch the ♣Q on an early round of the suit. When you attempt-ed the loser-on-loser play, leading dummy's ♣10 on the fourth round, East could then win with the ♣J.

Only one defender has cards left in the throw-in suit

Suppose you hold a side suit of ◇A-9-6-5 in dummy opposite a singleton ◇4 in your hand. You cash the ◇A and ruff two diamonds in your hand. If your left-hand opponent began with five diamonds, he will have to win the fourth round of diamonds as you make a loser-on-loser play. His partner, by this time, will have no cards left in the suit. Here is a full example of such a play:

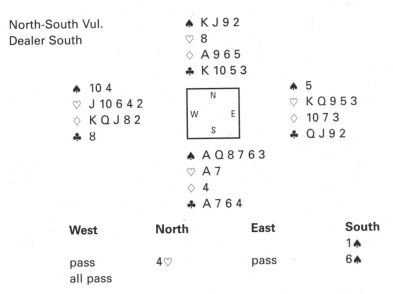

North-South Vul.
Dealer South

♠ K J 9 2
♡ 8
◇ A 9 6 5
♣ K 10 5 3

♠ 10 4
♡ J 10 6 4 2
◇ K Q J 8 2
♣ 8

♠ 5
♡ K Q 9 5 3
◇ 10 7 3
♣ Q J 9 2

♠ A Q 8 7 6 3
♡ A 7
◇ 4
♣ A 7 6 4

West	North	East	South
			1♠
pass	4♡	pass	6♠
all pass			

Right, we'll give you a bidding prize for the efficient splinter-bid auction. West leads the ◇K against the small slam. Can you also win a play prize for making the contract?

The contract is easy when clubs break 3-2. The same is true if West holds four clubs, since you can cash the ♣A and lead a club towards dummy, covering West's card. What if East holds four clubs? You may then survive with the aid of a loser-on-loser play.

You win the diamond lead and draw trumps with the ace and king. You ruff a diamond in your hand, cash the ♡A and ruff a heart in the dummy. Another diamond ruff in your hand removes East's last card in the suit. You now play the ♣A and lead another club, planning to insert dummy's ♣10 if West follows with a low card. No, West shows out. You rise with dummy's ♣K and survey this end position:

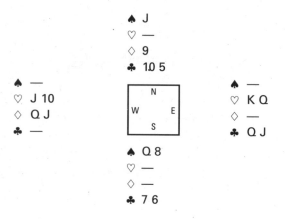

You lead the ◇9 and throw a club, a loser-on-loser play. Since East has no diamonds left, West has to win and must then deliver a ruff-and-sluff.

Discarding the third card from a 4-3 side suit

When you have a side suit such as A-x-x-x opposite K-x-x, there may be some benefit in discarding the third card from the three-card holding via a loser-on-loser play. When the side suit breaks 3-3, for example, you might then be able to establish the thirteenth card with a ruff. Let's see some examples of this technique:

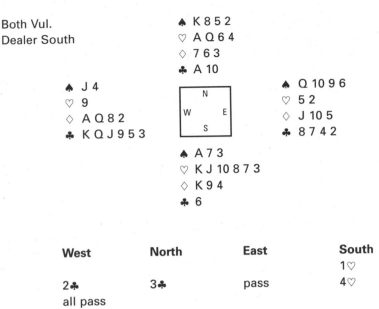

Both Vul.
Dealer South

North
♠ K 8 5 2
♡ A Q 6 4
◇ 7 6 3
♣ A 10

West
♠ J 4
♡ 9
◇ A Q 8 2
♣ K Q J 9 5 3

East
♠ Q 10 9 6
♡ 5 2
◇ J 10 5
♣ 8 7 4 2

South
♠ A 7 3
♡ K J 10 8 7 3
◇ K 9 4
♣ 6

West	North	East	South
			1♡
2♣	3♣	pass	4♡
all pass			

How will you play the heart game when West leads the ♣K?

First, let's see how the original declarer went down. Quite rightly, he expected West to hold the ◇A as part of his vulnerable overcall. There was a chance to discard a diamond loser if spades broke 3-3. Simply playing ace, king and another spade was risky because East might win the third round and lead through the ◇K. Declarer therefore ducked the ♣K lead and won the club continuation, discarding a spade. After drawing trumps, he played the ace and king of spades and ruffed a spade. It was clever play up to a point, since he would indeed have made the contract if spades had broken 3-3; however, they failed to oblige and he went one down.

A better line is a loser-on-loser elimination play, which will give you the contract when West holds three or fewer spades. You win the club lead, draw trumps and cash the ace and king of spades. You then lead the ♣10, throwing the last spade from the South hand, and West has to win the trick. Since he began with only two spades, he will have to lead a diamond or give you a ruff-and-sluff. If the spades were 3-3 all along, West could exit safely with a spade. You would then ruff in your hand and dummy's thirteenth spade would be established for a discard.

When the longer holding in the 4-3 side suit includes the jack or ten, your chances become even better. You may succeed even when the throw-in victim holds four cards in the suit. Look at the diamond suit in this similar deal:

Both Vul.
Dealer South

```
                      ♠ A 9 6 4
                      ♡ Q 10 2
                      ◇ A 10 4 3
                      ♣ 10 2
   ♠ K Q J 10 8                        ♠ 7 5 2
   ♡ 4                 ┌─────────┐     ♡ 9 5
   ◇ J 9 8 6          │    N    │     ◇ Q 5
   ♣ K 9 5           │ W     E │     ♣ J 8 7 6 4 3
                      │    S    │
                      └─────────┘
                      ♠ 3
                      ♡ A K J 8 7 6 3
                      ◇ K 7 2
                      ♣ A Q
```

West	North	East	South
			1♡
1♠	2♠	pass	4NT
pass	5♠	pass	6♡
all pass			

How will you play the small slam in hearts when West leads the ♠K?

You win with the ♠A and ruff a spade in the South hand. After drawing trumps with the ace and queen, you ruff another spade in your hand. Next, you cash the king and ace of diamonds, the queen appearing from East. This position is left:

```
                      ♠ 9
                      ♡ 10
                      ◇ 10 4
                      ♣ 10 2
   ♠ Q                                 ♠ —
   ♡ —                 ┌─────────┐     ♡ —
   ◇ J 9              │    N    │     ◇ —
   ♣ K 9 5           │ W     E │     ♣ J 8 7 6 4 3
                      │    S    │
                      └─────────┘
                      ♠ —
                      ♡ J 8 7
                      ◇ 7
                      ♣ A Q
```

If you ruff dummy's last spade now and lead towards the ◇10, East would enjoy the moment if he had falsecarded the queen from ◇Q-J-9-5! Instead, you should lead the ♠9 and throw the ◇7 from your hand (a loser-on-loser play). West wins with the ♠Q and you will make the contract however the diamond suit lies. After the fall of East's ◇Q, any diamond play from West will establish a trick for dummy's ◇10. A club exit will be into your tenace and a spade exit, if West still has one, would give you a ruff-and-sluff.

The presence of the ◇10 in dummy meant that the loser-on-loser play would succeed if West had started with ◇Q-x-x-x or ◇J-x-x-x. It would fail only when West had begun with ◇Q-J-x-x.

Transferring the guard to direct the throw-in

The maneuver known as 'transferring the guard' from one defender to the other is familiar in the world of squeezes. The same idea can be used when you have an endplay in mind and the wrong defender currently holds the top card or cards in the throw-in suit. Look at the diamonds on this deal:

Both Vul.
Dealer South

```
              ♠ A 7 4 3
              ♡ A 5 4
              ◇ Q J 7
              ♣ 7 5 4
♠ J 2                        ♠ 10 9 8 6
♡ 3              N           ♡ 7 2
◇ 10 9 8 6 4 3   W     E     ◇ A K 5 2
♣ K 9 8 2        S           ♣ J 10 6
              ♠ K Q 5
              ♡ K Q J 10 9 8 6
              ◇ —
              ♣ A Q 3
```

West	North	East	South
			1♡
pass	1♠	pass	3♣
pass	3♡	pass	5◇
pass	5NT	pass	6◇
pass	6♡	all pass	

South's 5◇ was Exclusion Blackwood, asking for keycards outside the diamond suit. North's 5NT (the equivalent of 5♡ over 4NT) showed two such keycards and 6◇ asked for side-suit kings, again excluding diamonds. When North denied the ♣K, the bidding ground to a halt in 6♡. How would you play this contract when West leads the ◇10?

You cover with dummy's ◇Q, East playing the ◇K. After ruffing in your hand, you draw trumps with the king and ace. Dummy's ◇J forces East to cover with the ace and you ruff in your hand. Do you see the purpose of this maneuver in diamonds? You have transferred the diamond guard to West. Now only West can beat dummy's ◇7 and you are moving towards a throw-in position.

When you play the king, queen and ace of spades, the suit fails to break 3-3. No matter! You lead the ◇7, throwing the ♣3 from your hand (a loser-on-loser play). West wins and must lead into your club tenace or give you a ruff-and-sluff.

Suppose you swap the North and South club holdings, West again leading the ◇10 against your heart slam. You would then ruff the ◇7 on the second round of the suit, planning to throw East on lead with dummy's ◇J on the third round.

Playing the throw-in suit correctly

On the next deal you have the chance of a loser-on-loser play, using the fourth round of diamonds to achieve the throw-in. You must calculate carefully how to play the early rounds of the diamond suit.

East-West Vul.
Dealer South

```
                  ♠ J 7 5 4 2
                  ♡ 9 8 4
                  ◇ J 3
                  ♣ 7 4 2
  ♠ 6 3                          ♠ —
  ♡ A Q 10 6          N          ♡ K J 7 5 3 2
  ◇ K 10 8 6    W         E      ◇ 9 5 2
  ♣ K 9 5           S            ♣ J 10 8 6
                  ♠ A K Q 10 9 8
                  ♡ —
                  ◇ A Q 7 4
                  ♣ A Q 3
```

West	North	East	South
			2♣
pass	2◇	pass	2♠
pass	4♠	pass	6♠
all pass			

North's leap to 4♠ (rather than the stronger move of 3♠) suggests a hand that is lacking in controls. Turning a blind eye to the five potential losers in the minor suits, you leap to the six-level nevertheless. How will you play the slam when West leads the ♠3?

All will be easy when East holds the ♣K, since the diamond suit can provide a discard for dummy's remaining club loser. What are your chances when West holds the ♣K? If your idea is to run the ◇J, using the ♠J as an entry, you will go down however the diamonds are placed. A much better idea is to lead towards the ◇J, which will allow an elimination play to succeed when West holds the ◇K. In the dangerous case where the ♣K is offside, you will then have a 50% chance of making the contract rather than no chance.

You win the trump lead with dummy's jack and ruff a heart, beginning the elimination process. You then draw West's second trump and lead a diamond towards the jack. If West rises with the ◇K, you will have two discards for dummy's club losers and make the slam easily. Let's say that West plays low instead and the ◇J wins. Taking advantage of the entry to dummy, you ruff another heart. When you continue with the ◇A and a diamond ruff, West's ◇K does not fall. You are in dummy again, however, and can ruff dummy's last heart, eliminating the suit. These cards remain:

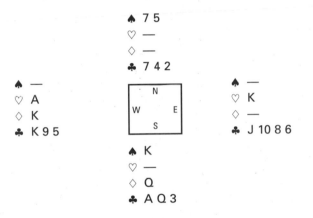

```
              ♠ 7 5
              ♡ —
              ◇ —
              ♣ 7 4 2
♠ —                        ♠ —
♡ A          ┌─────────┐   ♡ K
◇ K          │    N    │   ◇ —
♣ K 9 5      │ W     E │   ♣ J 10 8 6
             │    S    │
             └─────────┘
              ♠ K
              ♡ —
              ◇ Q
              ♣ A Q 3
```

You have worked hard and are about to receive a big paycheck. You lead the ◇Q to West's ◇K and discard a club from dummy, a loser-on-loser play. West has to return a club into your tenace or give you a ruff-and-sluff. The slam is yours.

The stars come out to play

loser-on-loser elimination play ⭐

The first deal in this 'all stars' section comes from the A-final of the 1999 Forbo-Krommenie teams. Teams from the Netherlands and Sweden faced each other and this was the layout:

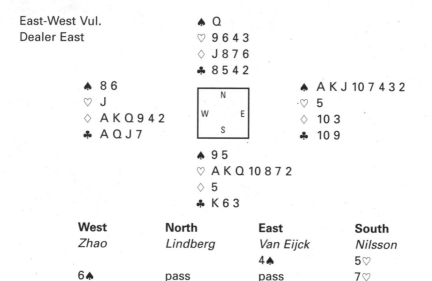

East-West Vul.
Dealer East

```
                          ♠ Q
                          ♡ 9 6 4 3
                          ◇ J 8 7 6
                          ♣ 8 5 4 2
      ♠ 8 6                              ♠ A K J 10 7 4 3 2
      ♡ J                  N             ♡ 5
      ◇ A K Q 9 4 2    W       E         ◇ 10 3
      ♣ A Q J 7            S             ♣ 10 9
                          ♠ 9 5
                          ♡ A K Q 10 8 7 2
                          ◇ 5
                          ♣ K 6 3
```

West	North	East	South
Zhao	*Lindberg*	*Van Eijck*	*Nilsson*
		4♠	5♡
6♠	pass	pass	7♡
dbl	all pass		

Nilsson decided to trust his opponents' bidding, a policy that is not always wise. He was on the money here, though, with 6♠ an easy make. West cashed the ◇K and switched to the ♠8, won by East. A club switch seems to be indicated and would indeed have picked up the 1100 that was the defenders' due. No, East preferred to lead a second round of diamonds. As declarer, how would you have taken advantage of this slip?

Nilsson ruffed in his hand and drew trumps. After ruffing a spade in dummy, he ruffed a third round of diamonds in his hand, East showing out. He then returned to dummy with a trump and led the ◇J, throwing a club from his hand (a loser-on-loser play). West won the trick and then had to open the club suit or give a ruff-and-sluff. Either way, the penalty was reduced to just 800. The auction at the other table was 4♠-5♡-5♠, with East-West collecting just 680. Nilsson's play reduced a potential 9-IMP loss into a 3-IMP loss.

In 2002, Canada won the Commonwealth Nations Bridge Championship. This fine deal comes from an exhibition match played a day or two later.

North-South Vul.
Dealer North

		♠ K 5 3 2	
		♡ A J 10 8	
		◇ K 7 2	
		♣ K 9	

♠ 7		♠ J 9 8 6
♡ K 9 5	N	♡ Q 7 6
◇ J 9 5 3	W E	◇ A Q 4
♣ Q J 8 6 5	S	♣ 10 7 3

	♠ A Q 10 4	
	♡ 4 3 2	
	◇ 10 8 6	
	♣ A 4 2	

West	North	East	South
Armstrong	*N.Gartaganis*	*Forrester*	*J.Gartaganis*
	1♣	pass	1♠
pass	2♠	pass	2NT
pass	3♣	pass	3NT
pass	4♠	all pass	

John Armstrong led the ♣Q and Judith Gartaganis won with dummy's king. A spade to the ace allowed her to lead a heart towards dummy. All would have been easy if West had followed with a low card, but Armstrong defended strongly by rising with the ♡K, forcing dummy's ♡A.

Declarer cashed the ♠K, discovering the 4-1 trump break, and continued with the ♡J. Anxious to avoid a later throw-in, Forrester took his ♡Q immediately and exited with a third round of hearts. It had been an immaculate defense, but declarer proved equal to it. She took a marked finesse of the ♠10, cashed the ♣A and ruffed a club. The lead was in dummy and these cards remained:

		♠ —	
		♡ 8	
		◇ K 7 2	
		♣ —	

♠ —		♠ J
♡ —	N	♡ —
◇ J 9 5	W E	◇ A Q 4
♣ Q	S	♣ —

	♠ Q	
	♡ —	
	◇ 10 8 6	
	♣ —	

When the ♡8 was led, Forrester ruffed with the ♠J in the East seat. Instead of overruffing, which would have resulted in defeat, declarer discarded a diamond (a loser-on-loser play). Forrester had to concede a trick to dummy's ◇K and the spade game was made.

NOW TRY THESE...

A.

    ♠ A Q 8 5
    ♡ A 6 4
    ◇ A K 6 2
    ♣ A 10

```
      N
   W     E
      S
```

♡ 10 led

    ♠ K J 10 9 7 6
    ♡ 3
    ◇ 10 5 4 3
    ♣ K 7

West	North	East	South
		3♡	pass
pass	dbl	pass	4♠
pass	6♠	all pass	

How will you tackle the spade slam when West leads the ♡10?

B.

    ♠ K J 10 7 4
    ♡ A
    ◇ A Q 8 5
    ♣ Q 5 2

```
      N
   W     E
      S
```

♣10 led

    ♠ A Q 9 5
    ♡ J 3
    ◇ 7 6 4
    ♣ A K J 7

West	North	East	South
			1NT
pass	2♡	pass	2♠
pass	3◇	pass	3♠
pass	6♠	all pass	

How will you play 6♠ when West leads the ♣10? (You will find that the trumps break 2-2.)

C.

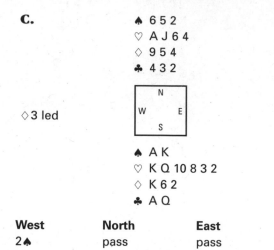

```
            ♠ 6 5 2
            ♡ A J 6 4
            ◊ 9 5 4
            ♣ 4 3 2
                ┌─────────┐
                │    N    │
◊ 3 led         │ W     E │
                │    S    │
                └─────────┘
            ♠ A K
            ♡ K Q 10 8 3 2
            ◊ K 6 2
            ♣ A Q
```

West	North	East	South
2♠	pass	pass	4♡
all pass			

West leads the ◊3 to East's ace. You cover the ◊Q return with the king and West ruffs. How will you continue when West switches to the ♠Q?

D.

```
            ♠ 10 8 5 4
            ♡ 9 5 2
            ◊ A 10
            ♣ 8 4 3 2
                ┌─────────┐
                │    N    │
♡K led          │ W     E │
                │    S    │
                └─────────┘
            ♠ A K Q J 7 3
            ♡ A
            ◊ K 7
            ♣ A Q 6 5
```

West	North	East	South
3♡	pass	pass	4♠
pass	5◊	pass	6♠
all pass			

Yes, your partner has faith in you! How will you play the spade slam when West leads the ♡K?

Answers ✐

A.

```
              ♠ A Q 8 5
              ♡ A 6 4
              ◇ A K 6 2
              ♣ A 10
♠ 2                           ♠ 4 3
♡ 10 9          N             ♡ K Q J 8 7 5 2
◇ Q J 9 8    W     E          ◇ 7
♣ J 9 5 4 3 2    S            ♣ Q 8 6
              ♠ K J 10 9 7 6
              ♡ 3
              ◇ 10 5 4 3
              ♣ K 7
```

West	North	East	South
		3♡	pass
pass	dbl	pass	4♠
pass	6♠	all pass	

How will you tackle the spade slam when West leads the ♡10?

You win with dummy's ♡A and draw trumps in two rounds. All will be well if diamonds break 3-2 and your next move therefore is to cash the ace and king of that suit. When East shows out on the second round, it seems that you have two certain losers in the diamond suit. How can you resolve the problem?

You should plan to throw in East at a time when he will have to give you a ruff-and-sluff. You ruff a heart in your hand and continue with the king and ace of clubs. Next, you throw East on lead with a third round of hearts, discarding a diamond from your hand. This is a loser-on-loser play. You lead one loser (dummy's last heart) and discard another loser (a diamond). The play gains nothing directly, but East will have to give you a trick with his return.

East's remaining cards are three hearts and the ♣Q. The return of any of these cards will give you a ruff-and-sluff. You will discard the last diamond from your hand and ruff in the dummy.

The winning play was possible only because East held seven hearts to West's two, as suggested by his opening preemptive bid. Had West held three or more hearts, the defenders could have arranged for him (rather than East) to win the third round of the suit. He would then have been able to cash a diamond winner.

B.

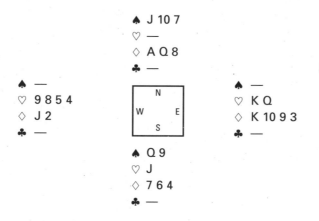

♠ K J 10 7 4
♥ A
♦ A Q 8 5
♣ Q 5 2

♠ 8 2
♥ 9 8 5 4 2
♦ J 2
♣ 10 9 8 3

♠ 6 3
♥ K Q 10 7 6
♦ K 10 9 3
♣ 6 4

♠ A Q 9 5
♥ J 3
♦ 7 6 4
♣ A K J 7

West	North	East	South
			1NT
pass	2♥	pass	2♠
pass	3♦	pass	3♠
pass	6♠	all pass	

North's 3♦ is forcing to game and South's 3♠ is more encouraging than a jump to 4♠ would have been. How will you play 6♠ when West leads the ♣10?

You win with the ♣A and play the ace and king of trumps, finding that the trump suit breaks 2-2. You cash the ♥A and continue with three more rounds of clubs, throwing a diamond from dummy. These cards remain:

♠ J 10 7
♥ —
♦ A Q 8
♣ —

♠ —
♥ 9 8 5 4
♦ J 2
♣ —

♠ —
♥ K Q
♦ K 10 9 3
♣ —

♠ Q 9
♥ J
♦ 7 6 4
♣ —

Suppose you ruff your last heart now, return to your hand with a third round of trumps and lead a diamond, intending to play dummy's ♦8 to endplay East. West can defeat you by rising with the ♦J!

When you lead the ♥J, intending to ruff in the dummy, you must halt in your tracks when West does not cover the ♥J. Instead of ruffing, you should throw the ♦8 from dummy (a loser-on-loser play). East wins the trick and has no safe return.

C.

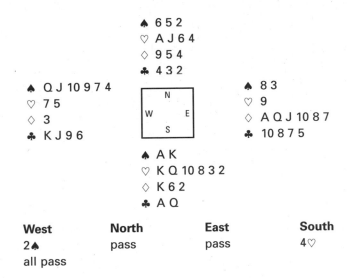

West	North	East	South
2♠	pass	pass	4♡
all pass			

West leads the ◇3 to East's ace. You cover the ◇Q return with the king and are disappointed to see West ruff. How will you continue when West switches to the ♠Q?

One possibility is to take an eventual club finesse, hoping to find East with the ♣K. It is not an attractive proposition. At the best of times, the play would require good luck. On this particular deal, West would have at most a 4-count if he did not hold the ♣K, so the club finesse is likely to fail. What else can you try?

The clue lies in the bidding. West's 2♠ opening strongly suggests a six-card spade suit. In that case, you can put West on lead with the third round of spades. You draw the outstanding trumps in one round and cash your other spade honor. You then cross to dummy with a trump and lead dummy's last spade. East shows out, as you expected, and you discard your remaining diamond. West wins the spade trick and is endplayed. He has only black cards in his hand. Since a spade will give you a ruff-and-discard, allowing you to ruff in the dummy and discard the ♣Q, he will no doubt switch to a club. With a modest yet masterly air, you table the ♣A-Q and claim the contract.

D.

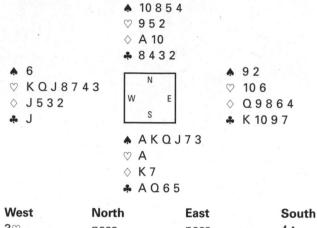

West	North	East	South
3♡	pass	pass	4♠
pass	5◇	pass	6♠
all pass			

Realizing that an ace is usually worth more than one trick, North makes a slam try. How will you play the resultant contract of 6♠ when West leads the ♡K?

You win the heart lead and draw trumps in two rounds with the ace and ten. A finesse of the ♣Q wins, West dropping the ♣J. When you continue with the ♣A, the good news dries up — West discards a heart. What now?

You can endplay West on the third round of hearts, forcing him to give you a ruff-and-sluff. You continue with the king and ace of diamonds, followed by a heart ruff with a top trump. You return to dummy by overtaking your last low trump. These cards are still out:

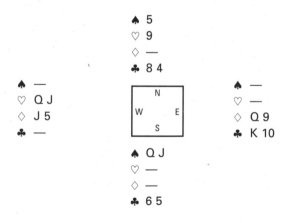

You lead the ♡9, throwing a club (a loser-on-loser play). West wins the trick and has to concede a ruff-and-sluff, allowing you to throw the last club from the South hand.

CHAPTER 4

Exiting in the Trump Suit

When your trumps are ♠A-9-7-5-3 opposite ♠K-8-6-2 and the suit breaks 3-1, you may be able to eliminate a couple of side suits and put a defender on lead with the third round of trumps. Nothing very special about that, you may be thinking. The very first deal of this book featured such a situation.

What if your trumps are ♡A-J-6-2 opposite ♡K-8-5-4? In a potential elimination setting, various interesting plays become possible. You may be able to eliminate a couple of side suits before playing the ♡K and finessing the ♡J. If this loses to a doubleton ♡Q, the defender may be endplayed. Alternatively, you may choose to play the ace and king of trumps. This will drop a doubleton queen offside, otherwise leaving you the chance of endplaying a defender who began with ♡Q-x-x. That sort of play is the subject of this chapter.

Declining a trump finesse

When you are missing three trumps to the king, it is usually right to finesse in the suit. Usually, yes, but not always! In an elimination setting, it may be a better idea to lay down the ace. If trumps break 2-1 but the king does not fall, you will then have the option of endplaying the defender who is left with the king. Look at this deal:

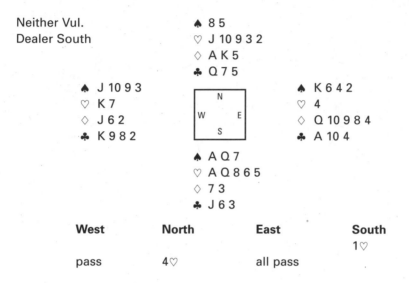

Neither Vul.
Dealer South

	♠ 8 5	
	♡ J 10 9 3 2	
	◇ A K 5	
	♣ Q 7 5	
♠ J 10 9 3		♠ K 6 4 2
♡ K 7		♡ 4
◇ J 6 2		◇ Q 10 9 8 4
♣ K 9 8 2		♣ A 10 4
	♠ A Q 7	
	♡ A Q 8 6 5	
	◇ 7 3	
	♣ J 6 3	

West	North	East	South
			1♡
pass	4♡	all pass	

West leads the ♠J and you win in hand with the ♠Q. Suppose you cross to dummy with a diamond and run the ♡J. You will make the contract when East holds the ♡K. If the finesse loses, you will have to play the club suit yourself and prospects will be poor. Is there a better line?

After winning the spade lead, you should cash the ♡A. If the ♡K falls singleton, you will be home and dry. When the ♡K does not fall and trumps break 2-1, you will eliminate spades and diamonds and exit with a trump. The defender who wins the trick will then have to make the first play in the club suit, guaranteeing you a trick there, or he will have to concede a ruff-and-sluff.

Playing in the recommended fashion gains against a singleton ♡K offside and a doubleton ♡K-7 or ♡K-4 offside. It loses (compared with a straightforward trump finesse) only when East holds ♡K-7-4. So in situations where your choice of play will make a difference, you will have odds of 3-to-1 in your favor.

You might make the same play when missing five trumps to the queen. Cash the ace and king of trumps. If the queen does not fall doubleton and trumps break 3-2, you plan to throw in the defender who is left with the bare queen of trumps.

Look at the next deal, a six-heart contract, and decide how you would have played the trump suit.

East-West Vul.
Dealer North

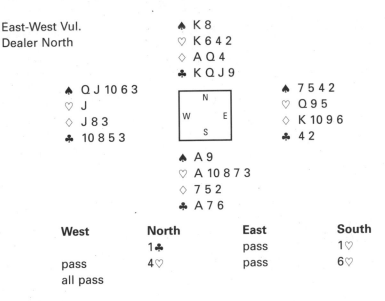

	♠ K 8	
	♡ K 6 4 2	
	◇ A Q 4	
	♣ K Q J 9	

♠ Q J 10 6 3   ♠ 7 5 4 2
♡ J   ♡ Q 9 5
◇ J 8 3   ◇ K 10 9 6
♣ 10 8 5 3   ♣ 4 2

♠ A 9
♡ A 10 8 7 3
◇ 7 5 2
♣ A 7 6

West	North	East	South
	1♣	pass	1♡
pass	4♡	pass	6♡
all pass			

West leads the ♠Q against your small slam. You win with dummy's king and play the ♡K, West dropping the ♡J. How will you continue?

The original declarer played a trump to the ten next, proudly informing the other three players that this was in accordance with Restricted Choice. He was amazed when no one congratulated him on his play. Do you see why?

Looking at the trump suit in isolation, declarer's play did indeed give him odds of 2-to-1 in his favor. However, had he played the ♡A on the second round, he would have given himself virtually a 100% chance of making the slam. Success would have been immediate if West had started with ♡Q-J and the trumps were picked up without loss. If instead the cards lay as in the diagram, East would have been left with the bare ♡Q. Declarer would cash the remaining spade honor, followed by four rounds of clubs for a diamond discard. If East declined to ruff any of the clubs, he would then be thrown on lead with a trump, forced to lead a diamond into dummy's tenace or concede a ruff-and-sluff.

Finessing into a bare trump honor

Even the best declarers take losing trump finesses and you may think there is nothing that can be done about it. Think again! Sometimes you can arrange that a defender will be endplayed if a trump finesse happens to lose to a bare honor. That is West's fate here:

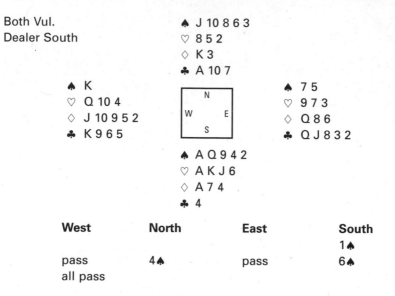

Both Vul.
Dealer South

♠ J 10 8 6 3
♡ 8 5 2
◇ K 3
♣ A 10 7

♠ K
♡ Q 10 4
◇ J 10 9 5 2
♣ K 9 6 5

♠ 7 5
♡ 9 7 3
◇ Q 8 6
♣ Q J 8 3 2

♠ A Q 9 4 2
♡ A K J 6
◇ A 7 4
♣ 4

West	North	East	South
			1♠
pass	4♠	pass	6♠
all pass			

How will you play the spade slam when West leads the ◇J?

You have finessing positions in both spades and hearts. How can you give yourself an extra edge in the case where both the ♠K and the ♡Q are offside? You should eliminate the minor suits before taking the trump finesse. West will then be endplayed if he happens to win with a singleton ♠K.

You win the diamond lead with the ace, cross to the ♣A and ruff a club. Re-entering dummy with the ◇K, you ruff dummy's last club with the ♠Q. You then ruff your diamond loser with the ♠8, everyone following. These cards remain:

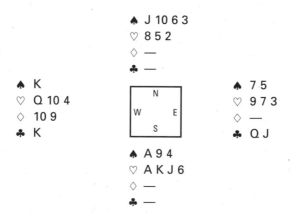

♠ J 10 6 3
♡ 8 5 2
◇ —
♣ —

♠ K
♡ Q 10 4
◇ 10 9
♣ K

♠ 7 5
♡ 9 7 3
◇ —
♣ Q J

♠ A 9 4
♡ A K J 6
◇ —
♣ —

With both minor suits eliminated, you run the ♠J. As it happens, the finesse loses, but West has no trump to return and is therefore endplayed. A heart will be into your tenace and a minor-suit return will give you a ruff-and-sluff.

If West had another trump to return, you would win in the dummy and take your remaining chance of the heart finesse. That's why you took one of the club ruffs with the ♠Q, to avoid being trapped in the South hand later.

Protecting yourself against a trump misguess

When you have a two-way guess for the queen of trumps, you may find that playing one particular defender for the queen will leave you an elimination play as a fallback should you guess wrongly. That's the case on this deal:

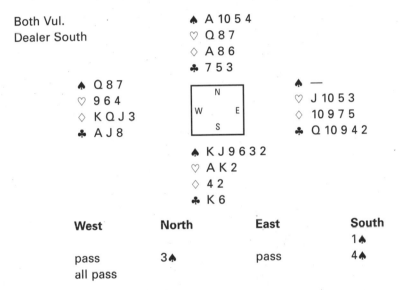

Both Vul.
Dealer South

	♠ A 10 5 4	
	♡ Q 8 7	
	◊ A 8 6	
	♣ 7 5 3	

♠ Q 8 7		♠ —
♡ 9 6 4		♡ J 10 5 3
◊ K Q J 3		◊ 10 9 7 5
♣ A J 8		♣ Q 10 9 4 2

	♠ K J 9 6 3 2	
	♡ A K 2	
	◊ 4 2	
	♣ K 6	

West	North	East	South
			1♠
pass	3♠	pass	4♠
all pass			

It is better than most of the contracts you reach, yes, but what is the safest line of play?

You can pick up a 3-0 break in the trump suit, provided you guess correctly which top honor to play first. Should you play the ♠A or the ♠K? It is better to play dummy's ♠A. If this turns out to be uninspired and West holds ♠Q-x-x, you will have a chance to catch West in an endplay.

Since you have no wish for East to gain the lead in diamonds to put a club through your king, you should duck the ◊K opening lead. You win the next round of diamonds with the ace and cash the ace of trumps. Not for the first time, you see that you have misguessed — East shows out. You draw a second round of trumps with the king, cross to the ♡Q and ruff dummy's last diamond. You then play your remaining two heart honors, not bothered whether West is able to ruff. When he follows suit, you throw him on lead with the trump queen and he has to give you a trick.

Suppose instead that you had played a low trump to your king after winning with the ◇A. If that proved to be a misguess, West showing out, no subsequent throw-in would assist you. You would make the contract only when the ♣A was onside.

Eliminating suits in the right order

When you are intending to put a defender on lead with a master trump, it may be important to eliminate two side suits in the right order. You cannot afford to have the defender ruff one of these suits and exit safely in the other suit. Look at this deal:

Both Vul.
Dealer South

```
              ♠ K 8 4 3
              ♡ A Q 8 5
              ◇ K 7 3
              ♣ J 6
♠ Q J 5                        ♠ 7 2
♡ 9 3            N              ♡ 10 6 4 2
◇ 9 8 5 2    W       E          ◇ J 10 4
♣ K 9 5 2        S             ♣ 10 8 7 4
              ♠ A 10 9 6
              ♡ K J 7
              ◇ A Q 6
              ♣ A Q 3
```

West	North	East	South
			2NT
pass	3♣	pass	3◇
pass	4◇	pass	4♠
pass	6♠	all pass	

A Puppet Stayman auction takes you to 6♠. (Your 3◇ denied a five-card major, but showed at least one four-card major. North's 4◇ indicated two four-card majors, allowing your good self to become the declarer.) How will you play the slam when West leads the ◇9?

You win the diamond lead and play the ace and king of trumps, both defenders following. The ♠Q is still out. If West holds that card, you may be able to throw him in with it, forcing him to lead a club or give you a ruff-and-sluff. First, you must remove West's cards in hearts and diamonds. Which red suit should you play first?

You can see from the diagram that cashing hearts first will cost the contract. West will ruff the third round with the ♠Q and exit safely in diamonds. When a subsequent club finesse loses, you will be one down. The winning line is to play two more rounds of diamonds first. West has to follow suit and you can then play your heart winners. You won't mind if West ruffs one of the hearts, because he will then have no safe exit card.

Why is it right to play diamonds first? Because you hold six cards in diamonds and seven cards in hearts. West is therefore slightly more likely to hold a doubleton heart than a doubleton diamond.

Retaining the top trump

Suppose you hold the ace of trumps and a defender may hold two trump tricks. Cashing the ace on the first round may prevent you from achieving a later endplay. You do better to concede one round of trumps, cash the ace next and eventually throw a defender in with the third round of trumps.

East-West Vul.
Dealer South

```
                    ♠ K 7
                    ♡ A 8 5 2
                    ◇ 8 4 2
                    ♣ A J 6 3
    ♠ Q J 10 4           N        ♠ 9 8 6 5 3
    ♡ K J 9                       ♡ 10 4
    ◇ K 9 5       W        E      ◇ J 10 6 3
    ♣ 10 7 5           S          ♣ 9 2
                    ♠ A 2
                    ♡ Q 7 6 3
                    ◇ A Q 7
                    ♣ K Q 8 4
```

West	North	East	South
			1NT
pass	2♣	pass	2♡
pass	4♡	all pass	

How will you play the heart game when West leads the ♠Q?

Suppose you win the spade lead and make the apparently natural continuation of cashing the ace of trumps. You will go down! When you play a second round of trumps to the queen and king, West will be able to cash the jack of trumps and exit safely in a black suit. You can eliminate the black suits and lead a diamond from dummy, but East will rise with the ◇J to prevent you from ducking the trick to West. Two losers in each red suit will put you one down.

A better line of play is to win the spade lead in dummy and lead a trump to the queen on the first round. You win West's round-suit return and cash the ace of trumps. You continue with your remaining spade winner, followed by four rounds of clubs. West will be in no hurry to ruff with his master trump and will discard on the fourth round of clubs. You can then throw him on lead with a trump, forcing him to lead into your diamond tenace or concede a ruff-and-sluff.

Here is another deal on the same theme:

```
North-South Vul.              ♠ K 10 7 5
Dealer South                  ♡ K 8 5
                              ◇ K Q 6
                              ♣ 8 4 2
         ♠ Q J 4        ┌─────────┐         ♠ 9
         ♡ A 9 3        │    N    │         ♡ 10 6 4 2
         ◇ 10 9 5       │ W     E │         ◇ 8 7 4 3
         ♣ A J 9 5      │    S    │         ♣ Q 10 7 3
                        └─────────┘
                              ♠ A 8 6 3 2
                              ♡ Q J 7
                              ◇ A J 2
                              ♣ K 6
```

West	North	East	South
			1♠
pass	3♠	pass	4♠
all pass			

West leads the ◇10 against your spade game. What is your plan?

You win the diamond lead and play the ♠A, no honor appearing. If your next move is a second round of trumps, you will go down. When West subsequently takes his ♡A, he will be able to cash his potentially embarrassing master trump and exit safely. You will then lose two tricks in the club suit.

Instead, you should retain dummy's top trump and knock out the ♡A. West can exit safely when he takes his heart trick, but after that he is doomed. You will play the ♠K, eliminate the red suits and endplay him on the third round of trumps. West will have to open the club suit, giving you a trick with the king, or deliver a ruff-and-sluff.

The stars come out to play:

Exiting in the trump suit

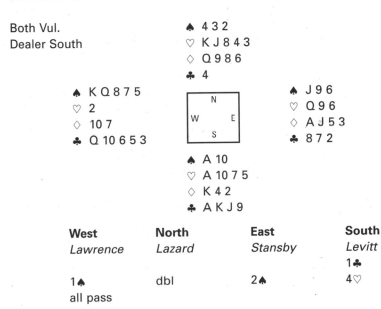

We will begin this section with a deal from the final of the 1967 Vanderbilt. It was a long time ago, yes, but some of you will recognize the names of the players involved.

Both Vul.
Dealer South

```
              ♠ 4 3 2
              ♡ K J 8 4 3
              ◇ Q 9 8 6
              ♣ 4
♠ K Q 8 7 5            ♠ J 9 6
♡ 2          N         ♡ Q 9 6
◇ 10 7    W     E      ◇ A J 5 3
♣ Q 10 6 5 3   S       ♣ 8 7 2
              ♠ A 10
              ♡ A 10 7 5
              ◇ K 4 2
              ♣ A K J 9
```

West	North	East	South
Lawrence	Lazard	Stansby	Levitt
			1♣
1♠	dbl	2♠	4♡
all pass			

Mike Lawrence led the ♠K and Paul Levitt allowed this to win. He won the low spade continuation, cashed the ♣A and ruffed a club. He then ruffed dummy's last spade, eliminating that suit.

A trump to the king was followed by a trump to the ten. As the cards lay, the finesse against the trump queen was successful. Declarer had his game with six trump tricks and four tricks in the side suits. Suppose the trump finesse had lost to a doubleton queen with West. He would then have been endplayed. A club return would be into the ♣K-J tenace and a spade would concede a ruff-and-sluff. West would therefore be forced to broach the diamonds and declarer could succeed by playing for the jack and ten to be in different hands. (If West switched to the ◇10, for example, declarer would cover with the ◇Q and subsequently finesse East for the ◇J.)

The next deal is slightly unusual because declarer could deduce that a finesse against the trump king was likely to lose. Taking advantage of this, he planned to endplay the defender who did hold the king of trumps.

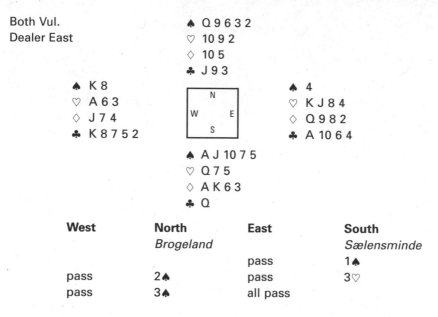

Both Vul.
Dealer East

	♠ Q 9 6 3 2
	♡ 10 9 2
	◇ 10 5
	♣ J 9 3

♠ K 8   ♠ 4
♡ A 6 3   ♡ K J 8 4
◇ J 7 4   ◇ Q 9 8 2
♣ K 8 7 5 2   ♣ A 10 6 4

	♠ A J 10 7 5
	♡ Q 7 5
	◇ A K 6 3
	♣ Q

West	North	East	South
	Brogeland		*Sælensminde*
		pass	1♠
pass	2♠	pass	3♡
pass	3♠	all pass	

The deal comes from an early round of the 2007 Spring Foursomes. Norway's Erik Sælensminde chose to make his game try in hearts, because that is where he needed the most help. Despite holding five-card support, Boye Brogeland did not like his 10-9-2 in the game-try suit and signed off. How would you play 3♠ when West leads a diamond to the queen and ace?

At Trick 2, Sælensminde led the ♣Q to East's ace. He won the diamond continuation with the king and paused to assess the situation. East, who had not opened the bidding, had already shown up with the ♣A and the ◇Q. He presumably held the ace or king of hearts too, or West would have led the suit. So, East could not hold the king of trumps!

Sælensminde cashed the ace of trumps, drawing two low cards. He could not restrict his heart losers to two with a straightforward finesse against the jack because the spot cards were inadequate (East would cover the ♡10 with the ♡J or ♡K). Instead, he ruffed two diamonds in dummy and two clubs in his hand, eliminating both suits. He then threw West on lead with a trump, forcing him to open the heart suit or give a ruff-and-sluff. West led a low heart to his partner's king and East returned a low heart. Sælensminde ran this to dummy's ten and the contract was made.

Did you notice something unusual about the last deal? It is the only partscore in the book! Some readers tend to switch off when the contract is a lowly partscore, so I have endeavored to hold your attention by using slam and game contracts.

We will visit the 2006 White House tournament for our final example of exiting in the trump suit. Poland faced France and Piotr Gawrys was sitting South.

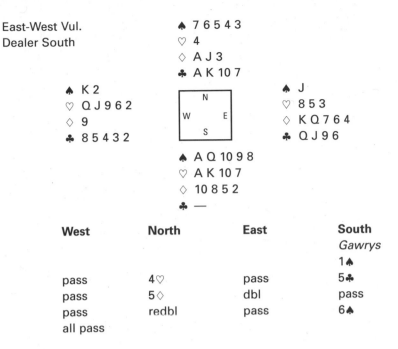

East-West Vul.
Dealer South

```
              ♠ 7 6 5 4 3
              ♡ 4
              ◇ A J 3
              ♣ A K 10 7

♠ K 2                           ♠ J
♡ Q J 9 6 2        N            ♡ 8 5 3
◇ 9           W         E       ◇ K Q 7 6 4
♣ 8 5 4 3 2        S            ♣ Q J 9 6

              ♠ A Q 10 9 8
              ♡ A K 10 7
              ◇ 10 8 5 2
              ♣ —
```

West	North	East	South
			Gawrys
			1♠
pass	4♡	pass	5♣
pass	5◇	dbl	pass
pass	redbl	pass	6♠
all pass			

Gawrys passed the double of his partner's diamond cuebid, requesting further definition of the control held. When the redouble confirmed first-round control, he leapt to a small slam. How would you play this when West leads the ◇9?

Gawrys rose with the ace of diamonds and continued with a trump to the ace, failing to drop the king. With a trump trick to be lost, it was now almost certain that declarer needed an endplay to avoid losing a diamond trick. Gawrys eliminated the hearts and clubs, discarding one diamond from dummy and two from his hand. When he exited with a trump, West won with the king and had no diamond to play. The ruff-and-sluff return allowed declarer to dispose of dummy's last diamond, and the slam was made.

In another match, Juan-Carlos Ventin followed the same successful line, again taking into account the lead-directing double from East. Both declarers gained a big swing when their counterparts finessed in trumps at the other table. Perhaps you think that the successful declarers were lucky to find West with a singleton diamond, since East might equally have doubled the diamond cuebid with only four diamonds to the king-queen. It's a good point, but remember that cashing the ♠A allows you to combine two different chances. Apart from the endplay possibility, you might drop a singleton ♠K offside.

NOW TRY THESE...

A.

```
              ♠ Q J 2
              ♡ A J 7
              ◇ A 9 6 2
              ♣ Q 5 2
```

```
              ┌─────────┐
              │    N    │
◇ Q led       │ W     E │
              │    S    │
              └─────────┘
```

```
              ♠ A K 10
              ♡ Q 10 9 5 4 2
              ◇ 4
              ♣ 7 6 4
```

West	North	East	South
		1◇	1♡
pass	2◇	pass	2♡
pass	3♡	pass	4♡
all pass			

How will you play the game in hearts when West leads the ◇Q?

B.

```
              ♠ K 7 4 2
              ♡ A K 2
              ◇ 8 6 4
              ♣ K J 6
```

```
              ┌─────────┐
              │    N    │
♡ Q led       │ W     E │
              │    S    │
              └─────────┘
```

```
              ♠ A J 9 6 5
              ♡ 8 4
              ◇ K 5 2
              ♣ A Q 7
```

West	North	East	South
	1♣	pass	1♠
pass	2♠	pass	4♠
all pass			

West leads the ♡Q against your spade game. How will you play the contract?

C.

        ♠ 10 6 4
        ♡ A 7 5 4
        ◇ A 6 3
        ♣ Q 9 7

```
        N
    W       E
        S
```

♠Q led

        ♠ A K 7 3
        ♡ 10 9 8 3 2
        ◇ K 4
        ♣ A 3

West	North	East	South
			1♡
1♠	2♠	pass	4♡
all pass			

West leads the ♠Q against your heart game. How will you play the contract?

D.

        ♠ K 5 3
        ♡ A K 9 8 2
        ◇ 7 4
        ♣ A 5 2

```
        N
    W       E
        S
```

◇K led

        ♠ A Q 8 6 4
        ♡ Q J
        ◇ A 9 3
        ♣ Q J 3

West	North	East	South
2◇	2♡	pass	2♠
pass	4♠	pass	4NT
pass	5♣	pass	6♠
all pass			

West opens a weak two in diamonds and eventually leads the ◇K against your small slam in spades. How will you play the contract?

Answers ✏

A.

<table>
<tr><td></td><td>♠ Q J 2
♡ A J 7
◇ A 9 6 2
♣ Q 5 2</td><td></td></tr>
<tr><td>♠ 9 7 5 3
♡ 8 3
◇ Q J 7
♣ J 9 8 3</td><td>N
W   E
S</td><td>♠ 8 6 4
♡ K 6
◇ K 10 8 5 3
♣ A K 10</td></tr>
<tr><td></td><td>♠ A K 10
♡ Q 10 9 5 4 2
◇ 4
♣ 7 6 4</td><td></td></tr>
</table>

West	North	East	South
		1◇	1♡
pass	2◇	pass	2♡
pass	3♡	pass	4♡
all pass			

How will you play the game in hearts when West leads the ◇Q?

    East, who opened the bidding, probably holds the ♡K. Forget about taking a trump finesse, then, and aim for an endplay on East. You win the diamond lead with dummy's ace and ruff a diamond. A trump to the ace fails to drop the king, but you use the entry to ruff another diamond with the ♡9. You cash the ace, king and queen of spades and continue with dummy's last diamond, ruffing with the ♡10 to avoid an overruff. These cards remain:

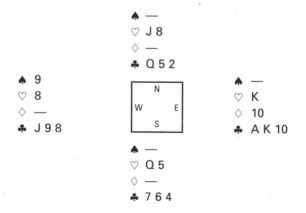

You put East on lead with a trump, pleased to see a 2-2 break. East is endplayed, forced to give a trick to dummy's ♣Q or to concede a ruff-and-sluff.

B.

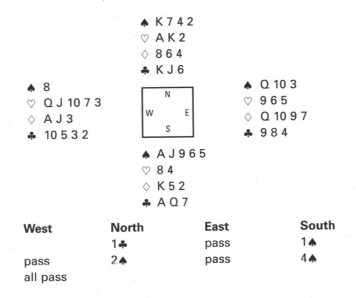

	♠ K 7 4 2		
	♡ A K 2		
	◇ 8 6 4		
	♣ K J 6		

♠ 8
♡ Q J 10 7 3
◇ A J 3
♣ 10 5 3 2

♠ Q 10 3
♡ 9 6 5
◇ Q 10 9 7
♣ 9 8 4

♠ A J 9 6 5
♡ 8 4
◇ K 5 2
♣ A Q 7

West	North	East	South
	1♣	pass	1♠
pass	2♠	pass	4♠
all pass			

West leads the ♡Q against your spade game. How will you play the contract?

You win in the dummy and play the ♠K, both defenders following low. If you play a second round of trumps immediately, the odds slightly favor playing for the drop (a 52% chance). If you guess wrongly and play a trump to the ace when East holds ♠Q-x-x, you will go down when there are three diamond tricks to be lost. A better idea is to eliminate hearts and clubs before taking a trump finesse. Then if you lose to a doubleton queen, West will be endplayed.

You cash a second top heart and ruff a heart. Next you play the ace, queen and king of clubs. When all follow, the contract is safe. You lead a second round of trumps and finesse the jack when East follows. The finesse wins, as it happens, but West would have been endplayed if he had won with an originally doubleton ♠Q. Had East shown out on the second round of trumps, you would have won with the ace and endplayed West with a third round of trumps.

You do not necessarily need a 4-3 club break for this line to work. If trumps are 2-2 and West ruffs the third round of clubs with his last trump, he will again be endplayed.

C.

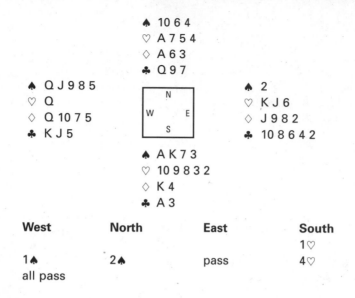

♠ 10 6 4
♡ A 7 5 4
◇ A 6 3
♣ Q 9 7

♠ Q J 9 8 5
♡ Q
◇ Q 10 7 5
♣ K J 5

♠ 2
♡ K J 6
◇ J 9 8 2
♣ 10 8 6 4 2

♠ A K 7 3
♡ 10 9 8 3 2
◇ K 4
♣ A 3

West	North	East	South
			1♡
1♠	2♠	pass	4♡
all pass			

West leads the ♠Q against your heart game. How will you play the contract?

Suppose you win the spade lead and continue with ace and another trump. East will take his two trump tricks and you will not be able to avoid two further losers in the black suits. Eliminating diamonds and playing ace and another club will do no good — West can rise with the ♣K and exit safely in the club suit.

Instead, you should play the ♣A at Trick 2 and then another club towards dummy. West rises with the ♣K, but he cannot damage the contract. If West plays a second round of spades, East will in effect be ruffing a loser with a natural trump trick.

Let's say that West exits passively with a third round of clubs to dummy's queen. You discard a spade from your hand, cash the ace of trumps and play three rounds of diamonds, eliminating the suit with a ruff. Only then do you play a second round of trumps. East scores his two trump winners, but will then have to give you a ruff-and-sluff by leading one of the minor suits. You will throw the remaining low spade from your hand and ruff in the dummy, claiming the contract.

D.

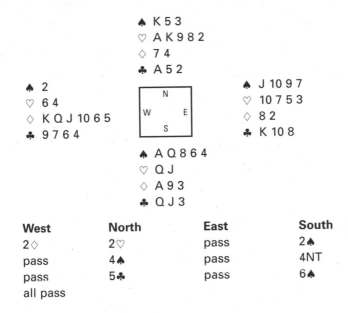

♠ K 5 3
♡ A K 9 8 2
♢ 7 4
♣ A 5 2

♠ 2
♡ 6 4
♢ K Q J 10 6 5
♣ 9 7 6 4

♠ J 10 9 7
♡ 10 7 5 3
♢ 8 2
♣ K 10 8

♠ A Q 8 6 4
♡ Q J
♢ A 9 3
♣ Q J 3

West	North	East	South
2♢	2♡	pass	2♠
pass	4♠	pass	4NT
pass	5♣	pass	6♠
all pass			

West opens with a weak two-bid in diamonds and North overcalls in hearts. Whether or not you normally play a change of suit as forcing opposite an overcall, it makes good sense to do so when partner has overcalled a weak two-bid. Roman Keycard Blackwood carries you to a small slam in spades and West leads the ◊K. How will you play the contract?

You win with the diamond ace and draw two rounds of trumps with the ace and queen. (Your intention was to use the king of trumps as an entry to the blocked heart suit.) As it happens, West shows out on the second round of trumps.

Even though you cannot now 'draw trumps, ending in the dummy', you continue with your plan. You cash the queen and jack of hearts and cross to dummy with the king of trumps. East follows to two more hearts and you throw your remaining cards in the diamond suit. A diamond ruff in the South hand removes East's last card in diamonds and the stage is set for a throw-in. When you exit with your last trump, East has to win and lead away from the ♣K. You win with the ♣Q, cross to the ♣A and cash the last heart for your twelfth trick.

CHAPTER 5

Partial Elimination Play

Many elimination plays are straightforward. You can see right from Trick 1 that you are certain to succeed however the cards lie. In this chapter, we will see some deals where life is not so perfect. You cannot eliminate one of the suits completely and will have to hope that your intended victim does not have a safe exit left when you throw him in. Since one or more suits have not been completely eliminated at the time of the throw-in, this technique is known as a 'partial elimination play'.

A side suit cannot be completely eliminated

We will start with a deal where, in an ideal world, you would like to eliminate the club suit completely. This is not possible, as we will see, but you can still catch West in an elimination play.

Both Vul.
Dealer South

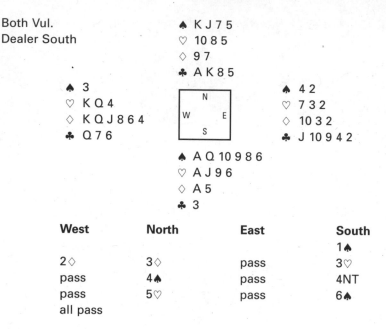

♠ K J 7 5
♡ 10 8 5
◇ 9 7
♣ A K 8 5

♠ 3
♡ K Q 4
◇ K Q J 8 6 4
♣ Q 7 6

♠ 4 2
♡ 7 3 2
◇ 10 3 2
♣ J 10 9 4 2

♠ A Q 10 9 8 6
♡ A J 9 6
◇ A 5
♣ 3

West	North	East	South
			1♠
2◇	3◇	pass	3♡
pass	4♠	pass	4NT
pass	5♡	pass	6♠
all pass			

How will you play the spade slam when West leads the ◇K?

You can discard the diamond loser on dummy's ♣K, so the contract is at risk only when West holds both the missing heart honors. What can you do in that case? With unlimited entries to dummy, you could ruff a diamond and two clubs in your hand, completely eliminating those suits. You could then return to dummy with a trump and finesse a heart into the West hand, leaving him endplayed.

To see whether you have enough entries for a 'perfect' elimination, you must project how the play will go. You win the diamond lead and play the two top clubs, throwing your diamond loser. You ruff dummy's remaining diamond with a high trump, cross to the ♠J and ruff a club high. You return to dummy by overtaking the ♠6 with the ♠7 and these cards remain:

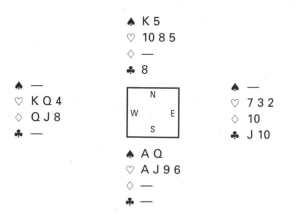

♠ K 5
♡ 10 8 5
◇ —
♣ 8

♠ —
♡ K Q 4
◇ Q J 8
♣ —

♠ —
♡ 7 3 2
◇ 10
♣ J 10

♠ A Q
♡ A J 9 6
◇ —
♣ —

You need to lead the first round of hearts from dummy in case East holds one of the heart honors. It follows that you cannot afford to ruff the ♣8 first, completing the elimination of that suit. If you did, you would have to return to dummy with the ♠K for the first heart lead and you would have no trumps left in your hand. (West could then exit safely in diamonds, since this would no longer give a ruff-and-sluff.)

You must therefore take the heart finesse now, while there are still two clubs out. The ♡10 runs to West's ♡Q and, luckily for you, he does not hold any more clubs. West is therefore endplayed. He must lead into your heart tenace or play a diamond, conceding a ruff-and-sluff.

The play was a 'partial elimination' because one suit (clubs, here) was only partly eliminated. Let's see another example of this style of play.

East-West Vul.		♠ 10 7 5 3	
Dealer South		♡ K Q 10 7	
		◇ A 6 5 4	
		♣ 5	
♠ K Q J 8 6			♠ 9 2
♡ 5 2			♡ 8 3
◇ 10 8			◇ Q J 9 2
♣ 10 6 3 2			♣ Q J 9 8 7
		♠ A 4	
		♡ A J 9 6 4	
		◇ K 7 3	
		♣ A K 4	

West	North	East	South
			1♡
pass	4♣	pass	6♡

North's 4♣ was a splinter bid. Although your ♣K may be wasted opposite partner's shortage, the overall strength of your hand justifies bidding a small slam. How will you play 6♡ when West leads the ♠K?

Bidding the slam seemed a good idea at the time, but how can you avoid a loser in both spades and diamonds? There is one card that offers hope of salvation — dummy's ♠10! You win the spade lead and draw trumps, pleased to see them break 2-2. You cash the ♣A-K, throwing a diamond from dummy, and ruff your last club. Next you play the ace and king of diamonds. You cannot completely eliminate the diamond suit, but you must hope that you have removed the diamonds from the West hand. These cards remain:

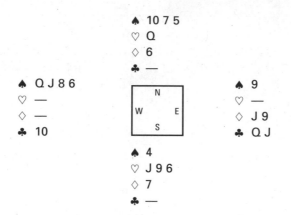

You lead the ♠4 and West wins with the ♠J. He is not a happy man. If he plays another spade, high or low, you will enjoy a diamond discard on dummy's ♠10. West's only alternative is a fourth round of clubs and this will give you a ruff-and-sluff.

The trump suit cannot be completely eliminated

A requirement of elimination play is that there should be at least one trump left in both your own hand and the dummy at the moment of the throw-in. When drawing all of the defenders' trumps would exhaust your own trumps or those of the dummy, you may have to perform the endplay while at least one trump is still out. That is the winning line on this slam:

North-South Vul.
Dealer East

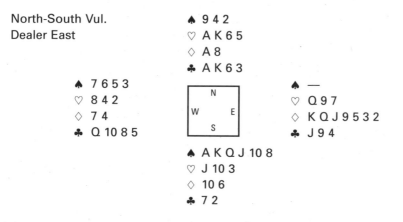

West	North	East	South
		3◇	3♠
pass	4NT	pass	5♠
pass	5NT	pass	6♠
all pass			

West leads the ◇7 against your spade slam. You win with dummy's ◇A and play a trump to the ace, East discarding a diamond. How will you play the contract?

One obvious chance is to draw trumps and run the ♡J. Such a move will fail on this occasion and it will be a case of 'That was unlucky, partner!'

A much better idea is a partial elimination play, aiming to put East on lead with a second round of diamonds. Your first move is to eliminate East's clubs. You cash the ace and king of clubs and ruff a club. A heart to the ace is followed by another club ruff (just in case East began with four clubs). The scene is now set for the throw-in. These cards remain:

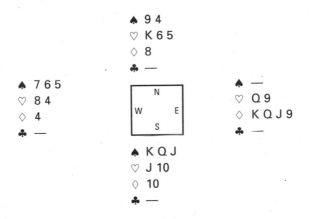

```
              ♠ 9 4
              ♡ K 6 5
              ◇ 8
              ♣ —
  ♠ 7 6 5                    ♠ —
  ♡ 8 4         N            ♡ Q 9
  ◇ 4      W        E        ◇ K Q J 9
  ♣ —          S            ♣ —
              ♠ K Q J
              ♡ J 10
              ◇ 10
              ♣ —
```

You eliminate-exit in diamonds, putting East on lead. If he returns a heart, you will score two tricks in the suit. His only alternative is to lead a third round of diamonds, giving you a ruff-and-sluff. Since your trumps are solid, this will present no problem. You will discard a heart from your hand and ruff in the dummy, overruffing West if necessary.

The stars come out to play:

partial elimination play

For our first all-stars deal, we will visit the 11th Team Olympiad in Maastricht, where the women's teams of Germany and South Africa faced each other. Pony Nehmert was declarer in the promising-looking contract of 5◊.

```
                    ♠ K Q J 5 3
                    ♡ A Q 10
                    ◇ J 9 7 2
                    ♣ A
   ♠ 10 8 7 6 4                          ♠ A
   ♡ 8 4          ┌──────────┐          ♡ K J 9 2
   ◇ 10 6 3       │ N        │          ◇ 8
   ♣ 9 8 5        │ W      E │          ♣ K Q J 10 7 3 2
                  │     S    │
                  └──────────┘
                    ♠ 9 2
                    ♡ 7 6 5 3
                    ◇ A K Q 5 4
                    ♣ 6 4
```

West	North	East	South
Mansell	Rauscheid	Modlin	Nehmert
		1♣	1◇
pass	1♠	3♣	pass
pass	dbl	pass	3♡
pass	5◇	all pass	

Petra Mansell led the ♣8, won in the dummy. When Nehmert played the ace and king of trumps, East showed out on the second round. How would you have continued?

If declarer had drawn a third round of trumps next and played a spade to the king, the 5-1 spade break, coupled with the adverse position of the two missing heart honors, would have defeated her. Seeing no hurry to draw the last trump, Nehmert ruffed her remaining club and led the ♠K to East's ♠A. If Merle Modlin had been able to lead back a spade at this stage, the suit would have broken 4-2 at worst and declarer would have been able to establish a long spade as her eleventh trick. The ♠A was singleton, however, so East had no spade to play. A heart into dummy's tenace was hardly attractive and East played back the ♣K.

Nehmert discarded the last spade from her hand and ruffed in the dummy. She could then return to her hand with a spade ruff to draw the last trump.

Eleven tricks were guaranteed. A finesse of the ♡Q failed, as expected, but that was still a very satisfying +600. The German East-West pair bought the contract in 4♣ at the other table, going one down, so that was a gain of 9 IMPs.

Our second deal arose in the 1993 European Championship in Menton. Both Bauke Muller of the Netherlands and Daniela von Arnim of the German women's team arrived in 6♠ on this deal:

Both Vul.
Dealer South

```
                    ♠ A J 8 4
                    ♡ A 4
                    ◇ 10 2
                    ♣ K 8 6 3 2
  ♠ 5 3                              ♠ 10 9 2
  ♡ K Q 8 7 3 2          N           ♡ J 10 9 6
  ◇ K 7 6          W           E     ◇ J 9 5 3
  ♣ Q J                  S           ♣ 9 4
                    ♠ K Q 7 6
                    ♡ 5
                    ◇ A Q 8 4
                    ♣ A 10 7 5
```

West	North	East	South
Lesniewski	De Boer	Martens	Muller
			1♣
1♡	dbl	pass	3♠
pass	4♣	pass	4◇
pass	4♡	pass	4♠
pass	4NT	pass	5♣
pass	6♠	all pass	

North's negative double showed precisely four spades. A comprehensive auction ensued and Marcin Lesniewski led the ♡K against Muller's spade slam. How would you have played the deal?

With the ◇K offside, it seemed to onlookers that everything would hinge on the play of the clubs. To make use of the ♣10 in his hand, declarer would surely cash dummy's ♣K on the first round of the suit. After the fall of an honor from West, the Principle of Restricted Choice would suggest that the honor was twice as likely to be a singleton as a chosen card from ♣Q-J doubleton. If declarer followed this generally admirable dictum, he would go down.

Muller proceeded to prove his doubters wrong. His intention was indeed to follow Restricted Choice, but he gave himself an extra chance—he arranged for West to be endplayed if a second-round club finesse should lose. He needed to ruff a heart in his hand to eliminate that suit. He could therefore afford to play only two rounds of trumps before the club play (a partial elimination), so that he would still have at least one trump left in each hand.

Muller won the heart lead, played the king and ace of trumps and ruffed dummy's last heart. He then crossed to the king of clubs, noting that West did indeed follow with one of the honors. A club to the ten lost to West's other honor, but West did not hold the last trump and was therefore endplayed. He had to play a diamond into South's tenace or concede a ruff-and-sluff.

In another match, Germany's Daniela von Arnim followed the same impressive line of play.

The next deal comes from the 2005 South-West Pacific Teams and was played by Australia's David Hoffman:

Both Vul.
Dealer East

```
                    ♠ A
                    ♡ K 8 6 5
                    ◇ A Q 3 2
                    ♣ A Q 4 2
  ♠ K Q 8 4 2                        ♠ J 10 6 5
  ♡ J 7 4 3          N               ♡ A Q 9 2
  ◇ 10 9         W       E           ◇ K J 6 4
  ♣ 8 6              S               ♣ 3
                    ♠ 9 7 3
                    ♡ 10
                    ◇ 8 7 5
                    ♣ K J 10 9 7 5
```

West	North	East	South
	Julia Hoffman		David Hoffman
		1◇	pass
1♠	dbl	2♠	3♣
pass	5♣	all pass	

North's double strongly suggested at least four cards in clubs, so South was fully entitled to bid 3♣ on his 4-point hand. How would you play the resultant club game when West leads the ♠K?

West's opening lead implied 5 points in the spade suit, so Hoffman could place East with both the ♡A and the ◇K. Hoffman won the spade lead with dummy's ♠A and called for the ♡5. East won with the queen and switched to the ♣3. Declarer now aimed for an elimination play. Since two spades would have to be ruffed in dummy, and declarer needed there to be a trump in dummy for the end position, it would have to be a partial elimination with one trump still out.

Hoffman won the trump switch in dummy and crossruffed two hearts and two spades to reach the following position:

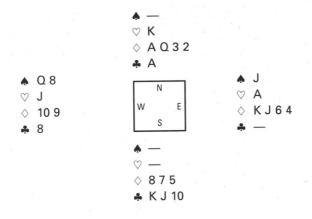

'King of hearts, please,' said declarer. East produced the ace and a low diamond was thrown from the South hand (a loser-on-loser play). Since declarer had left a trump in dummy, East could not return his last spade without giving a ruff-and-sluff. A diamond return would be into dummy's tenace, so that was eleven tricks and the contract. Well played!

We will end this section with an 'extra chance' play found by Eric Rodwell in the Life Master Pairs at the 2006 NABC in Chicago:

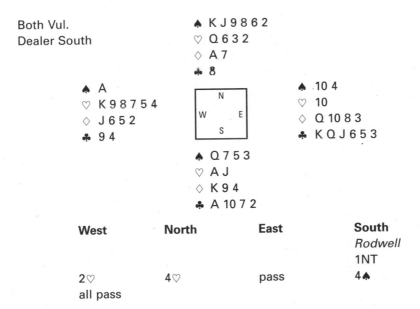

West	North	East	South
			Rodwell
			1NT
2♡	4♡	pass	4♠
all pass			

North's 4♡ was a transfer bid, showing long spades, and West led the ◇2 against the resultant spade game. Bearing in mind that it was a matchpoint event, can you see any way to make twelve tricks when the bidding has indicated that the ♡K is with West?

Rodwell aimed to endplay West if he held a singleton ♠A. He won the diamond lead in dummy, played a club to the ace and ruffed a club. He then crossed to his hand with the ◇K. This was the last convenient entry to his hand, since he needed to keep the heart tenace intact. He could therefore take only one more ruff in this attempted partial elimination. Since West had led the ◇2, followed by the ◇5 on the second round, it was clear that he had at least one diamond remaining. Rodwell therefore took the second ruff in diamonds rather than clubs.

After ruffing his last diamond, eliminating that suit, Rodwell led the king of trumps to West's ace. Not only was West's trump ace singleton, he had also started with only two clubs. With no safe exit available, he had to lead a heart into declarer's tenace or concede a ruff-and-sluff. Declarer had his twelfth trick and an excellent score on the board.

(A singleton ace of trumps is always a potential hazard. Had West chosen to lead this card, he would have avoided the endplay and lived to score his ♡K.)

NOW TRY THESE...

A.

        ♠ K 7 5
        ♡ 5 4
        ◇ A 6 5 2
        ♣ 9 7 6 3

♡K led

```
    N
 W     E
    S
```

        ♠ A Q J 10 4 3
        ♡ A 10
        ◇ K 7
        ♣ K 4 2

West	North	East	South
1♡	pass	pass	dbl
pass	2◇	pass	2♠
pass	4♠	all pass	

How will you play the spade game when West leads the ♡K?

B.

        ♠ 9 6 3 2
        ♡ J 7 6 2
        ◇ 10 5
        ♣ A 4 3

♣9 led

```
    N
 W     E
    S
```

        ♠ A K Q J
        ♡ A K 8 5 3
        ◇ A Q 2
        ♣ 5

West	North	East	South
			2♣
pass	2◇	3♣	3♡
pass	4♣	pass	6♡
all pass			

West leads the ♣9 against your small slam. How will you play the contract?

C.

        ♠ 6 5 3
        ♡ J 9 4 2
        ◇ 9 8 7 2
        ♣ J 4

♣ 10 led

```
      N
  W       E
      S
```

        ♠ A Q 9
        ♡ A K Q 10 6 3
        ◇ A
        ♣ A K 2

West	North	East	South
			2♣
pass	2◇	pass	2♡
pass	4♡	pass	6♡
all pass			

How will you play the heart slam when West leads the ♣10?

D.

        ♠ A Q 7 4 3 2
        ♡ A 8 3
        ◇ A 5 2
        ♣ A

♡ K led

```
      N
  W       E
      S
```

        ♠ K 9 8 6
        ♡ J 5 4
        ◇ K 8 6
        ♣ Q J 4

West	North	East	South
1♡	dbl	pass	2♠
pass	6♠	all pass	

The auction is short, yes. Perhaps you can make equally short work of the play when West leads the ♡K against your small slam.

Answers ✏

A.

```
              ♠ K 7 5
              ♡ 5 4
              ◇ A 6 5 2
              ♣ 9 7 6 3
♠ 6                          ♠ 9 8 2
♡ K Q J 8 3                  ♡ 9 7 6 2
◇ Q 9 8 3        N           ◇ J 10 4
♣ A Q 5       W     E        ♣ J 10 8
                 S
              ♠ A Q J 10 4 3
              ♡ A 10
              ◇ K 7
              ♣ K 4 2
```

West	North	East	South
1♡	pass	pass	dbl
pass	2◇	pass	2♠
pass	4♠	all pass	

How will you play the spade game when West leads the ♡K?

You can expect West to hold the ♣A. On a lucky day, the card might be doubleton. On every other day of the month, you should aim to endplay West with the ♡10, forcing him to play a club or give you a ruff-and-sluff.

You win the heart lead and draw one round of trumps with the ace. Your next task is to eliminate the diamonds. Since you will need the ♠K as an entry to take the second diamond ruff, you cannot afford to play another trump at this stage. You cash the king and ace of diamonds and ruff a diamond high. You cross to the ♠K, West showing out, and ruff dummy's last diamond. These cards remain:

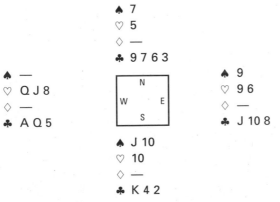

```
              ♠ 7
              ♡ 5
              ◇ —
              ♣ 9 7 6 3
♠ —                          ♠ 9
♡ Q J 8          N           ♡ 9 6
◇ —           W     E        ◇ —
♣ A Q 5          S           ♣ J 10 8
              ♠ J 10
              ♡ 10
              ◇ —
              ♣ K 4 2
```

You exit with the ♡10 and West is endplayed. It is a partial elimination because you have not drawn all of the trumps. Ten tricks are ten tricks just the same!

B.

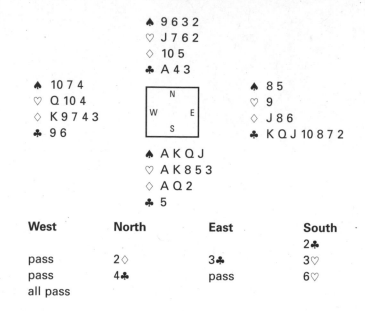

West	North	East	South
			2♣
pass	2◇	3♣	3♡
pass	4♣	pass	6♡
all pass			

West leads the ♣9 against your small slam. How will you play the contract?

If the ♡Q falls in two rounds or the diamond finesse works, everything will be easy. Have any of the other problems in this book been easy? No, so you must make a plan for dealing with the situation where both red suits lie poorly.

Your aim is to endplay West with a trump in the case where he started with three trumps to the queen. East's 3♣ overcall suggests that he holds seven clubs, so you ruff a club at Trick 2. When you continue with the ace and king of trumps, East shows out on the second round. You play all four top spades and West declines to ruff. These cards remain:

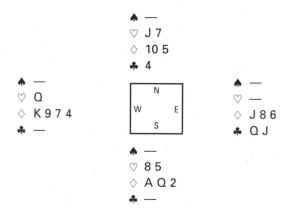

You throw West in with a trump and he has to lead into your diamond tenace. You can then ruff your remaining diamond with dummy's last trump. The play was a partial elimination because you were unable to ruff dummy's last club.

C.

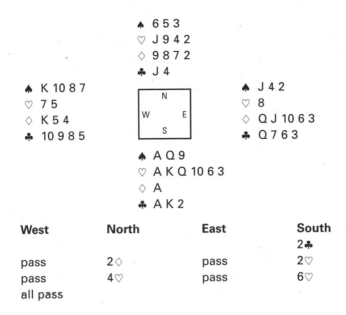

	West	North	East	South
	----------	-------	------	-------
				2♣
	pass	2◇	pass	2♡
	pass	4♡	pass	6♡
	all pass			

West leads the ♣10 against your heart slam. How will you play the contract?

Spades is the problem suit and you would like to eliminate both minors before playing a spade to the nine. However, there is no practical way to ruff three rounds of diamonds. (You could do it by overtaking the ♡10, the ♡6 and the ♡3 in turn, finally ruffing a club with the ♡2, but that would leave you with no trumps in dummy.) You must be content with ruffing only two diamonds.

The ♣10 lead is covered by the jack, queen and ace. You cash the ◇A and overtake the ♡10 with the ♡J. A diamond ruff high is followed by the ♡6 to the ♡9 and another diamond ruff with a high trump. You cash the ♣K and ruff your last club with the ♡2, leaving these cards to be played:

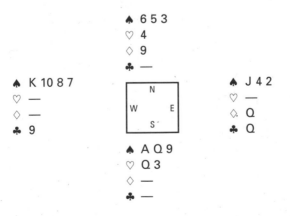

After a spade to the nine and ten, West is endplayed. If he had a diamond to return, you would ruff high and cross to the ♡4 to finesse the ♠Q.

D.

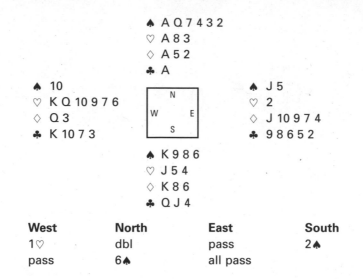

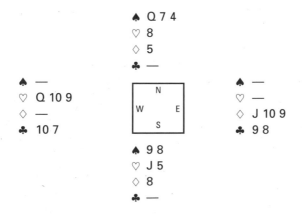

	♠ A Q 7 4 3 2	
	♡ A 8 3	
	◇ A 5 2	
	♣ A	
♠ 10		♠ J 5
♡ K Q 10 9 7 6		♡ 2
◇ Q 3		◇ J 10 9 7 4
♣ K 10 7 3		♣ 9 8 6 5 2
	♠ K 9 8 6	
	♡ J 5 4	
	◇ K 8 6	
	♣ Q J 4	

West	North	East	South
1♡	dbl	pass	2♠
pass	6♠	all pass	

It's all very well for partner to leap to 6♠ in such cavalier fashion. You are the one who will have to land twelve tricks. How will you set about it when West leads the ♡K?

Ducking the opening lead in the hope that West will gift you a second heart trick is a forlorn prospect. As the cards lie, East would ruff the second heart anyway. You might set up a red-suit squeeze by ducking the first trick, but this would require West to hold five of the seven outstanding diamonds, despite holding several more hearts than East. A better chance is to find West with six hearts and only two diamonds, in which case you can arrange an endplay on East.

You win the heart lead and play dummy's two black aces. You then cross to your hand with the ♠K and lead the ♣Q for a ruffing finesse. When West covers with the ♣K, you ruff in the dummy. The ace and king of diamonds return the lead to your hand and you cash the established ♣J, discarding a heart from dummy. These cards remain:

	♠ Q 7 4	
	♡ 8	
	◇ 5	
	♣ —	
♠ —		♠ —
♡ Q 10 9		♡ —
◇ —		◇ J 10 9
♣ 10 7		♣ 9 8
	♠ 9 8	
	♡ J 5	
	◇ 8	
	♣ —	

A third round of diamonds forces East to win and give you a ruff-and-sluff.

Advanced Elimination Play

It is a long climb up Elimination Mountain. In the final stretch to the snow-clad peak, we will see some advanced applications of this technique that are well worthy of our attention.

Exiting in a suit where a defender holds a singleton

It is often effective to exit in a side suit where one of the defenders holds a singleton. If that defender wins the trick, he will have to play some different suit, to your benefit. If instead his partner wins, he may not be able to continue the suit safely. This technique is not so easy to describe in words, so let's look at an example.

North-South Vul.
Dealer South

```
                      ♠ A 6 4
                      ♡ K Q 10 7
                      ◇ A 9
                      ♣ A Q 6 2
  ♠ K J 10 8 3 2      ┌─────────┐      ♠ 9
  ♡ 8                 │    N    │      ♡ 6 3 2
  ◇ Q J 10 6          │ W     E │      ◇ K 8 7 5 4 2
  ♣ 4 3               │    S    │      ♣ 10 9 7
                      └─────────┘
                      ♠ Q 7 5
                      ♡ A J 9 5 4
                      ◇ 3
                      ♣ K J 8 5
```

West	North	East	South
			1♡
2♠	4NT	pass	5◇
pass	6♡	all pass	

How will you play the heart slam when West leads the ◇Q?

You win with dummy's ◇A and draw trumps in three rounds. You then play three rounds of clubs, ending in the dummy. When you lead the ◇9, East rises with the ◇K (otherwise you could have discarded the ♠5, endplaying West). East is only postponing the defenders' fate. You ruff in your hand and lead the ♠5, calling for dummy's ♠4. With spades breaking 6-1, as you expect from the bidding, it makes no difference which defender wins the trick. If East wins with the ♠9, he will have to give you a ruff-and-sluff. If instead West puts up the ♠10 and wins the trick, he will have to lead a spade from the king or play a third round of diamonds, again giving you a ruff-and-sluff.

Exiting in a suit where a defender has length

Suppose a defender has advertised length in a suit by making a preemptive bid. You can often take advantage of this knowledge by throwing him in to lead in that suit. Look at this deal, where East has opened with a weak 2♡:

North-South Vul.
Dealer East

```
                        ♠ K 10 9 4
                        ♡ A Q 4 3
                        ♢ 4
                        ♣ A K J 4

    ♠ 7 3                                   ♠ 6
    ♡ 8              ┌─────────┐            ♡ K J 10 9 6 2
    ♢ K J 9 8 6 3 2  │    N    │            ♢ Q 7 5
    ♣ 10 8 3         │ W     E │            ♣ Q 9 7
                     │    S    │
                     └─────────┘
                        ♠ A Q J 8 5 2
                        ♡ 7 5
                        ♢ A 10
                        ♣ 6 5 2
```

West	North	East	South
		2♡	2♠
pass	4NT	pass	5♠
pass	6♠	all pass	

West leads the ♡8 against your 6♠. How will you play the contract?

An inexperienced player might rely on a finesse of the ♣J. A slightly better player might take advantage of the known 1-6 heart distribution by cashing the ♣A-K, gaining against ♣Q-x offside, and then leading towards the ♣J. Neither of these lines would succeed. With six trumps opposite four, it is natural to look instead for an elimination play.

You win the opening lead with dummy's ♡A, cross to the ♢A and eliminate the diamond suit with a ruff. You draw trumps with the king and ace, leaving these cards still to be played:

```
                        ♠ 10
                        ♡ Q 4 3
                        ♢ —
                        ♣ A K J 4

    ♠ —                                     ♠ —
    ♡ —              ┌─────────┐            ♡ K J 10 9
    ♢ K J 9 8 6      │    N    │            ♢ Q
    ♣ 10 8 3         │ W     E │            ♣ Q 9 7
                     │    S    │
                     └─────────┘
                        ♠ Q J 8 5
                        ♡ 7
                        ♢ —
                        ♣ 6 5 2
```

You lead the ♡7, West showing out (as expected), and duck in the dummy. East wins and has no safe return. He cannot continue hearts without giving you a trick with the ♡Q. A club will be into dummy's tenace and a diamond will give you a ruff-and-sluff.

Defensive blockage in the exit suit

Sometimes the defenders cannot avoid a blockage in a suit where you hold several losers and have chosen to exit. Suppose this is your intended exit suit:

	♣ 10 8 4	
♣ A Q	▭	♣ K 9 5
	♣ J 7 6 3 2	

When you duck a round of clubs, you are happy to see West take his ace and queen of clubs in either order. East cannot overtake the ♣Q with the ♣K on the second round or the defenders will score only two club tricks. When West is left on lead after two rounds of clubs, he may have to give you a ruff-and-sluff, allowing you to throw the last club from the North hand.

A defender with a doubleton honor in your three-loser exit suit will often be in trouble. Look at West's predicament here:

East-West Vul.
Dealer South

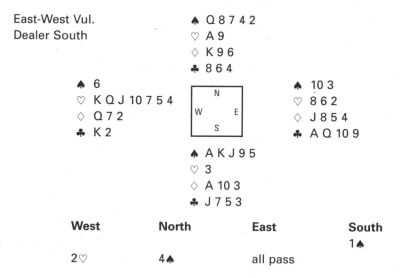

	♠ Q 8 7 4 2	
	♡ A 9	
	◇ K 9 6	
	♣ 8 6 4	

♠ 6		♠ 10 3
♡ K Q J 10 7 5 4		♡ 8 6 2
◇ Q 7 2		◇ J 8 5 4
♣ K 2		♣ A Q 10 9

	♠ A K J 9 5
	♡ 3
	◇ A 10 3
	♣ J 7 5 3

West	North	East	South
			1♠
2♡	4♠	all pass	

How will you play the spade game when West leads the ♡K?

If you can force the defenders to open the diamonds for you, there is a good chance of avoiding a loser in the suit. (You will play for the missing honors to be split.) You win the heart lead, draw trumps in two rounds and ruff dummy's remaining heart. Next, you lead a low club from the South hand. What are your prospects?

With the club suit lying as in the diagram, West has to decide whether to play his ♣K on the first round. If he does, and plays another club, you will be able to set up a discard on the ♣J. If instead West plays low on the first round of clubs, he will have to win the second round and then open the diamonds. Whether West chooses to exit with the ◇Q or a low diamond, you will make three diamond tricks by playing for the diamond honors to be divided.

Similarly, you would be in good shape if the club suit broke 3-3. Since the defenders could not cash three rounds of clubs without setting up a club trick for you, they would again have to make the first play in the diamond suit.

Elimination play to assist suit establishment

As we have seen, the idea of elimination play is to present an opponent with two or more losing options. Let's look at a deal now where one of those options is to set up a long card in dummy's main side suit.

```
Neither Vul.              ♠ 7 4
Dealer South              ♡ Q 9 3
                          ◇ 10 8 5 3 2
                          ♣ 6 4 2

        ♠ K 10 6                          ♠ J 9 8 5 3 2
        ♡ 8 4           ┌──────────┐      ♡ 6 5
        ◇ Q J 9 4       │    N     │      ◇ 7
        ♣ Q J 10 5      │ W     E  │      ♣ 9 8 7 3
                        │    S     │
                        └──────────┘
                          ♠ A Q
                          ♡ A K J 10 7 2
                          ◇ A K 6
                          ♣ A K
```

West	North	East	South
			2♣
pass	2◇	pass	2♡
pass	4♡	pass	6♡
all pass			

How will you play the small slam in hearts when West leads the ♣Q?

One straightforward line is to draw trumps in two rounds and continue with ace, king and another diamond. If the diamond suit fails to deliver a twelfth trick, you can fall back on the spade finesse. This would be good enough much of the time, but not when the cards lie as in the diagram. Can you see anything better?

After winning the club lead, you should cash the ♡A and take the small risk of playing your remaining club winner. You cross to dummy with the ♡9, pleased to see a 2-2 break, and ruff dummy's last club. With the club suit eliminated, you play ace, king and another diamond. When West wins the third round, his options will include two familiar ones: he can lead into the ♠A-Q or give you a ruff-and-sluff in clubs. On this occasion, there will a third, must less common option: he can play his remaining diamond honor, setting up the ◇10 in dummy. You will ruff the trick in your hand and cross to the ♡Q to discard your ♠Q on the established long diamond.

Elimination play to protect you from a ruff

Sometimes you cannot prevent the defenders from scoring a ruff. You may, however, be able to arrange for the defender who takes the ruff to find himself endplayed. Here is a straightforward example of this technique. Would you have spotted the winning line?

Neither Vul.
Dealer South

	♠ K 9 6 5	
	♡ A 3	
	◇ 6 5 2	
	♣ Q 9 8 4	

♠ 8 2		♠ A 4
♡ K Q J 9 8 5 4	N	♡ 10 7 6
◇ K 4 3	W E	◇ J 10 9 7
♣ 6	S	♣ 10 5 3 2

	♠ Q J 10 7 3	
	♡ 2	
	◇ A Q 8	
	♣ A K J 7	

West	North	East	South
			1♠
3♡	3♠	pass	4♠
all pass			

How would you play the spade game when West leads the ♣6?

The original declarer played with impressive speed. He won the club lead with the ace and led a trump to the king and ace. East returned a club for his partner to ruff and West was able to exit safely with the ♡K. Declarer won with the ♡A, ruffed a second round of hearts and drew the outstanding trump. He then played the remaining club winners and led a diamond towards his hand, hoping to insert the eight, thereby endplaying West. It wasn't to be. East rose with the ◇J in the second seat and there was no way for declarer to avoid two diamond losers. That was one down.

Impressive skill is more valuable than impressive speed. Before playing a trump, you should cash the ♡A and ruff a heart in your hand, eliminating the suit. East wins the first round of trumps, as before, and gives his partner a club ruff. You can see the difference that your early heart ruff makes. After taking the club ruff, West has no safe return. A diamond return will be into your ace-queen and a third round of hearts will give you a ruff-and-sluff.

Exiting in an ace-opposite-singleton suit

Suppose you hold a singleton in dummy opposite A-J-10 or A-Q-9 in your hand. You could easily win the first round with the ace and ruff the other two cards, losing no trick in the suit. However, it will sometimes be better to play low to the jack (or low to the nine with the second combination). By doing so, you may be endplaying your left-hand opponent to give you a trick. Since the ace will still be alive, this can easily represent a net gain. Let's see two examples of this style of play.

East-West Vul.	♠ A K Q 10 9 4		
Dealer South	♡ 4		
	◇ K J		
	♣ 9 6 5 4		

	♠ 6 3 2	N	♠ —
	♡ K Q 6 2	W E	♡ 9 8 7 5 3
	◇ Q 9 5 3 2	S	◇ 10 8 6 4
	♣ 2		♣ Q J 10 8

	♠ J 8 7 5		
	♡ A J 10		
	◇ A 7		
	♣ A K 7 3		

West	North	East	South
			1NT
pass	2♡	pass	3♠
pass	4NT	pass	5♣
pass	6♠	all pass	

West leads the ♣2 against your spade slam. You win East's ♣8 with the ♣A and play a trump to the ace, East showing out. How will you continue?

All will be easy if clubs break 3-2, but the first trick gives you a clear warning that this is unlikely to be the case. What can be done when East holds ♣Q-J-10-8?

You draw trumps in two further rounds and cash the ♣K, confirming the bad split in that suit. You then play the ace and king of diamonds to leave this position:

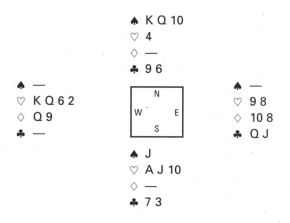

A heart to the jack leaves West endplayed. If he leads into your ♡A-10, you will have two discards for dummy's clubs. If instead he plays a diamond, giving a ruff-and-sluff, you will throw one of dummy's clubs on that trick and another on the ♡A. The play would be similarly successful when the king and queen of hearts were split between the defenders.

The next deal features a slightly more complex position in the throw-in suit:

North-South Vul.
Dealer South

```
                    ♠ Q
                    ♡ A J 10 9 5 2
                    ♢ 7 4 2
                    ♣ A 7 3
    ♠ J 8 6 2           N           ♠ K 9 7 5 3
    ♡ 7                              ♡ 8 6
    ♢ K 9 6 5      W       E         ♢ J 10 8
    ♣ 10 9 8 5         S             ♣ J 6 2
                    ♠ A 10 4
                    ♡ K Q 4 3
                    ♢ A Q 3
                    ♣ K Q 4
```

West	North	East	South
			2NT
pass	3◇	pass	3♡
pass	4NT	pass	5♣
pass	6♡	all pass	

It is a matter of partnership agreement whether 4NT, after a transfer bid, is Blackwood or a natural slam try. Here North-South played it as RKCB and South duly showed three keycards. How would you play 6♡ when West leads the ♣10?

You win the club lead in your hand, draw trumps with the king and ace and cash the remaining clubs, ending in the dummy. Your next move is to lead the ♠Q, planning to run the card. If West wins with the king, he will be end-played, forced to lead into one of your tenaces or to give you a ruff-and-sluff in clubs. (In the latter case, you will throw one diamond from dummy immediately and another on the ♠A.) As the cards lie, East may well cover the ♠Q with the ♠K. What then?

You win with the ♠A and see that you still have a chance of endplaying West on the third round of spades. You ruff the ♠4 in dummy, return to your hand with a third round of trumps and survey this end position:

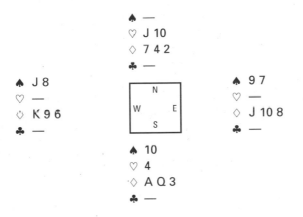

You lead the ♠10 and your prayers are answered when West covers with the ♠J. You discard a diamond from dummy and West has to give you a trick with his return. (If West plays low on the spade, you will again throw a diamond. Should East win with the ♠J, you will have to finesse the queen on a diamond return.)

Choosing which defender to endplay

Some deals offer you a choice of endplays. See how you fare on this slam contract:

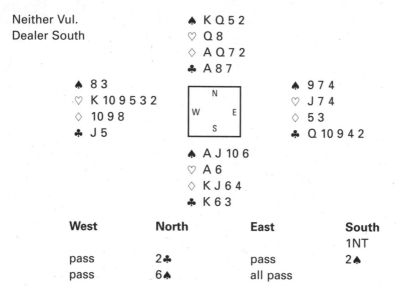

Neither Vul.
Dealer South

♠	K Q 5 2
♡	Q 8
◊	A Q 7 2
♣	A 8 7

West:
♠ 8 3
♡ K 10 9 5 3 2
◊ 10 9 8
♣ J 5

East:
♠ 9 7 4
♡ J 7 4
◊ 5 3
♣ Q 10 9 4 2

South:
♠ A J 10 6
♡ A 6
◊ K J 6 4
♣ K 6 3

West	North	East	South
			1NT
pass	2♣	pass	2♠
pass	6♠	all pass	

How will you play the spade slam when West leads the ◊ 10?

You win the diamond lead and draw trumps in three rounds. With potential losers in clubs and hearts, only an endplay can rescue the contract. You eliminate the diamond suit and ponder the situation. One chance is to play ace, king and another club, hoping that the defender who wins will have to lead away from the ♡K. This line has little chance of success, however, when the clubs break 4-3. A defender holding the ♡K along with ♣Q-x-x or ♣Q-J-x will surely unblock his club honor(s), allowing his partner to win the third round. If you assume that the defenders are skilful enough to do that, what conclusion should you draw?

You should reason that a genuine endplay is likely only when the clubs divide 5-2 (or 6-1). In that case, the defender with the club length will have to win the third round of clubs. If he also holds the ♡K, he will be endplayed.

When you play the spades and diamonds, you will find that each defender holds five cards in those suits. A defender holding five clubs will therefore have only three hearts to his partner's six and be '2-to-1 against' to hold the ♡K. When you play the top two clubs, these cards remain:

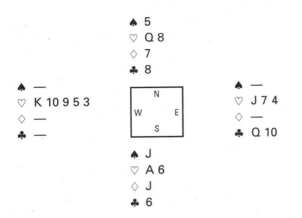

```
              ♠ 5
              ♡ Q 8
              ◇ 7
              ♣ 8
♠ —                          ♠ —
♡ K 10 9 5 3      N          ♡ J 7 4
◇ —          W       E       ◇ —
♣ —              S           ♣ Q 10
              ♠ J
              ♡ A 6
              ◇ J
              ♣ 6
```

Exiting with a club will not succeed because East (who was dealt only three hearts) does not hold the ♡K. Instead, you should eliminate-exit with ace and another heart. West (who started with six hearts) has to win the second round of hearts and is then forced to give you a ruff-and-sluff.

Discarding on the attempted exit card

In the situation where a defender has only one safe exit card, it can pay you to discard a loser when he plays it. By leaving him on lead, you can force him to give you a trick with his next play.

Neither Vul.
Dealer South

```
                    ♠ Q 9 7 6
                    ♡ 8 6 2
                    ◇ A 10 6
                    ♣ 8 5 2
♠ 5                                 ♠ J 8
♡ K Q 10 9 7 3       N              ♡ 5 4
◇ Q 5 4          W       E          ◇ J 9 7 3 2
♣ A 10 3             S              ♣ Q J 9 4
                    ♠ A K 10 4 3 2
                    ♡ A J
                    ◇ K 8
                    ♣ K 7 6
```

West	North	East	South
			1♠
2♡	2♠	pass	4♠
all pass			

How will you play the spade game when West leads the ♡K?

You win with the ♡A and draw trumps. After eliminating diamonds, you put West on lead with the ♡J. He wins with the ♡Q and plays the ♡10. What now?

If you ruff this trick, you will have to play clubs yourself and will lose three tricks in the suit, going one down. Instead, you should discard a club from your hand, leaving West on lead. He must open the club suit or give you a ruff-and-sluff. Either way, you will lose just one further club trick and make the contract.

Here is a more exotic version of this technique:

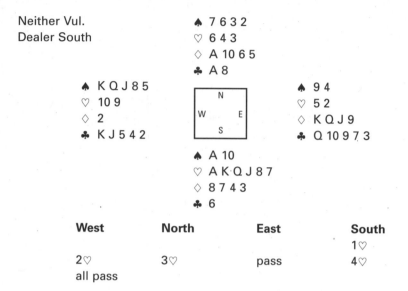

Neither Vul.
Dealer South

```
              ♠ 7 6 3 2
              ♡ 6 4 3
              ◇ A 10 6 5
              ♣ A 8
♠ K Q J 8 5              ♠ 9 4
♡ 10 9          N       ♡ 5 2
◇ 2          W     E    ◇ K Q J 9
♣ K J 5 4 2     S       ♣ Q 10 9 7 3
              ♠ A 10
              ♡ A K Q J 8 7
              ◇ 8 7 4 3
              ♣ 6
```

West	North	East	South
			1♡
2♡	3♡	pass	4♡
all pass			

West's Michaels cuebid shows at least 5-5 shape in spades and one of the minor suits. How will you play the heart game when West leads the ◇2?

It does not take a genius to read the opening lead as a singleton. You face the loss of three diamond tricks and a spade. What can be done? You win the lead with dummy's ◇A and draw trumps, relieved to see a 2-2 break. The ace of clubs and a club ruff eliminates that suit. You cash the ♠A and these cards remain:

```
              ♠ 7 6 3
              ♡ 6
              ◇ 10 6 5
              ♣ —
♠ K Q J 8               ♠ 9
♡ —            N        ♡ —
◇ —         W     E     ◇ K Q J
♣ K J 5        S        ♣ Q 10 7
              ♠ 10
              ♡ Q J 8
              ◇ 8 7 4
              ♣ —
```

Exiting with a diamond would not be productive. East would cash three winners in the suit and then play a spade. Instead, you should exit with the ♠10 to West's ♠J. When he returns the ♠K, you discard a diamond from the South hand. West persists with the ♠Q and you ditch another diamond. Dummy is now out of spades and a fifth round of the suit will give you a ruff-and-sluff. West has, at last, run out of safe exit cards and the contract is yours.

Ducking a round of the exit suit

Before we admire the play of our world-ranking stars, let's see a rather unusual technique: with A-x-x opposite x-x-x in your intended exit suit, you have to duck the first round, intending to exit to a particular defender on the third round. Such a move is needed here:

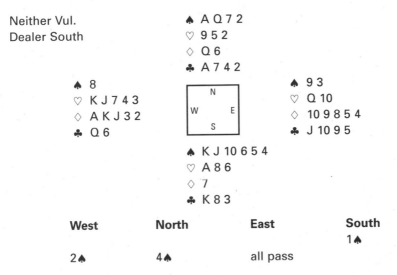

Neither Vul.
Dealer South

```
                 ♠ A Q 7 2
                 ♡ 9 5 2
                 ◇ Q 6
                 ♣ A 7 4 2
  ♠ 8                            ♠ 9 3
  ♡ K J 7 4 3         N          ♡ Q 10
  ◇ A K J 3 2    W         E     ◇ 10 9 8 5 4
  ♣ Q 6               S          ♣ J 10 9 5
                 ♠ K J 10 6 5 4
                 ♡ A 8 6
                 ◇ 7
                 ♣ K 8 3
```

West	North	East	South
			1♠
2♠	4♠	all pass	

As on the previous deal, West intervenes with a Michaels cuebid. His 2♠ overcall shows at least 5-5 shape in hearts and one of the minor suits. How will you play the spade game when West leads the ace and king of diamonds?

You ruff the second diamond and draw trumps in two rounds, noting that you have three apparent further losers in the round suits. West's bidding tells you that clubs cannot possibly break 3-3 and provide a heart discard. You must aim to endplay West on the third round of hearts, having eliminated his black suits. How can this be achieved?

Suppose you cash the ace and king of clubs and play ace and another heart. That's no good. East will win, cash one club winner and exit safely with another top club. You will have no way to dispose of your remaining heart loser.

The only solution is to duck a round of hearts early in the play. Whoever wins this trick and whichever round suit he returns, you will cash your remaining top cards in the side suits and exit with a third round of hearts. West will have to win this trick, as the bidding tells you, and he will then have to award you a ruff-and-sluff. Your potential club loser will vanish into the mists and the spade game will be yours.

The stars come out to play:
advanced elimination play

The women's teams of France and Germany faced each other in the 2006 European championships, contested in Warsaw. Sabine Auken found herself in very much the second-best contract on the next deal, but she managed to rescue the situation with an elimination play.

East-West Vul.
Dealer North

```
                      ♠ 7 5 2
                      ♡ A 8 5
                      ◇ A 6 5
                      ♣ Q 7 4 3
    ♠ K 8 6 4                          ♠ A Q
    ♡ Q 4 3            ┌─────────┐     ♡ K J 10 9 6 2
    ◇ Q J 10 4 3       │    N    │     ◇ 9 8 7 2
    ♣ 6             W  │       E │     ♣ J
                       │    S    │
                      └─────────┘
                      ♠ J 10 9 3
                      ♡ 7
                      ◇ K
                      ♣ A K 10 9 8 5 2
```

West	North	East	South
Willard	*von Arnim*	*Cronier*	*Auken*
	1NT	2◇	5♣
all pass			

Germany's Daniela von Arnim opened with a mini-notrump and East's 2◇ overcall showed hearts. As you can see, 3NT was a good spot for North-South (it was duly bid by the French at the other table, for a score of +430). Sabine Auken leapt to 5♣, however, and the ♡3 was led. How would you play this contract?

Three spade losers loom. The only apparent chance is to eliminate the red suits and then find that the defenders' spades are blocked. Auken won the heart lead and ruffed a heart in her hand. Then she led the ♣8 to dummy's ♣Q and ruffed dummy's last heart with the ♣9. The ◇K was followed by the ♣2

112 • **Bridge Endplays for Everyone**

to dummy's ♣4. Declarer could then cash the ◇A and ruff dummy's last diamond, eliminating the suit. These cards remained:

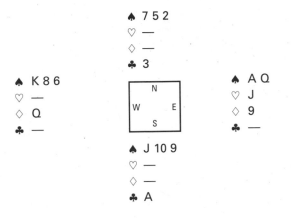

$$\spadesuit \;7\;5\;2$$
$$\heartsuit \;—$$
$$\diamond \;—$$
$$\clubsuit \;3$$

♠ K 8 6   ♠ A Q

With both red suits eliminated, Auken exited with a spade. Bénédicte Cronier (East) defended well by winning the first round with the ace of spades, continuing with the spade queen. If West had held ♠K-J-6, she could have overtaken the queen and beaten the contract. Declarer held the ♠J, though. West could not afford to overtake and East had to give a ruff-and-sluff on the next trick, allowing declarer to throw her remaining spade. That was +400 and Auken had restricted the damage to just 1 IMP.

NOW TRY THESE...

A.

      ♠ Q 10 7 6 5
      ♡ A Q 8
      ◇ A Q 9 2
      ♣ 3

```
        N
    W       E
        S
```

♣K led

      ♠ A K J 8 4 2
      ♡ 6 5 2
      ◇ 4
      ♣ A 8 4

West	North	East	South
			1♠
pass	4♣	pass	4◇
pass	4NT	pass	5♣
pass	5NT	pass	6♠
all pass			

How will you play the spade slam when West leads the ♣K?

B.

      ♠ 7 5 3 2
      ♡ K 10 7 6
      ◇ A 9 4
      ♣ K 5

```
        N
    W       E
        S
```

◇Q led

      ♠ A 10 4
      ♡ A Q 9 8 4 3
      ◇ K 7
      ♣ A 4

West	North	East	South
			1♡
1♠	2♠	pass	4NT
pass	5♡	pass	6♡
all pass			

West leads the ◇Q against your heart slam. How will you play?

C.

                    ♠ 10 7 6 5
                    ♡ 5 3 2
                    ◇ 9 3 2
                    ♣ A 8 5

                    ┌─────────┐
                    │   N   │
♠K led   │ W   E │
                    │   S   │
                    └─────────┘

                    ♠ A 8
                    ♡ A K Q J 8 6
                    ◇ K 6 4
                    ♣ K 6

West	North	East	South
1♠	pass	pass	dbl
pass	2♣	pass	3♡
pass	4♡	all pass	

It's just possible that 3NT might have been a better spot. No one's bidding is perfect, however, and you arrive in 4♡. How will you play this when West leads the ♠K? (You will find that the trumps break 2-2.)

D.

                    ♠ A 6
                    ♡ K J 7 4
                    ◇ 10 8 7 2
                    ♣ A 4 2

                    ┌─────────┐
                    │   N   │
♠2 led   │ W   E │
                    │   S   │
                    └─────────┘

                    ♠ 5 3
                    ♡ A Q 10 8 5
                    ◇ A Q
                    ♣ K Q J 10

West	North	East	South
			1♡
pass	2NT	4♠	5♣
pass	6♡	all pass	

North's Jacoby 2NT showed a sound heart raise to at least the three-level. Sitting South, you are strong enough to visualize a slam but cannot use Blackwood with two top losers in the suit bid by East. You cuebid 5♣, denying a spade control, and North has an obvious raise to 6♡.

West leads the ♠2 against the slam. You win with the ace and play a round of trumps, East showing out. How will you continue?

Answers 🖉

A.

```
                    ♠ Q 10 7 6 5
                    ♡ A Q 8
                    ◇ A Q 9 2
                    ♣ 3
    ♠ —                              ♠ 9 3
    ♡ 10 9 4 3          N            ♡ K J 7
    ◇ J 8 6 5      W       E         ◇ K 10 7 3
    ♣ K Q J 7 5        S             ♣ 10 9 6 2
                    ♠ A K J 8 4 2
                    ♡ 6 5 2
                    ◇ 4
                    ♣ A 8 4
```

West	North	East	South
			1♠
pass	4♣	pass	4◇
pass	4NT	pass	5♣
pass	5NT	pass	6♠
all pass			

How will you play the slam when West leads the ♣K?

You win with the ♣A, ruff a club high, cross to the ♠A and ruff your last club high. A trump to the king draws East's remaining trump. These cards remain:

```
                    ♠ 7
                    ♡ A Q 8
                    ◇ A Q 9 2
                    ♣ —
    ♠ —                              ♠ —
    ♡ 10 9 4           N            ♡ K J 7
    ◇ J 8 6 5      W       E         ◇ K 10 7 3
    ♣ Q                S             ♣ 10
                    ♠ J 8 4 2
                    ♡ 6 5 2
                    ◇ 4
                    ♣ —
```

At this stage, you play a diamond, inserting the nine from dummy. East wins with the ◇10 and is endplayed. The return of either red suit will allow you to dispose of your two heart losers. If East gives a ruff-and-sluff instead, you will discard one heart from your hand on that trick and another heart on dummy's ◇A.

If West rises with the ◇J on the first round, you will cover with the ◇Q. Dummy's ◇A-9 will then be an effective tenace against East's ◇10.

B.

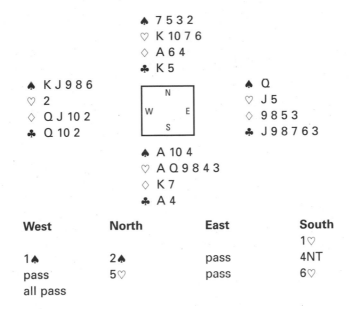

♠ 7 5 3 2
♡ K 10 7 6
◇ A 6 4
♣ K 5

♠ K J 9 8 6
♡ 2
◇ Q J 10 2
♣ Q 10 2

♠ Q
♡ J 5
◇ 9 8 5 3
♣ J 9 8 7 6 3

♠ A 10 4
♡ A Q 9 8 4 3
◇ K 7
♣ A 4

West	North	East	South
			1♡
1♠	2♠	pass	4NT
pass	5♡	pass	6♡
all pass			

West leads the ◇Q against your heart slam. How will you play?

Somehow you must avoid two spade losers. West would probably have led the suit if he held ♠K-Q-J, so the odds are good that East holds a singleton honor. You win the diamond lead with the king and draw trumps in two rounds. You eliminate clubs by playing the ace and king and continue with the ◇A and a diamond ruff, eliminating that suit too. These cards remain:

♠ 7 5 3 2
♡ 10 7
◇ —
♣ —

♠ K J 9 8
♡ —
◇ J
♣ Q

♠ Q
♡ —
◇ 9
♣ J 9 8 7

♠ A 10 4
♡ Q 9 8
◇ —
♣ —

With both minor suits eliminated, you exit with the ♠4. If East wins the trick with the singleton ♠Q, he will have to give you a ruff-and-sluff. You will discard the ♠10 and ruff in the dummy. Nor can West save the situation by rising heroically with the ♠K to save his partner from being endplayed. With the king and queen of spades departing on a single trick, West would then have to lead a spade into your ♠A-10 tenace or give a ruff-and-sluff.

C.

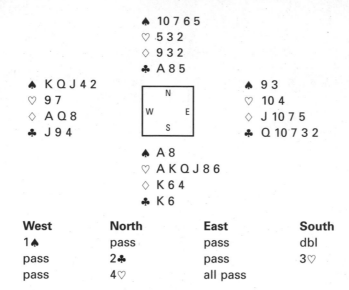

West	North	East	South
1♠	pass	pass	dbl
pass	2♣	pass	3♡
pass	4♡	all pass	

Respecting your bidding (indeed, why not?) and expecting his ♣A to be worth more than one trick, North raises you to the heart game. How will you play this contract when West leads the ♠K?

You win with the ♠A and draw trumps, pleased to see the 2-2 break. You continue with the king and ace of clubs, ruffing the third round to eliminate the suit. These cards remain:

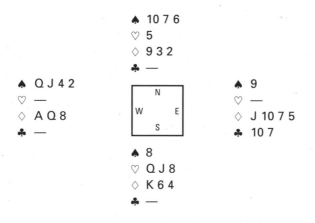

If West is not looking worried by this stage, he should be! You lead the ♠8 and he wins with the ♠J. When he continues with the ♠Q, you throw a low diamond from your hand. (There is no point in ruffing, since you have no entry to dummy to reach the established ♠10.) West has no good continuation. He must open the diamond suit or give a trick to dummy's ♠10.

D.

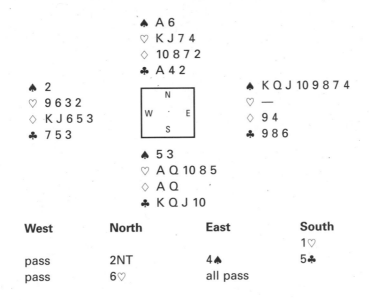

	♠ A 6		
	♡ K J 7 4		
	◇ 10 8 7 2		
	♣ A 4 2		

♠ 2
♡ 9 6 3 2
◇ K J 6 5 3
♣ 7 5 3

♠ K Q J 10 9 8 7 4
♡ —
◇ 9 4
♣ 9 8 6

♠ 5 3
♡ A Q 10 8 5
◇ A Q
♣ K Q J 10

West	North	East	South
			1♡
pass	2NT	4♠	5♣
pass	6♡	all pass	

West leads the ♠2 against the slam. You win with the ace and play a round of trumps, East showing out. How will you continue?

If West holds four or more clubs, you will be able to throw dummy's spade loser on the fourth round of the suit and ruff a spade in dummy. Even if West holds fewer than four clubs, you can arrange for him to be endplayed should he ruff an early club. After three rounds of trumps, you play three rounds of clubs, the suit breaking. These cards are still to be played:

	♠ 6		
	♡ K		
	◇ 10 8 7 2		
	♣ —		

♠ —
♡ 9
◇ K J 6 5 3
♣ —

♠ Q J 10 9
♡ —
◇ 9 4
♣ —

♠ 5
♡ 10 8
◇ A Q
♣ J

What can West do when you lead the ♣J? If he ruffs with his last trump, you will throw the ♠6 from dummy. West will then have to play a diamond into your tenace, after which you can ruff your remaining spade in the dummy.

Suppose instead that West declines to ruff the fourth club. You will again discard a spade from dummy and ruff your spade loser, eventually conceding just one trick in diamonds.

C H A P T E R 7

The Throw-In

The time has come to move away from potential ruff-and-sluff end positions. Now we will look at the situation where you endplay a defender at notrump or in a suit contract where you do not have at least one trump remaining in each hand. It is more awkward to operate in such an environment and you will sometimes have to read exactly which cards a defender has chosen to retain. The throw-in is an underrated technique, despite its relative difficulty. Perhaps this is because it has never been awarded a glamorous name.

Let's start with a straightforward example of the throw-in:

```
Both Vul.              ♠ 8 7 3
Dealer South           ♡ 10 7 4 2
                       ◇ A Q 5
                       ♣ K 7 5
        ♠ K Q J 10 5       ┌─────┐        ♠ 9 4
        ♡ K 8 5            │  N  │        ♡ J 9 3
        ◇ 9 2             │W   E│        ◇ 10 8 6 4
        ♣ 10 6 4           │  S  │        ♣ Q J 9 2
                           └─────┘
                       ♠ A 6 2
                       ♡ A Q 6
                       ◇ K J 7 3
                       ♣ A 8 3
```

West	North	East	South
			1◇
1♠	dbl	pass	2NT
pass	3NT	all pass	

How will you play the notrump game when West leads the ♠K?

You duck the first round of spades and win the second, leaving open the possibility of throwing West in to lead with a third round of the suit. When you play four rounds of diamonds, let's say that West throws the ♡5 and the ♣4. You have eight tricks on top and a successful heart finesse would bring you a ninth. West's overcall makes him the favorite to hold the ♡K, however, and you may well decide to catch this card with a throw-in.

If West has kept three winning spades and ♡K-x, he will have only two cards left in clubs. You can remove these by playing the ace and king of clubs. The lead is in dummy and these cards remain:

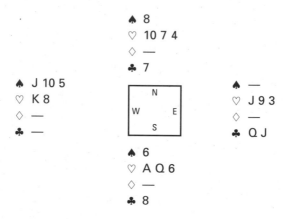

You put West on lead with a spade. After cashing two further winners in the suit, he does indeed have to lead away from the ♡K and the contract is yours.

'What was difficult about that?' you may be thinking. The answer is that you needed to read how the cards lay. Suppose West had not been dealt the ♡K and had kept: ♠J-10-5 ♡8 ♣J. You would then need to finesse the ♡Q to make the contract; an attempted throw-in would allow West to beat you by cashing four more tricks. Suppose instead that West had retained ♠J-10-5 ♡K ♣10. To succeed then, you would have to play a heart to the ace, dropping the singleton ♡K.

Counting the hand to read the end position

When you are not protected by a ruff-and-sluff environment, you will often need to read the cards correctly. Counting the hands becomes even more important than usual. Test yourself on this deal:

Both Vul.
Dealer South

```
                    ♠ 7 5 2
                    ♡ A 5 4 3
                    ◇ A 9 8
                    ♣ K J 5
    ♠ K 10 4 3                      ♠ J 9 8
    ♡ J 10 9 8 6      N             ♡ 2
    ◇ 7 3          W     E          ◇ J 10 6 5 2
    ♣ 10 3            S             ♣ 9 7 6 4
                    ♠ A Q 6
                    ♡ K Q 7
                    ◇ K Q 4
                    ♣ A Q 8 2
```

West	North	East	South
			2NT
pass	4NT	pass	6NT
all pass			

West leads the ♡J against 6NT. How will you play the slam?

You win with the ♡K and cash the ♡Q, East discarding a diamond. Seeking further information, you play four rounds of clubs, throwing a spade from dummy, and continue with the top three diamonds. What is the result of this industrious research? You discover that West began with 4-5-2-2 shape. He holds four spades to East's three and is therefore a '4-to-3 on' favorite to hold the ♠K.

Meanwhile, you have been noting West's discards. Suppose he has thrown two spades and a heart. This will be the end position:

```
                    ♠ 7 5
                    ♡ A 5
                    ◇ —
                    ♣ —
    ♠ K 10                            ♠ J 9 8
    ♡ 10 9           N                ♡ —
    ◇ —           W     E             ◇ J
    ♣ —              S                ♣ —
                    ♠ A Q 6
                    ♡ 7
                    ◇ —
                    ♣ —
```

Regardless of who holds the ♠K, you are certain to make the contract by playing ace and another heart, putting West on lead. You know from your count of the hand that West will then have to lead a spade into your tenace.

A skilled defender in the West seat will realize that he is giving himself no chance by reducing to two cards in each major suit. He may keep all his hearts and bare the ♠K, leaving this position:

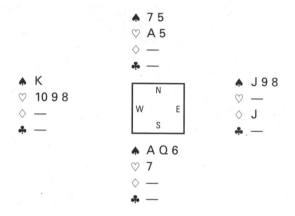

When you are facing top-class defenders, life is not so pleasant. If East holds the ♠K, you must cross to the ♡A and finesse the ♠Q. If instead West holds the ♠K, you will have to lay down the ♠A. What guess should you make? In the absence of any other clue, still assuming that West is competent enough to bare his king, you should refer back to the original count in the spade suit. The odds are '4-to-3 on' that West holds the ♠K and you should therefore play for the drop.

Note that West should reduce to one spade and three hearts even when he does not hold the ♠K. By doing so, he will give you the losing option of playing to drop the ♠K offside. If he keeps two spades and two hearts, you can, as we saw earlier, guarantee the contract with a throw-in.

Removing the safe exit cards

There are various ways of removing a defender's safe exit cards and we will see some of them in this section. On the next deal, East is your intended throw-in victim. The bidding suggests that he will hold a singleton in spades, the suit that his partner has bid. This potential exit card must be removed at an early stage.

North-South Vul.
Dealer West

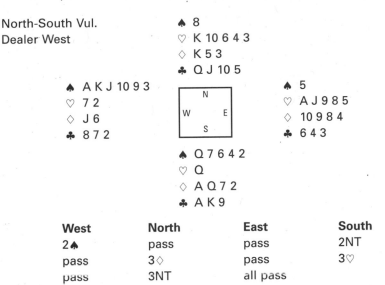

```
                      ♠ 8
                      ♡ K 10 6 4 3
                      ◇ K 5 3
                      ♣ Q J 10 5
  ♠ A K J 10 9 3                        ♠ 5
  ♡ 7 2                                 ♡ A J 9 8 5
  ◇ J 6           N                     ◇ 10 9 8 4
  ♣ 8 7 2      W     E                  ♣ 6 4 3
                   S
                      ♠ Q 7 6 4 2
                      ♡ Q
                      ◇ A Q 7 2
                      ♣ A K 9
```

West	North	East	South
2♠	pass	pass	2NT
pass	3◇	pass	3♡
pass	3NT	all pass	

North uses a transfer sequence to offer a choice of games. Unwilling to give declarer a spade trick, West leads a passive ♣7 against 3NT. How will you play the contract?

There are seven top tricks in the minors and it will be easy to establish an eighth trick in hearts. A ninth trick might arrive from a 3-3 diamond break. Failing that, it may be possible to endplay East with the fourth round of diamonds, forcing him to concede a second heart trick.

You win the club lead in your hand and lead a low spade. Do you see the point of this? You expect spades to break 6-1 and want to remove East's singleton, which constitutes a safe exit card. West wins the trick with the ♠9 and cannot afford to cash the top two spades, since this will set up the ♠Q as your ninth trick. He can guess, from your play in the spade suit, that East holds only one spade. Let's say that he cashes one top spade, East showing out, and switches to the ♡7.

You win with the ♡Q (East fares no better by playing the ♡A) and then cash three more clubs, followed by the king, ace and queen of diamonds. These cards remain:

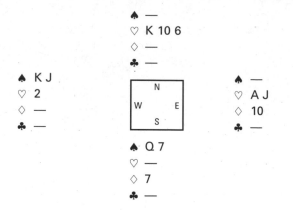

```
                         ♠ —
                         ♡ K 10 6
                         ◇ —
                         ♣ —
      ♠ K J                              ♠ —
      ♡ 2            ┌─────────┐         ♡ A J
      ◇ —           │    N    │          ◇ 10
      ♣ —           │  W   E  │          ♣ —
                     │    S    │
                     └─────────┘
                         ♠ Q 7
                         ♡ —
                         ◇ 7
                         ♣ —
```

East's safe exit cards in the black suits have been extracted. You throw him in with a diamond and he has to give dummy a heart trick.

On the next deal, it is West's clubs that have to be removed. You must manage the entries to dummy carefully.

North-South Vul.
Dealer East

```
                         ♠ 9 2
                         ♡ Q 10 6 4
                         ◇ 9 7 4
                         ♣ J 9 7 4
      ♠ 7 6 4                            ♠ 5 3
      ♡ K 9 8 5 2    ┌─────────┐         ♡ 3
      ◇ 2           │    N    │          ◇ K Q J 10 8 6 5
      ♣ Q 6 3 2     │  W   E  │          ♣ 10 8 5
                     │    S    │
                     └─────────┘
                         ♠ A K Q J 10 8
                         ♡ A J 7
                         ◇ A 3
                         ♣ A K
```

West	North	East	South
		3◇	dbl
pass	3♡	pass	4NT
pass	5♣	pass	6♠
all pass			

The auction was not entirely satisfactory. To investigate a potential grand slam, South bid Roman Keycard Blackwood with hearts agreed. If partner had shown the king and queen of hearts, South would have bid 7NT. When the first response denied the king of hearts, there was no sound way to determine whether a small slam was playable. South followed a well-trodden path when he shut his eyes and leapt to 6♠ anyway. How would you play this contract when West leads the two of diamonds, an obvious singleton?

Since the nine of trumps is an entry to dummy, one possibility is to finesse East for the ♡K. However, the fact that he has seven diamonds to West's one makes West a big favorite to hold the heart king. What else could you try?

The original declarer won the diamond lead and played the ace of trumps. He then cashed the ace and king of clubs, everyone following. A trump to the nine was followed by a club ruff, East following for the third time. The queen still refused to show. Declarer now drew West's last trump and played the ace and jack of hearts. If West were to win the second heart, declarer would make the contract easily, throwing his diamond loser on the fourth round of hearts. West therefore had to hold up his king of hearts for one round. Declarer overtook with dummy's queen of hearts and ruffed the jack of clubs, removing West's last card in the suit.

West now had nothing but hearts left. When declarer led a third round of the suit from his hand, West had to win with the king and then surrender a trick to dummy's ten of hearts. Away went South's diamond loser and the slam was made. Declarer would have gone down if East had held the king of hearts, of course, but the chosen line was a better prospect.

Sometimes you have to duck a round or two of a suit in order to remove a defender's exit cards there. Again, on the next deal, it is West's clubs that have to be removed.

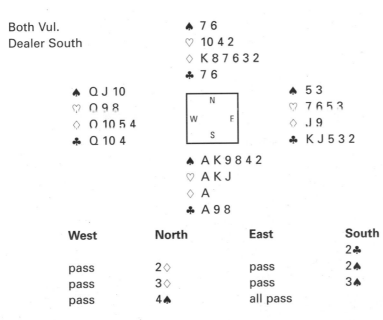

Both Vul.
Dealer South

North
♠ 7 6
♡ 10 4 2
◇ K 8 7 6 3 2
♣ 7 6

West
♠ Q J 10
♡ Q 9 8
◇ Q 10 5 4
♣ Q 10 4

East
♠ 5 3
♡ 7 6 5 3
◇ J 9
♣ K J 5 3 2

South
♠ A K 9 8 4 2
♡ A K J
◇ A
♣ A 9 8

West	North	East	South
			2♣
pass	2◇	pass	2♠
pass	3◇	pass	3♠
pass	4♠	all pass	

West leads the trump queen and you win with the ace. It's an annoying lead because it prevents you from ruffing a club, thereby reaching the ◇K for an overtrick. How will you continue?

You must aim to endplay West. This can be done when he holds no more than three clubs. You win the trump lead, duck a club and win the trump continuation, pleased to see that the suit breaks 3-2. You unblock the ◊A and play ace and another club. With West holding only three cards in the club suit, the contract cannot be beaten.

Suppose West wins the third round of clubs and cashes his master trump. He will then have to lead a heart into your A-K-J tenace or act as a stepping stone to dummy's ◊K. The defenders will not fare any better if East wins the third round of clubs. If he switches to a heart, you will rise with the ace and throw West in with a trump. The only other possibility is that East will win and play a fourth round of clubs. You will then ruff in the South hand, knowing that West will be endplayed if he overruffs. If he declines to overruff, you will throw him in with a trump on the next trick anyway.

Forcing the defenders to assist in the strip

Sometimes it is not possible to strip a defender's last safe exit card under your own steam. The solution may be to throw him in twice. The first time, he exits safely. The second time, he has to give you a trick. That's what happens here:

East-West Vul.
Dealer South

		♠ K 10 5 3	
		♡ 6	
		◊ 9 7 5 3 2	
		♣ 10 6 3	

♠ 9 7 2		♠ Q J 8 6 4
♡ J 9 8 3	N	♡ 7
◊ K Q J	W E	◊ 10 8 6
♣ K 7 4	S	♣ Q 9 8 2

		♠ A	
		♡ A K Q 10 5 4 2	
		◊ A 4	
		♣ A J 5	

West	North	East	South
			2♣
pass	2◊	pass	2♡
pass	2NT	pass	3♡
pass	3♠	pass	4♡
all pass			

West leads the ◇K and you win with the ace. When you start to draw trumps, East throws a spade on the second round. There is no entry to dummy's ♠K, so you have four potential losers — one trump, one diamond and two clubs. What can you do about it?

Prospects are not especially bright, but there is some chance of endplaying West with the fourth round of trumps. You cash the ♠A and exit with your remaining diamond. West wins and cannot safely play a spade, heart or club. Like it or not, West has to return the jack of diamonds, burning his last safe exit card.

When East follows suit to this trick, a smile comes to your lips. You ruff in the South hand, draw a third round of trumps and put West on lead with his jack of trumps. Two poisons lie before him. He can lead a club, giving you two tricks in the suit, or he can act as a stepping stone to dummy's apparently isolated ♠K. Ten tricks to you either way. You would make the contract even if West had led from ◇K-Q-x and East could win the second round of diamonds. He could play one club through, to the king, but this would not stop the subsequent endplay on West.

Throw-in with no side suits eliminated

There are few boundaries for the throw-in play. Let's see a deal where all three side suits are still alive but the defender still has no safe return when he is put on lead.

Neither Vul.
Dealer North

```
                    ♠ K 9
                    ♡ K Q 7
                    ◇ A K J 5 3
                    ♣ Q 7 4
♠ Q J 8 6 5 3              N         ♠ 4
♡ 9                                 ♡ 10 8 4 2
◇ 10           W         E          ◇ Q 9 8 7 4
♣ A 10 8 3 2              S         ♣ K 9 6
                    ♠ A 10 7 2
                    ♡ A J 6 5 3
                    ◇ 6 2
                    ♣ J 5
```

West	North	East	South
	1◇	pass	1♡
1♠	dbl	pass	3♡
pass	4♡	all pass	

You arrive in 4♡ after a Support Double from North showed three-card heart support. How will you play the contract when West leads the ◇10?

You win with the ◇A and draw trumps in four rounds. Your next move is both simple and elegant — you lead a second round of diamonds, West showing out, and duck in the dummy. East wins cheaply with the ◇9 but he has no safe return.

If the defenders take their two club tricks, you will have discards for your spade losers — one on the ♣Q and one on the ◇K. A diamond return into dummy's K-J tenace will obviously be fatal for the defense. East's only other choice is to play a spade. You would win West's jack with the king and discard one of your club losers on the ◇K. Then you would run the ♠9 to West's ♠Q, setting up the ♠10 in your hand. That would give you the game, for a loss of one spade, one diamond and one club.

Preserving two tenaces

When you have two tenaces waiting for your intended victim, you must make sure that you will not be embarrassed for discards when the defender cashes his winners. Take the South cards here:

```
North-South Vul.              ♠ J 3
Dealer South                  ♡ 10 7 6 4
                              ◇ K Q J 6 5
                              ♣ J 9
        ♠ A 10 8 7 5      ┌──────────┐      ♠ K 9
        ♡ K 9             │    N     │      ♡ J 8 5 3 2
        ◇ 7 3             │ W     E  │      ◇ 9 8 2
        ♣ K 10 3 2        │    S     │      ♣ 8 6 5
                          └──────────┘
                              ♠ Q 6 4 2
                              ♡ A Q
                              ◇ A 10 4
                              ♣ A Q 7 4
```

West	North	East	South
			1♣
1♠	dbl	pass	2NT
pass	3NT	all pass	

West leads the ♠7 against 3NT, East winning with the king and returning the suit. West wins the second round with the ace and persists with the ♠10 to force out your ♠Q. How will you continue?

With eight tricks on top, you would like to put West on lead with a spade, forcing him to lead into one of your A-Q tenaces. There are two good reasons why you cannot afford to play five rounds of diamonds first, discarding the two low clubs from your hand. The first is that you would then be in the wrong hand to throw West in with a spade. Even if this were not the case, you would have no safe discard from the South hand when West cashed his last spade. You would have to throw the ♡Q or the ♣Q, allowing West to exit safely to your bared ace.

So, you cash just ace and ten of diamonds, trusting that West began with no more than two cards in the suit. These cards remain:

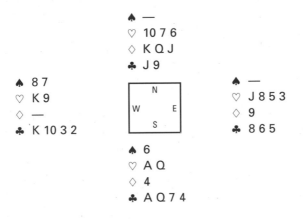

```
              ♠ —
              ♡ 10 7 6
              ◇ K Q J
              ♣ J 9
  ♠ 8 7                        ♠ —
  ♡ K 9          N             ♡ J 8 5 3
  ◇ —       W        E         ◇ 9
  ♣ K 10 3 2       S           ♣ 8 6 5
              ♠ 6
              ♡ A Q
              ◇ 4
              ♣ A Q 7 4
```

You exit with a spade and throw a low club from your hand when West cashes his last spade. Since he does not hold the last diamond, West will then have to lead a heart or a club. A ninth trick is yours.

The stars come out to play:

the throw-in

Up goes the curtain and out stride our star players, ready to demonstrate their impressive throw-in technique. The first deal may seem relatively easy, but several declarers went astray in the quarterfinals of the 1991 Bermuda Bowl and Venice Cup, played in Yokohama.

North-South Vul.
Dealer South

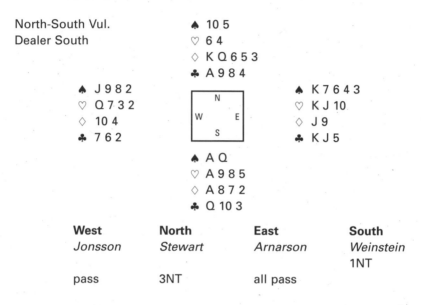

```
                    ♠ 10 5
                    ♡ 6 4
                    ◇ K Q 6 5 3
                    ♣ A 9 8 4
  ♠ J 9 8 2                        ♠ K 7 6 4 3
  ♡ Q 7 3 2           N            ♡ K J 10
  ◇ 10 4         W        E        ◇ J 9
  ♣ 7 6 2            S             ♣ K J 5
                    ♠ A Q
                    ♡ A 9 8 5
                    ◇ A 8 7 2
                    ♣ Q 10 3
```

West	North	East	South
Jonsson	*Stewart*	*Arnarson*	*Weinstein*
			1NT
pass	3NT	all pass	

West leads the ♡2 against 3NT, East playing the ♡K. In order to appreciate Steve Weinstein's line of play, let's first see how some other stars tackled it. In the Venice Cup, O'Yang for Chinese Taipei won the first round of hearts and passed the ♣Q to the ♣K. East cashed the jack and ten of hearts and switched to a spade. A second club finesse appeared to be a better prospect than the spade finesse, so declarer rose with the ♠A and ran the ♣10, going three down. Nell Kahn (representing USA II in the Venice Cup) played the same way, but she judged to finesse the ♠Q and made the contract.

Steve Weinstein, playing for USA II against Iceland, will now demonstrate how the contract should be played. He won the third round of hearts and cashed three rounds of diamonds, retaining a fourth-round entry to the dummy. When he exited with his last heart, West won and had to play one of the black suits. Declarer was assured of a ninth trick however the remaining cards lay.

The next deal arose in the 2002 World Bridge Championships in Montreal. During the qualifying rounds for the Rosenblum, Israel's David Birman arrived in 3NT on this deal:

North-South Vul.
Dealer South

```
                    ♠ A 4
                    ♡ 9 7 3 2
                    ◇ 8 6 4
                    ♣ K Q J 5
   ♠ J 9 7 5 3                        ♠ K Q 8
   ♡ Q J 6          N                 ♡ 10 8 5
   ◇ K 9 3      W       E             ◇ J 7 5 2
   ♣ 8 6            S                 ♣ 10 7 2
                    ♠ 10 6 2
                    ♡ A K 4
                    ◇ A Q 10
                    ♣ A 9 4 3
```

West	North	East	South
	Sagiv		*Birman*
			1NT
pass	2♣	pass	2◇
pass	3NT	all pass	

West, who was supposedly playing fourth-best leads, led the ♠3 against 3NT. When East won with the ♠Q and returned the ♠K, the odds were high that spades were in fact breaking 5-3 (rather than 4-4, as suggested by the opening lead).

Birman won with dummy's ♠A and marked time by cashing four rounds of clubs. West discarded an encouraging ◇9 and then the ♡6. Reading the cards well, Birman crossed to his hand with the ♡A, cashed the ♡K and then led the ♠10 to put West on lead. West was able to cash two more spades, but at Trick 12, he had to lead away from his ◇K-3 into declarer's ◇A-Q.

It was somewhat naïve of West to signal his ◇K. Had he chosen a low diamond as his first discard, declarer would have been hard-pressed to read the lie of the cards so well. Another possibility was for West to discard the ◇3 and the ◇9. If declarer followed his original line, cashing two rounds of hearts, West could unblock the ♡Q and the ♡J. To make the contract then, declarer would have to diagnose that the ◇K had been bared offside. Not easy.

We will end the section with a spade game played by Tim Seres in the final of the 1975 Australian Interstate Teams. It is an unusual situation because the 'problem suit', the one that declarer needed the defenders to open, is the trump suit!

Both Vul.
Dealer West

```
                        ♠ K 7 6
                        ♡ K 9 7 6
                        ◇ A Q
                        ♣ 10 9 6 3
     ♠ Q 4                              ♠ J 8 5
     ♡ J 10 8 3          N              ♡ Q 5 4
     ◇ J 7 5 2       W       E          ◇ K 9 8 6
     ♣ K J 7             S              ♣ Q 8 4
                        ♠ A 10 9 3 2
                        ♡ A 2
                        ◇ 10 4 3
                        ♣ A 5 2
```

West	North	East	South
			Seres
pass	1♣	pass	1NT
pass	2NT	pass	3♠
pass	4♠	all pass	

In the New South Wales system, the 1NT response is an artificial game force. West led the ♡J, won with the ace, and Seres took an immediate diamond finesse. When this lost to the king, he was faced with three losers in the minor suits and could not therefore afford a loser in the trump suit.

A club was returned, to the jack, and West continued with the ♣K. Seres won with the ♣A, cashed dummy's ◇A and ♡K and then ruffed a heart in his hand. A diamond ruff was followed by a fourth round of hearts. East showed out and declarer was able to ruff cheaply in his hand. These cards remained:

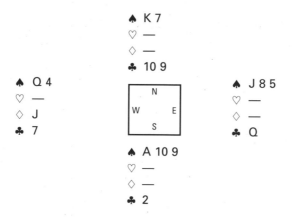

```
                        ♠ K 7
                        ♡ —
                        ◇ —
                        ♣ 10 9
     ♠ Q 4                              ♠ J 8 5
     ♡ —                N              ♡ —
     ◇ J            W       E          ◇ —
     ♣ 7                  S              ♣ Q
                        ♠ A 10 9
                        ♡ —
                        ◇ —
                        ♣ 2
```

Time to exit with a club! East won and returned the ♠5, covered by the ten, queen and king. A finesse of the ♠9 then gave Seres his contract. If East had returned the ♠J instead, Seres would have had to read the position — dropping the ♠Q on the second round. The same situation would have arisen if West had retained the top club, allowing him to win the third round. He could not safely return a trump or a diamond without giving declarer a chance to pick up the trumps.

NOW TRY THESE...

A.

    ♠ K Q 6 5 3
    ♡ 6 4
    ◇ J 10 2
    ♣ J 10 6

```
      N
  W       E
      S
```

♠2 led

♠ —
♡ A K Q J 9 7 2
◇ A K 4
♣ A K 3

West	North	East	South
		3♠	6♡
all pass			

Suppressing the urge to make a once-in-a-lifetime overcall at the seven-level, you bid a modest 6♡. How will you play this contract when West leads the ♠2, an obvious singleton?

B.

    ♠ J 8 3
    ♡ 10 5 2
    ◇ 5 3
    ♣ J 9 7 4 2

```
      N
  W       E
      S
```

♡K led

♠ A Q
♡ A 6 4
◇ A K Q 6 4
♣ A K 3

West	North	East	South
			2♣
pass	2◇	pass	3NT
all pass			

West leads the ♡K against 3NT. How will you play the contract?

C.

             ♠ 6 3
             ♡ K J 7 6 2
             ♦ 6 5 2
             ♣ A Q 4

           ┌─────────┐
           │   N   │
♡9 led   │ W   E │
           │   S   │
           └─────────┘

             ♠ A Q 9
             ♡ A Q 10
             ♦ A Q 3
             ♣ K 7 3 2

West	North	East	South
			2NT
pass	3◊	pass	3♡
pass	3NT	pass	4♣
pass	6♡	all pass	

How will you play the heart slam when West leads the nine of trumps?

D.

             ♠ 10 5
             ♡ 6 3
             ♦ A 10 9 7 3 2
             ♣ 9 6 2

           ┌─────────┐
           │   N   │
♠3 led   │ W   E │
           │   S   │
           └─────────┘

             ♠ A J 8 6
             ♡ A K Q J 10 4 2
             ♦ —
             ♣ K 5

West	North	East	South
		2♠	4♡
all pass			

East's weak-two opening shows 5-9 points. How will you play the heart game when West leads the ♠3, East playing the ♠Q?

Answers ✎

A.

```
              ♠ K Q 6 5 3
              ♡ 6 4
              ◇ J 10 2
              ♣ J 10 6
  ♠ 2                          ♠ A J 10 9 8 7 4
  ♡ 10 8 3        N            ♡ 5
  ◇ 9 7 5 3   W     E          ◇ Q 8 6
  ♣ Q 9 7 5 2      S           ♣ 8 4
              ♠ —
              ♡ A K Q J 9 7 2
              ◇ A K 4
              ♣ A K 3
```

West	North	East	South
		3♠	6♡

all pass

How will you play the heart slam when West leads the ♠2, an obvious single-ton?

Dummy's ♠K is covered by the ♠A and you take care to ruff this with the ♡7, retaining the ♡2. When you continue with the ace and king of trumps, East shows out on the second round, throwing a spade. What now?

Even if West has been alert enough to follow with the ♡8 and ♡10 on the first two rounds, you will still be able to throw him in, provided you retained the ♡2 on the first trick. West wins the third round of trumps and has to exit in one of the minors. Whether it is East or West who holds the queen of the suit West decides to play, you will not only score three tricks in the suit played, you will also gain access to the ♠Q. You can then discard your loser in the other minor suit and claim the slam.

Is there any hope if the trump suit breaks 2-2, preventing you from throwing West in with a trump? Yes, you can run all of your trumps, hoping to reduce West to Q-x-x in both of the minors. You can then throw him in on the third round of one suit, forcing a lead away from the queen in the other suit. He is unlikely to fool you by reducing to Q-x-x-x in one minor suit and Q-x in the other, because you will play ace and king and another of the suit in which West has made more discards. Unless he began with a huge disparity in his minor-suit lengths, you will drop the doubleton queen.

B.

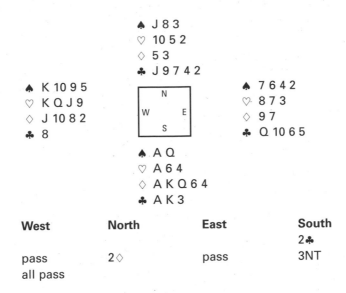

West	North	East	South
			2♣
pass	2◇	pass	3NT
all pass			

West leads the ♡K against 3NT. How will you play the contract?

There is not much point in winning the second round of hearts, planning to put West on lead with the third round if he holds five cards in the suit. You will have nine tricks anyway if the diamonds break 3-3. On any other diamond break, putting West on lead to give you one extra trick in the black suits will bring your total to only eight tricks. You should win the third round of hearts, discovering that the suit breaks 4-3. What now?

You test the diamond suit, finding that West holds four diamonds. When you continue with the ace and king of clubs, West shows out on the second round. These cards remain:

```
              ♠ J 8
              ♡ —
              ◇ —
              ♣ J 9 7
  ♠ K 10 9      ┌─────────┐      ♠ 7 6 4
  ♡ 9          │    N    │      ♡ —
  ◇ J          │ W     E │      ◇ —
  ♣ —          │    S    │      ♣ Q 10
               └─────────┘
              ♠ A Q
              ♡ —
              ◇ 6 4
              ♣ 3
```

If you lead a club now, putting East on lead, you will succeed only when East holds the ♠K. A better idea is to exit with a diamond, endplaying West. When he cashes the ♡9, you will discard your club loser. West will then have to lead into your spade tenace and you will have nine tricks whoever holds the ♠K.

C.

```
              ♠ 6 3
              ♡ K J 7 6 2
              ◇ 6 5 2
              ♣ A Q 4
♠ K J 4 2          N          ♠ 10 8 7 5
♡ 9 8 5                       ♡ 4 3
◇ K 8 4     W         E       ◇ J 10 9 7
♣ 10 6 5          S           ♣ J 9 8
              ♠ A Q 9
              ♡ A Q 10
              ◇ A Q 3
              ♣ K 7 3 2
```

West	North	East	South
			2NT
pass	3◇	pass	3♡
pass	3NT	pass	4♣
pass	6♡	all pass	

North was initially prepared to let the bidding die at the game level. South's 4♣ indicated a good heart fit, not quite good enough for an original transfer break, and North bid 6♡. How would you play this contract on a trump lead?

You win the trump lead and draw trumps in two further rounds. Next, you play the ace, king and queen of clubs. The suit breaks 3-3, fortunately, and you are conveniently in the North hand. These cards remain:

```
              ♠ 6 3
              ♡ J 7
              ◇ 6 5 2
              ♣ —
♠ K J 4 2          N          ♠ 10 8 7
♡ —                           ♡ —
◇ K 8 4     W         E       ◇ J 10 9 7
♣ —               S           ♣ —
              ♠ A Q 9
              ♡ —
              ◇ A Q 3
              ♣ 7
```

You play a spade to the nine and jack, forcing West to lead into one of your ace-queen tenaces. The slam is yours. If clubs had not broken 3-3, you would need two extra tricks from spades and diamonds. You would again play a spade to the nine, gaining when East held the ♠J-10. Failing that, you would need both the spade king and the diamond king onside. West would have to lead into one tenace. You would then cross to dummy with a club ruff and finesse in the other pointed suit.

D.

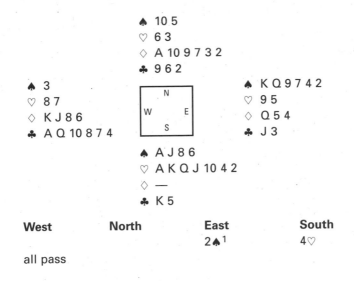

	♠ 10 5	
	♡ 6 3	
	◇ A 10 9 7 3 2	
	♣ 9 6 2	

♠ 3		♠ K Q 9 7 4 2
♡ 8 7		♡ 9 5
◇ K J 8 6		◇ Q 5 4
♣ A Q 10 8 7 4		♣ J 3

	♠ A J 8 6
	♡ A K Q J 10 4 2
	◇ —
	♣ K 5

West	North	East	South
		2♠[1]	4♡
all pass			

1. 5-9.

How will you play when West leads the ♠3 to East's ♠Q and your ♠A?

You draw trumps in two rounds. What now? If East holds the ♣A, you can simply play a spade to dummy's ten. East would have to win to prevent you from enjoying the ◇A and would then be endplayed. A diamond return would give you access to the ◇A and a black-suit return would provide your tenth trick.

There is just room for the ♣A in East's proclaimed 5-9 range, but it is ten times more likely that West holds that card. What are your chances in that case?

You can still succeed when East has no more than two clubs. After drawing trumps, you exit with the ♣K West wins with the ♣A and has no major-suit card to return. A diamond would give you access to dummy's ◇A. Suppose that West plays the queen and ten of clubs, stripping East's holding. You ruff, leaving:

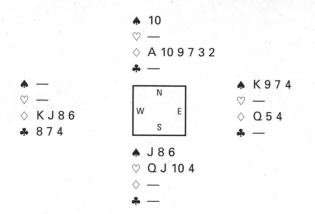

♠ 10
♡ —
◇ A 10 9 7 3 2
♣ —

♠ —
♡ —
◇ K J 8 6
♣ 8 7 4

N
W   E
S

♠ K 9 7 4
♡ —
◇ Q 5 4
♣ —

♠ J 8 6
♡ Q J 10 4
◇ —
♣ —

A spade to the ten endplays East.

Think back to the moment when West won the ♣K with the ♣A. Even if he plays an imaginative low club to East's bare jack on the second round, this will not assist the defense. Since East began with only two clubs, he will have to play a spade or a diamond next, giving you the contract.

The Strip Squeeze

Sometimes you are prevented from performing a throw-in because the defender has too many winners to cash. You may then need to play some winners of your own, to squeeze the defender out of one or more of his winners. This technique is known as a strip squeeze, even though it may end up being a simple throw-in play.

Squeezing the defender out of a winner

Let's see a full-deal example of a strip squeeze straight away.

Both Vul.
Dealer West

	♠ A 10 5	
	♡ 9 7 4	
	◇ Q 4 2	
	♣ Q 5 4 3	

♠ K 6		♠ 9 7 4 3 2
♡ K Q J 10 5 3	N	♡ 2
◇ 8 7	W E	◇ 10 9 6 5 3
♣ K J 8	S	♣ 10 7

	♠ Q J 8	
	♡ A 8 6	
	◇ A K J	
	♣ A 9 6 2	

West	North	East	South
1♡	pass	pass	2NT
pass	3NT	all pass	

West leads the ♡K against 3NT. How will you play the contract?

After West's opening bid, it is reasonable to hope that the ♠K is onside. In that case you have eight top tricks (three spades, three diamonds and two aces). You cannot simply lead towards the ♣Q for a ninth trick, of course, since West would rise with the ♣K and cash too many hearts. Instead, you must aim to throw West in with a heart, forcing him to lead away from the ♣K.

You duck the first round of hearts and West persists with another heart, East discarding a spade. You win the second round with the ace, preserving a potential throw-in card in the suit. What now?

You lead the ♠Q, covered by the king and ace. Suppose you simply extract West's spades and diamonds, playing two rounds of each suit, and then throw him in with a heart. That's no good! He will be able to cash four more hearts, beating the contract, before having to lead away from the ♣K. Instead, you must cash every one of your spade and diamond winners, forcing West to a critical discard. This will be the position as you lead your last pointed-suit winner:

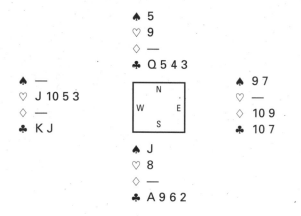

West has to find a discard when you lead the ♠J. If he throws the ♣J, you will drop his ♣K on the next round and score two overtricks. No doubt he will prefer to throw a heart instead. Since he now holds only three heart winners to go with the one that he scored at Trick 1, you can afford to throw him in with a heart. After cashing his hearts, he will have to lead away from the ♣K at Trick 12 and the game will be yours.

You can see why this style of play is classified as a squeeze. When you cash the ♠J, West has to retain his club guard and is squeezed out of a winner.

On the next deal, East is forced to dispose of both a winner and a safe exit card in order to retain his guard in another suit.

North-South Vul.
Dealer West

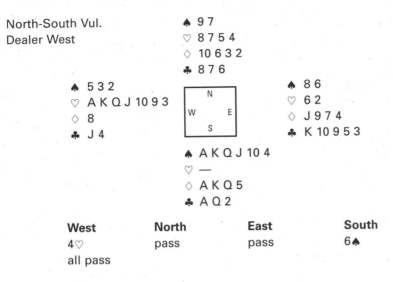

♠ 9 7
♡ 8 7 5 4
◇ 10 6 3 2
♣ 8 7 6

♠ 5 3 2
♡ A K Q J 10 9 3
◇ 8
♣ J 4

♠ 8 6
♡ 6 2
◇ J 9 7 4
♣ K 10 9 5 3

♠ A K Q J 10 4
♡ —
◇ A K Q 5
♣ A Q 2

West	North	East	South
4♡	pass	pass	6♠
all pass			

How will you play the spade slam when West leads the ♡K?

Anyone who has battled through to this stage of the book will find it easy to ruff the heart lead with a high trump, retaining the ♠4 as a means of entering the dummy. You draw two rounds of trumps with the ace and nine and feel there is still some justice in the world when a finesse of the ♣Q proves successful. You draw the last trump and turn to the diamond suit. Justice proves to be limited when West shows out on the second round of diamonds. What next?

West is marked with 3-7-1-2 shape, leaving East with 2-2-4-5. You must aim to put East on lead with a third round of clubs at a time when he will have to lead away from his ◇J-9. At the moment, East has spare cards in hearts and clubs; these must be squeezed away by running your trumps. This is the position you will reach:

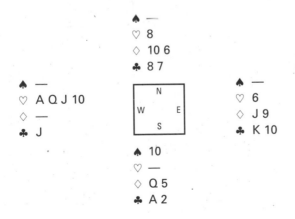

♠ —
♡ 8
◇ 10 6
♣ 8 7

♠ —
♡ A Q J 10
◇ —
♣ J

♠ —
♡ 6
◇ J 9
♣ K 10

♠ 10
♡ —
◇ Q 5
♣ A 2

East has already had to ditch two clubs. You lead your last trump, throwing the ♡8 from dummy, and East is not a happy man. If he throws a minor-suit card, he will give you a twelfth trick directly. He therefore has to throw his last heart, the link to the winners in partner's hand. You continue with ace and another club, putting East on lead. He has to play a diamond from his ◇J-9 and you score both the ◇10 and the ◇Q.

Squeeze out one exit card and ruff the other

Let's look at a special form of the strip squeeze where the defender has two spare cards in a side suit in which he hopes to exit safely. To succeed with your intended throw-in, you must squeeze the defender out of one exit card and then ruff out his remaining exit card. Here is a straightforward example:

Neither Vul.
Dealer South

	♠ J 8 7 5	
	♡ A K 10	
	◇ A K 8	
	♣ K 9 5	
♠ K Q 9 6 3		♠ 10
♡ 3		♡ 9 6 5 4
◇ Q J 10 7		◇ 9 6 4 3
♣ J 8 6		♣ 10 7 4 2
	♠ A 4 2	
	♡ Q J 8 7 2	
	◇ 5 2	
	♣ A Q 3	

West	North	East	South
			1♡
1♠	dbl	pass	1NT
pass	2♣	pass	2♡
pass	4NT	pass	5♠
pass	6♡	all pass	

North's 2♣ asks for further information and he launches Roman Keycard on the next round. An unimpressive auction, perhaps, but how will you play the heart slam when West leads the ◇Q?

West is likely to hold the king and queen of spades for his overcall. If you can strip his non-spades, it will then be a simple matter to lead towards dummy's ♠J. West can win with one spade honor but will then have to lead away from the other honor. All will be easy if West holds no more than three cards in each minor. Unfortunately, his opening lead of the ◇Q suggests that he may hold four diamonds. How can you remove the diamonds from his hand in that case?

You win the diamond lead with the ace and draw trumps in four rounds. West can spare two low spades and we will say that his third discard is the ♣6. If your next move is to cross to the ◇K and ruff a diamond, hoping that West started with only three diamonds, you will go down. (It would be no use cashing the last trump — West would throw a spade, retaining ♠K-Q and a diamond winner.) You may cash the ◇K if you like, but you must then play three rounds of clubs. This will be the position after two high clubs:

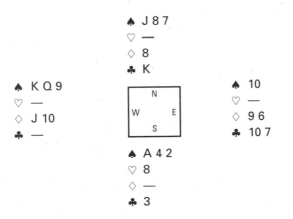

What can West throw when you lead to the ♣K? A spade will allow you to set up a winner in the suit. He is therefore forced to discard one of his two safe exit cards in diamonds. You promptly ruff dummy's ◇8, removing West's remaining safe exit card. In the three-card ending, you lead a low spade from your hand. As you had hoped, West has to win with one honor and lead into your split spade tenace. Forget about the unimpressive auction. You made the contract!

Here is another example of this style of play:

East-West Vul.
Dealer East

```
              ♠ A 10 2
              ♡ 9 5 4
              ◇ A Q 10
              ♣ A Q 9 3
♠ 8 7 5 4                      ♠ 6
♡ J 8 2          N             ♡ K Q 10 7 6 3
◇ 8 7 4 3 2   W     E          ◇ 9 6
♣ 2              S             ♣ K 10 8 5
              ♠ K Q J 9 3
              ♡ A
              ◇ K J 5
              ♣ J 7 6 4
```

West	North	East	South
		2♡	2♠
pass	3♡	pass	4♡
pass	6♠	all pass	

North's 3♡ shows (at least) a sound raise in spades and South cuebids his heart control in case North has a slam in mind. His intentions do indeed lie in that direction and West leads the ♡2 against your small slam in spades. How would you play the contract?

You win the heart lead and draw trumps in four rounds, throwing a heart from dummy. East, meanwhile, discards three hearts. All will be well unless East holds ♣K-10-x-x, but it would be premature to tackle the club suit at this stage. Instead, you should play your diamonds, reaching this position:

```
              ♠ —
              ♡ 9
              ◇ Q
              ♣ A Q 9 3
♠ —                           ♠ —
♡ J 8            N             ♡ K 10
◇ 8 7 4      W     E           ◇ —
♣ 2              S             ♣ K 10 8 5
              ♠ 9
              ♡ —
              ◇ J
              ♣ J 7 6 4
```

When you lead the ◇Q, East cannot afford a club and must release a heart winner. East can be counted for 1-6-2-4 shape. You therefore lead dummy's ♡9, ruffing out East's last card in hearts and reducing him to his four clubs. Then you lead a club towards dummy and finesse the queen. East wins with the king and has to return a club away from the ten. Three club tricks come home and the slam is yours.

Squeezing the defender down to one safe exit card

Suppose you can reduce a defender to one safe exit card by running a long suit. He will be able to exit safely when thrown in, yes, but maybe you can throw him in again and he will have to give you a trick. That is what happens here:

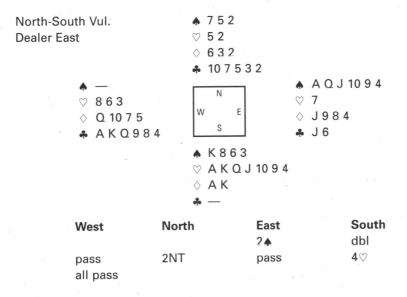

North-South Vul.
Dealer East

♠ 7 5 2
♡ 5 2
◇ 6 3 2
♣ 10 7 5 3 2

♠ —
♡ 8 6 3
◇ Q 10 7 5
♣ A K Q 9 8 4

♠ A Q J 10 9 4
♡ 7
◇ J 9 8 4
♣ J 6

♠ K 8 6 3
♡ A K Q J 10 9 4
◇ A K
♣ —

West	North	East	South
		2♠	dbl
pass	2NT	pass	4♡
all pass			

North's 2NT was part of the Lebensohl convention and showed a weak hand in the 0-7 point range. How will you play the heart game when West leads the ♣K?

At first glance it seems that you are certain to lose four spade tricks unless the defenders make a mistake. After this helpful club lead, you can in fact make the contract, provided East holds no more than two clubs. You aim to endplay East in spades at a time when he will have to allow you to score the ♠K.

You ruff the club lead and run the trump suit. This will be the position with two trumps still to be played:

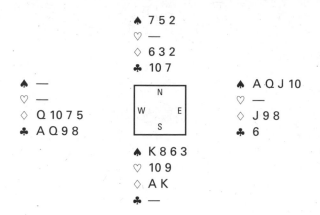

♠ 7 5 2
♥ —
♦ 6 3 2
♣ 10 7

♠ —
♥ —
♦ Q 10 7 5
♣ A Q 9 8

♠ A Q J 10
♥ —
♦ J 9 8
♣ 6

♠ K 8 6 3
♥ 10 9
♦ A K
♣ —

When you lead the ♥10, East cannot afford to throw a spade. If he does, you will give up a spade and ruff the club return with your last trump. When you give up another spade, East will have no club to play. He will have to return a diamond, allowing you to play yet another spade and set up the king. Again, East will have to play a diamond and you can then cash the established ♠K.

So, East has to release a minor-suit card. Let's say he throws the ♦8. You cash the top two diamonds, leaving East with a single safe exit card (the ♣6). You exit with a spade to East's ♠10 and ruff the club return. Once more, you put East on lead with a spade—what a tormenter you are! East's remaining two cards are the ♠A-Q and he has to give you a trick with the ♠K.

Strip squeeze after an enforced hold-up

When a defender holds up an ace for a round or two in order to keep you out of the dummy and any potential winners there, all may not be lost. You may be able to strip him down to the bare ace and a vulnerable honor holding such as K-x in a different suit. That's what happens here:

North South Vul.
Dealer South

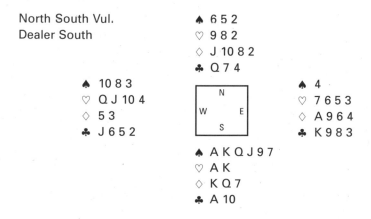

♠ 6 5 2
♥ 9 8 2
♦ J 10 8 2
♣ Q 7 4

♠ 10 8 3
♥ Q J 10 4
♦ 5 3
♣ J 6 5 2

♠ 4
♥ 7 6 5 3
♦ A 9 6 4
♣ K 9 8 3

♠ A K Q J 9 7
♥ A K
♦ K Q 7
♣ A 10

West	North	East	South
			2♣
pass	2♢	pass	2♠
pass	4♠	pass	6♠
all pass			

You and your partner have different ideas of what a raise to 4♠ shows. How will you retrieve the situation when West leads the ♡Q to your ♡A?

You draw trumps in three rounds. When you lead the king and queen of diamonds, East takes note of his partner's count signal in the suit and holds up the ♢A for two rounds. What now?

You will have to hope that the defender with the ♢A (you can probably tell from the table reactions that this is East) also holds the ♣K. You cash the ♡A and play your remaining trumps, reaching this position with one trump to be played:

```
              ♠ —
              ♡ —
              ♢ J 10
              ♣ Q 7
♠ —                        ♠ —
♡ J          ┌─────────┐   ♡ 7
♢ —          │   N     │   ♢ A
♣ J 6 5      │ W     E │   ♣ K 9
             │   S     │
             └─────────┘
              ♠ 7
              ♡ —
              ♢ 7
              ♣ A 10
```

You lead your last trump and throw the ♢10 from dummy. East is caught in a strip squeeze. He cannot throw the ♢A, obviously. If he throws the ♡7, you will throw him in with the ♢A to lead away from his presumed ♣K.

What if East is a tricky customer and throws the ♣9? Dummy play in such positions is not a precise art. You will have to diagnose what has happened and cash the ♣A to drop the bare ♣K.

What clues will there be on this particular deal? You can probably read the diamond position. West will have played high-low and East will have subsequently discarded the ♢9. Although, in theory, West might play high-low from ♢A-5-3, few players do this in practice. So, you can place East with the ♢A. The situation is similar in hearts, where West has discarded the ♡10. He might have thrown this card from a remaining holding of ♡J-10-7, yes, and a top-class defender would doubtless do so now and again. It would not occur to most of the world's defenders! So, East is likely to hold the ♡7. Indeed, he may well have given a high-low count signal at Trick 1, before any need for disguise became apparent.

You get the general idea. Once in a while, you will be caught out by some clever defender who bares a king, after he and his partner have managed to prevent you from reading their distribution. Much more often, you will be able to gather sufficient clues to read how the cards lie.

Many defenders (would it be rude of me to say 'most defenders'?) would never dream of baring their king. They will come down to K-x and a winner, allowing your throw-in to succeed without any real effort on your part.

The stars come out to play:
the strip squeeze

I will now ask Geir Helgemo to step forward and play the first deal, from the 2000 European Mixed Pairs.

```
Both Vul.              ♠ Q J 6 5 3
Dealer South           ♡ K 5
                       ◇ A 9 7
                       ♣ Q 6 2

        ♠ K 10                          ♠ A 8 7 2
        ♡ 10 8 7 4 3      N             ♡ Q
        ◇ Q 10 6 5 2   W     E          ◇ J 4 3
        ♣ 10              S             ♣ J 9 8 4 3

                       ♠ 9 4
                       ♡ A J 9 6 2
                       ◇ K 8
                       ♣ A K 7 5
```

West	North	East	South
	Langeland		Helgemo
			1♡
pass	1♠	pass	2♣
pass	2◇	pass	2NT
pass	3NT	all pass	

West led the ◇5 and Helgemo won East's jack with the king. A heart to the king brought interesting news, the queen dropping from East. Helgemo led a second heart to the ace, East throwing a club. When a spade was led towards dummy, West defended strongly by playing the ♠10, retaining the ♠K as a possible entry. East won with the ♠A and returned a diamond.

Helgemo ducked the second round of diamonds and won the third round, throwing a heart from his hand. When the three top clubs were played, West showed out on the second round and discarded a heart followed by a diamond winner. These cards remained:

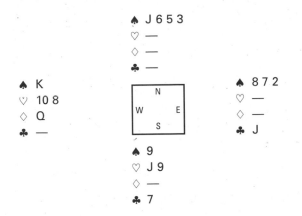

```
              ♠ J 6 5 3
              ♡ —
              ◊ —
              ♣ —
♠ K                              ♠ 8 7 2
♡ 10 8          N                ♡ —
◊ Q          W     E             ◊ —
♣ —             S                ♣ J
              ♠ 9
              ♡ J 9
              ◊ —
              ♣ 7
```

West was known to hold two hearts, a diamond and a spade. Helgemo needed to judge which defender held the ♠K. If it was East, the winning play would be to cash the ♡J and exit with the ♠9. After scoring his master club, East would have to give dummy the last trick with the ♠J. If instead West held the ♠K, the winning play would be to exit with a spade immediately. West could cash his one remaining diamond, but he would then have to lead into the ♡J-9.

Helgemo took little time to read the cards. It was unlikely that West would waste the ♠10 on the first round from ♠10-x. Also, if East held the ace and king of spades, he might have won the first round with the king instead of the ace. Helgemo duly exited with a spade and made his contract.

The USA's Tobi Sokolow won the 2004 Women's World Individual Championship in Verona. She read the cards well on this pairs deal:

North-South Vul.
Dealer North

```
                         ♠ Q 6 2
                         ♡ A Q J 8 6 4
                         ◊ Q 7 4
                         ♣ 4
    ♠ 9 8 7 3                              ♠ A J 10 4
    ♡ 9 7          N                       ♡ K 10 5 2
    ◊ K 10 8 6 2   W     E                 ◊ J 3
    ♣ 8 2             S                     ♣ 7 5 3
                         ♠ K 5
                         ♡ 3
                         ◊ A 9 5
                         ♣ A K Q J 10 9 6
```

West	North	East	South
			Sokolow
	1♡	pass	2♣
pass	2♡	pass	4♣
pass	4♡	pass	6NT
all pass			

Sokolow's 4♣ was Roman Keycard Blackwood for clubs and the response showed one or four keycards. What do you make of West's ◇6 lead against the eventual contract of 6NT? It is usually wise to choose a passive lead against 6NT and, after most auctions, it would be foolish to lead from a K-10 combination. Here, perhaps, there was some excuse for West because the opponents were likely to hold two long suits. At matchpoints, they might have taken a risk to play in the higher-scoring notrump slam. Anyway, how would you have played the contract?

Hoping for the best, Sokolow called for the ◇Q. It won the trick and she could now count ten tricks on top. A certain eleventh trick could be generated from the spade suit. She would then need either a heart finesse or an endplay. At Trick 2, declarer played a spade to her king, which won. There was no hurry to finesse the ♡Q, so she proceeded to run her clubs. This was the end position:

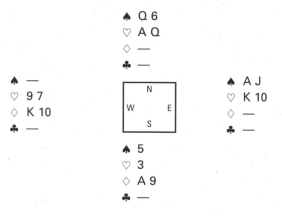

Sokolow played the ◇A, throwing the ♠6 from dummy, and East decided to throw the ♠J. It was not a difficult task to read the lie of the cards and declarer exited with a spade to the bare ace, endplaying East to lead back into dummy's ♡A-Q.

Suppose East had discarded the ♡10 instead. Declarer would then have had to guess whether to finesse in hearts, to play for the drop in hearts or to attempt an endplay. If she were confident of the count — East starting with four hearts to West's two — the odds would be 2-to-1 in favor of East's last heart being the king.

We will end the section with a deal from the 2007 Spring Foursomes in Stratford, England. Top pairs from Norway and England face each other.

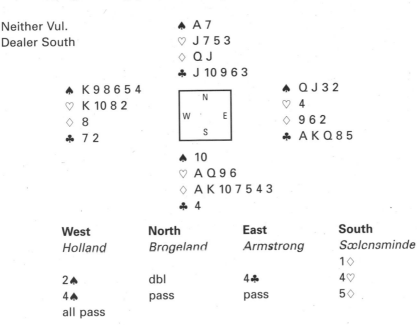

Neither Vul.
Dealer South

♠ A 7
♡ J 7 5 3
◇ Q J
♣ J 10 9 6 3

♠ K 9 8 6 5 4
♡ K 10 8 2
◇ 8
♣ 7 2

♠ Q J 3 2
♡ 4
◇ 9 6 2
♣ A K Q 8 5

♠ 10
♡ A Q 9 6
◇ A K 10 7 5 4 3
♣ 4

West	North	East	South
Holland	Brogeland	Armstrong	Sælensminde
			1◇
2♠	dbl	4♣	4♡
4♠	pass	pass	5◇
all pass			

Boye Brogeland's double was negative and John Armstrong's 4♣ was a 'fit jump', showing a good spade fit and a side suit of clubs. How would you play 5◇ when West leads the ♣7 to the jack and queen, East switching to the ♡4?

Sælensminde avoided immediate defeat by rising with the ♡A. To prevent the loss of two tricks in the heart suit, he now had to arrange an endplay on the West hand. Aiming to remove West's clubs, he crossed to the queen of trumps and ruffed a club. A trump to the jack was followed by another club ruff, West throwing a spade.

John Holland (West) still had several safe exit cards in spades, so Sælensminde played off his remaining trumps. On the last of these, Holland had to find a discard from ♠K-9 ♡K-10-8. He could not spare a heart, since declarer could then easily set up two more heart tricks. When Holland threw a spade, Sælensminde removed West's last spade by leading to the ♠A. These cards remained:

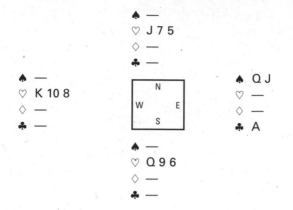

Leading the ♡J would not be good enough — West would duck, scoring the last two tricks with his ♡K-10. Sælensminde instead played a low heart to his queen. It was the end of the road for West. He had to win with the king and lead away from the ♡10. A fine piece of card play!

NOW TRY THESE...

A.

    ♠ K J 9 7
    ♡ 5 3 2
    ♢ Q J 2
    ♣ A K 4

♡Q led

```
      N
  W       E
      S
```

    ♠ A Q 4 3
    ♡ A K 9
    ♢ A K 7
    ♣ J 7 6

West	North	East	South
			2N I
pass	6NT	all pass	

West leads the ♡Q against 6NT. How will you play the contract?

B.

    ♠ K Q J
    ♡ Q J 10 2
    ♢ Q 2
    ♣ A Q J 7

♢J led

```
      N
  W       E
      S
```

    ♠ A 9 8
    ♡ A 8 4 3
    ♢ A 7 6 5
    ♣ K 4

West	North	East	South
			1NT
pass	6NT	all pass	

With a full 18 points facing a strong 1NT, North leaps directly to 6NT rather than seeking a 4-4 fit. How will you play the slam when West leads the ♢J?

C.

♠ A K
♡ 9 8 2
◇ A Q J 2
♣ A K 10 6

♠J led

```
      N
  W       E
      S
```

♠ 8 5 4
♡ A Q 3
◇ K 8 6
♣ Q J 4 3

West	North	East	South
2♡	dbl	pass	3NT
pass	6NT	all pass	

West leads the ♠J against 6NT. How will you play the contract?

D.

♠ 6 4 3
♡ A K 5
◇ A Q J 8
♣ 10 9 6

♠Q led

```
      N
  W       E
      S
```

♠ A K
♡ Q J 8
◇ K 2
♣ A K 8 5 3 2

West	North	East	South
			2NT
pass	6NT	all pass	

How will you play 6NT when West leads the ♠Q?

Answers ✐

A.

                    ♠ K J 9 7
                    ♡ 5 3 2
                    ◇ Q J 2
                    ♣ A K 4

    ♠ 6 2   ♠ 10 8 5
    ♡ Q J 10 8 7   ♡ 6 4
    ◇ 8 4   ◇ 10 9 6 5 3
    ♣ Q 10 5 2   ♣ 9 8 3

                    ♠ A Q 4 3
                    ♡ A K 9
                    ◇ A K 7
                    ♣ J 7 6

West	North	East	South
			2NT
pass	6NT	all pass	

With an unattractive 4-3-3-3 shape and enough points to suggest good play for 6NT, North sees no advantage in seeking a 4-4 spade fit. How will you play the notrump slam when West leads the ♡Q?

Despite the healthy point-count, you have only eleven top tricks and no especially good prospect for a twelfth trick. The chance of the ♣Q dropping in two rounds is very small. It is more likely that West will hold the club queen and can be endplayed.

You win the heart lead with the ace and cash four rounds of spades, West throwing two hearts and East throwing one diamond. When you continue with three rounds of diamonds, West throws a club on the third round. West has shown up with only four cards in spades and diamonds. He has already thrown two hearts, not including the jack or ten, so it is very likely that his last five cards are two hearts and three clubs. You play the king of hearts and the ten falls from West, East following suit. Continuing with your original plan, you exit at Trick 10 with a heart. West wins with the bare jack and has to lead a low club. You run this successfully to your jack and the small slam is made.

The play was a strip squeeze because West was squeezed out of two potential winners in hearts in order to retain his club guard.

B.

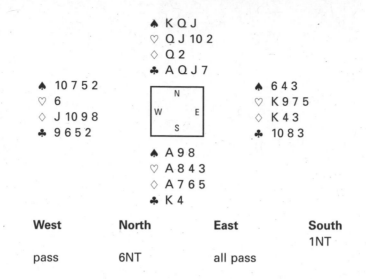

♠ K Q J
♡ Q J 10 2
◇ Q 2
♣ A Q J 7

♠ 10 7 5 2
♡ 6
◇ J 10 9 8
♣ 9 6 5 2

♠ 6 4 3
♡ K 9 7 5
◇ K 4 3
♣ 10 8 3

♠ A 9 8
♡ A 8 4 3
◇ A 7 6 5
♣ K 4

West	North	East	South
			1NT
pass	6NT	all pass	

As on the previous problem, North leaps directly to 6NT rather than seeking a 4-4 fit. How will you play the slam when West leads the ◇J?

Only a madman would lead from a K-J-10 combination against 6NT, so (unless you are playing in an asylum) you can be almost certain that East holds the ◇K. You should play low from the dummy, preserving the queen, and win with the diamond ace. You cross to dummy with a spade and run the ♡Q successfully. When you lead the ♡J, a cloud appears on the horizon. East covers with the king, won with the ace, but West discards a club. What now?

The answer is that you are about to benefit from your sensible play of withholding the ◇Q at Trick 1. The next step is to cash your black-suit winners. This is the end position you will reach:

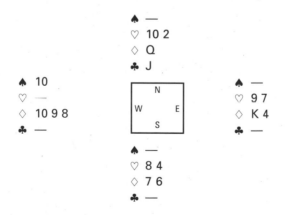

♠ —
♡ 10 2
◇ Q
♣ J

♠ 10
♡ —
◇ 10 9 8
♣ —

♠ —
♡ 9 7
◇ K 4
♣ —

♠ —
♡ 8 4
◇ 7 6
♣ —

When you lead the ♣J, East is caught in a strip squeeze and is forced to throw the ◇4. You then lead the ◇Q to his ◇K and collect the last two tricks with the ♡8 and the ♡10. Try to look casual about it!

C.

```
                    ♠ A K
                    ♡ 9 8 2
                    ◇ A Q J 2
                    ♣ A K 10 6
  ♠ J 10 7            ┌─────────┐        ♠ Q 9 6 3 2
  ♡ K J 10 7 5 4      │   N     │        ♡ 6
  ◇ 10 4 3           │ W     E │        ◇ 9 7 5
  ♣ 8               │   S     │        ♣ 9 7 5 2
                     └─────────┘
                    ♠ 8 5 4
                    ♡ A Q 3
                    ◇ K 8 6
                    ♣ Q J 4 3
```

West	North	East	South
2♡	dbl	pass	3NT
pass	6NT	all pass	

West has read the text books that recommend a safe lead against 6NT. Pushing his heart suit to one side, he leads the ♠J. How will you play the contract?

You have eleven top tricks and can be fairly certain, even nowadays, that West holds the ♡K. Where is your twelfth trick coming from? You must aim for a three-card end position where West holds three hearts. You can then pass the ♡9 to his hand. If West started with only two spades, it will be child's play to strip him of his non-hearts. If West started with three or more spades, you can catch him in a strip squeeze by playing your minor-suit winners.

You win the spade lead in dummy and play four rounds of clubs and three rounds of diamonds, ending in the dummy. These cards remain:

```
                    ♠ A
                    ♡ 9 8 2
                    ◇ J
                    ♣ —
  ♠ J 10              ┌─────────┐        ♠ Q 9 6 3
  ♡ K J 10            │   N     │        ♡ 6
  ◇ —               │ W     E │        ◇ —
  ♣ —               │   S     │        ♣ —
                     └─────────┘
                    ♠ 8 5
                    ♡ A Q 3
                    ◇ —
                    ♣ —
```

You throw a spade on the ◇J, catching West in a strip squeeze. Since he presumably held six hearts for his weak two-bid, you know his shape. If he throws a spade, you will cash the ♠A and run the ♡9 to endplay him. (If East's singleton was the ♡J or the ♡10, you would cover with the ♡Q and again endplay West.) If instead West throws a heart, ace and another heart will set up an extra heart trick.

D.

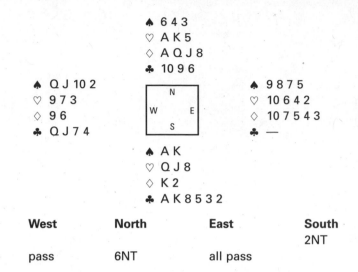

West	North	East	South
			2NT
pass	6NT	all pass	

How will you play 6NT when West leads the ♠Q?

You win with the ♠A and play the ♣A, following with the ♣6 from dummy. Or do you? In that case, you will not make the contract! The slam is at risk only if West holds ♣Q-J-x-x. You can then catch West in a strip squeeze, but only if you unblock the ♣10-9, freeing the path to your ♣K-8 tenace.

You cash the ♣A, following with the ♣10 from dummy, and East does indeed show out. Your intention now is to strip West of his non-clubs. You begin with four rounds of diamonds, throwing two clubs from your hand. West discards a spade and a heart. You then turn to the heart suit, arriving at this position:

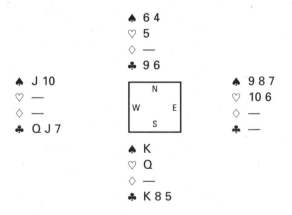

When you lead the ♡Q, West cannot throw a club or you will simply duck a round of the suit. He therefore throws a spade. You cash the ♠K and lead the ♣5. West rises with the ♣Q and you unblock dummy's ♣9. West can then enjoy the moment as he leads into your ♣K-8. If dummy's last club was the ten or nine, the suit would be blocked and you would have to concede a spade at Trick 13.

CHAPTER 9

Avoidance Play to Set Up an Endplay

In this chapter, we will see how to make use of avoidance play to set up an end position for a successful throw-in. For example, you may wish to keep a particular defender off lead as you eliminate a side suit — to prevent him from attacking the problem suit from his side of the table.

Finessing into the safe hand as you eliminate a suit

Suppose that you need to eliminate a side suit of ◊A-4-2 in the dummy opposite ◊K-10-5 in your hand. If you cannot afford your right-hand opponent to gain the lead, it makes good sense to play low to the ten on the first or second round. Unless the danger hand holds both the ◊Q and ◊J, you will be able to eliminate the diamond suit without allowing him on lead.

Let's see an example of this style of play.

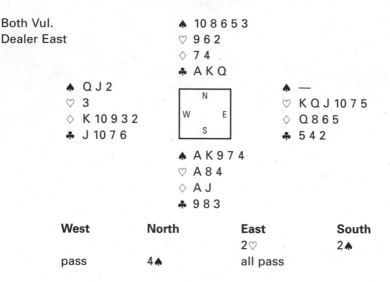

Both Vul.
Dealer East

♠ 10 8 6 5 3
♡ 9 6 2
◇ 7 4
♣ A K Q

♠ Q J 2
♡ 3
◇ K 10 9 3 2
♣ J 10 7 6

♠ —
♡ K Q J 10 7 5
◇ Q 8 6 5
♣ 5 4 2

♠ A K 9 7 4
♡ A 8 4
◇ A J
♣ 9 8 3

West	North	East	South
		2♡	2♠
pass	4♠	all pass	

East opens with a weak two-bid in hearts and West leads the ♡3, an obvious singleton, against your eventual game in spades. You win with the ace and play the ace of trumps, East discarding a heart. How will you continue?

If you can eliminate the minor suits without East gaining the lead, you will be able to endplay West with a third round of trumps. He will then have to give you a ruff-and-sluff. Playing the ace and jack of diamonds would be risky, of course, because East might win the second round and cash his two heart winners. Instead, you should cross to dummy with a club and lead a diamond, finessing the jack (into the safe hand) when East follows with a spot card.

West wins with the ◇K and exits safely in clubs. You cash the other high trump, followed by the remaining minor-suit winners. Finally, you put West on lead with a third round of trumps, forcing him to give you a ruff-and-sluff. Away goes one of your heart losers and the game is made. (You could attempt the same play with ◇A-10, or even ◇A-9, succeeding when East held no more than one of the missing diamond honors.)

On the next deal your aim is a partial elimination, one that will work if a particular defender began with only two clubs. To remove his doubleton club, you must duck a round of the suit into the safe defender's hand.

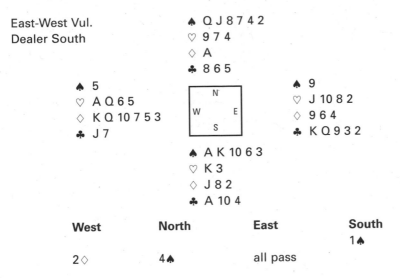

East-West Vul.
Dealer South

```
                      ♠ Q J 8 7 4 2
                      ♡ 9 7 4
                      ◇ A
                      ♣ 8 6 5
    ♠ 5                                  ♠ 9
    ♡ A Q 6 5         ┌──────────┐       ♡ J 10 8 2
    ◇ K Q 10 7 5 3    │    N     │       ◇ 9 6 4
    ♣ J 7             │ W     E  │       ♣ K Q 9 3 2
                      │    S     │
                      └──────────┘
                      ♠ A K 10 6 3
                      ♡ K 3
                      ◇ J 8 2
                      ♣ A 10 4
```

West	North	East	South
			1♠
2◇	4♠	all pass	

How will you play the spade game when West leads the ◇K?

The ♡A is likely to be with West, after his overcall, so it seems that you might lose two clubs and two hearts. The best chance of survival is to find West with a doubleton club honor. Your aim will be to remove West's club holding and to endplay him with your ◇J on the third round of the suit. However, you will need to extract West's club holding without allowing East (the danger hand who can lead through your ♡K) to gain the lead.

You win the diamond lead, draw the defenders' trumps with the queen and lead a club from dummy. Let's suppose first that East plays low. West wins your ♣10 with the ♣J and cannot safely play either red suit. He therefore exits with a club. You win with the ace, ruff the ◇8 and return to your hand with a trump. These cards remain:

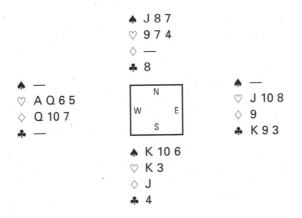

```
                      ♠ J 8 7
                      ♡ 9 7 4
                      ◇ —
                      ♣ 8
    ♠ —                                  ♠ —
    ♡ A Q 6 5         ┌──────────┐       ♡ J 10 8
    ◇ Q 10 7          │    N     │       ◇ 9
    ♣ —               │ W     E  │       ♣ K 9 3
                      │    S     │
                      └──────────┘
                      ♠ K 10 6
                      ♡ K 3
                      ◇ J
                      ♣ 4
```

You lead the ◇J to West's ◇Q, discarding the last club from dummy (a loser-on-loser play). Since West has no clubs left, he must open the heart suit or lead a fourth round of diamonds, giving you a ruff-and-sluff. Either way, you will lose just one heart, one diamond and one club, making the game.

What happens if instead East decides to split his ♣K-Q on the first round? You win with the ace and lead a second round of clubs. West's jack appears and East cannot overtake or he will set up your ♣10. Once again, West is endplayed. He has to exit in one of the red suits and this will give you an extra trick.

Ducking the lead to protect the elimination position

When you have two losers in your exit suit, it can pay to duck an opening lead in that suit. By doing so, you may prevent the danger hand from gaining the lead.

East-West Vul.
Dealer South

	♠ 7 6 4	
	♡ A 10 4 2	
	◇ A Q J	
	♣ A 7 3	
♠ A J 10 5 3 2		♠ Q 9
♡ —	N	♡ 8 7 6 5
◇ 9 6 3	W E	◇ 7 5 4 2
♣ K Q J 4	S	♣ 9 8 6
	♠ K 8	
	♡ K Q J 9 3	
	◇ K 10 8	
	♣ 10 5 2	

West	North	East	South
			1♡
1♠	2♠	pass	3♡
pass	4♡	all pass	

How will you play the heart game when West leads the ♣K?

Suppose you win the first trick with the ♣A and play a round of trumps, discovering the 4-0 break. West's overcall makes it very likely that he holds the ♠A. To make the contract in that case, you must remove his red-card holdings and endplay him with a club. You will not be able to draw trumps before the throw-in, since you will need at least one trump in both your own hand and the dummy. You play three rounds of diamonds, all following, and exit with a club. Unfortunately, you cannot prevent East from gaining the lead with his ♣9-8. You cover his ♣9 with the ♣10 on the first round, but a skilful West will win with the ♣J and return the ♣4 to East's ♣8. A spade switch will then sink the contract.

It is easy enough to prevent East from gaining the lead in clubs. You must duck the opening lead, allowing West's ♣K to win. Whichever minor suit West chooses for his continuation, you will make the contract. You will draw one round of trumps, discovering the break, and play your remaining minor-suit winners. A club to the ten will then endplay West and he will have to give you a spade trick or concede a ruff-and-sluff.

Let's see a more difficult example of this technique, one where you cannot afford to let your right-hand opponent gain the lead twice in the suit that has been led.

North-South Vul.
Dealer South

```
                      ♠ Q 10 8 7
                      ♡ 6 5 3
                      ◇ 10 6 5
                      ♣ A 8 7
    ♠ 3                                    ♠ 9 5 2
    ♡ J 10 8 2            N                ♡ K Q 7
    ◇ K Q 7 2       W          E           ◇ 9 8 3
    ♣ J 5 3 2            S                 ♣ Q 10 9 4
                      ♠ A K J 6 4
                      ♡ A 9 4
                      ◇ A J 4
                      ♣ K 6
```

West	North	East	South
			2NT
pass	3♣	pass	3♠
pass	4♠	all pass	

How will you play the spade game when West leads the ♡J?

Let's suppose first that you win immediately with the ♡A. You draw trumps in three rounds, eliminate the club suit and exit with a heart, hoping that the defenders will be forced to assist you in diamonds. East wins the second round of hearts with the queen and sends the ◇9 through. West wins with the ◇Q and plays another heart to his partner's king. East plays another diamond and you finesse again, cursing your luck when West turns up with the ◇K as well. That's one down.

When both diamond honors are offside, you cannot allow East to gain the lead twice in hearts and play diamonds from his side of the table. Look back to the first trick. You should allow West's ♡J to win. He cannot play a diamond profitably from his side and will doubtless continue with another heart. You win East's ♡Q with the ♡A, draw trumps and eliminate the club suit. These cards remain:

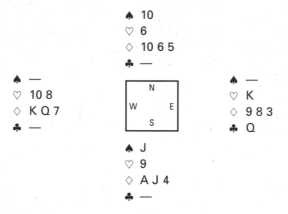

```
              ♠ 10
              ♡ 6
              ◇ 10 6 5
              ♣ —
♠ —                              ♠ —
♡ 10 8        ┌─────────┐        ♡ K
◇ K Q 7       │    N    │        ◇ 9 8 3
♣ —           │ W     E │        ♣ Q
              │    S    │
              └─────────┘
              ♠ J
              ♡ 9
              ◇ A J 4
              ♣ —
```

You exit with a third round of hearts and East wins with the king. He leads the ◇9 to partner's ◇Q, but West is now endplayed. He will have to return a diamond into your tenace or give you a ruff-and-sluff.

Suppose that East takes positive steps to gain the lead in order to play diamonds through your holding. What will you do if East overtakes the ♡J with the ♡Q at Trick 1? You must win immediately with the ♡A; otherwise, East will play a diamond though and destroy your position in that suit. Later you will lead towards the ♡9, ensuring that East does not gain the lead twice in the suit.

Ducking the lead to eliminate a different suit safely

Suppose West leads the ◇K and you hold ◇A-8-2 in the dummy opposite the ◇7 in your hand. Occasionally, it will pay to duck the first trick, allowing West's king to win. The safe hand will be left on lead and the discard that has become available on the ◇A may benefit you tactically. If you are planning an elimination, ducking may allow you to eliminate some other suit without allowing the danger hand to gain the lead.

An example will make this technique easier to visualize:

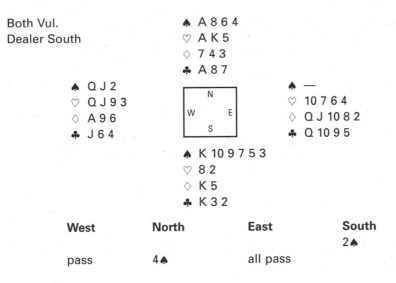

Both Vul.
Dealer South

♠ A 8 6 4
♡ A K 5
◇ 7 4 3
♣ A 8 7

♠ Q J 2
♡ Q J 9 3
◇ A 9 6
♣ J 6 4

♠ —
♡ 10 7 6 4
◇ Q J 10 8 2
♣ Q 10 9 5

♠ K 10 9 7 5 3
♡ 8 2
◇ K 5
♣ K 3 2

West	North	East	South
			2♠
pass	4♠	all pass	

How will you play the spade game when West leads the ♡Q?

The contract is in danger only when trumps break 3-0 and West holds the ◇A. When West holds three trumps, you can survive by throwing him in with the third round of trumps. You will need to eliminate the club suit, however, and this must be done without allowing East (the danger hand) to gain the lead. Imagine, for a moment, that you had forgotten the title of this section. Would you see how to play the deal?

You must allow West's lead of the ♡Q to win the trick! Let's say he plays another heart. You win in the dummy and play the ♠A, East discarding a diamond. You are not in the least distressed by the bad trump break because your clever move at Trick 1 is about to pay dividends.

You draw a second round of trumps with the king, cash the king and ace of clubs and then play dummy's remaining top heart, throwing the last club from your hand. You can then ruff dummy's last club and put West on lead with a third round of trumps. He will either have to open the diamond suit, allowing you to score your king, or give you a ruff-and-sluff.

Look back at the full diagram and imagine that you mistakenly win the first round of hearts. You will not then be able to eliminate the club suit without allowing East to gain the lead. (If, at any stage, you lead dummy's ♡5, hoping to throw a club and have West win the trick, East can thwart you by rising with the ♡10.)

Morton's Fork to prepare an elimination

One of the most famous avoidance plays is Morton's Fork, where you lead a low card through a defender's ace and present him with a no-win situation. West is your intended victim here:

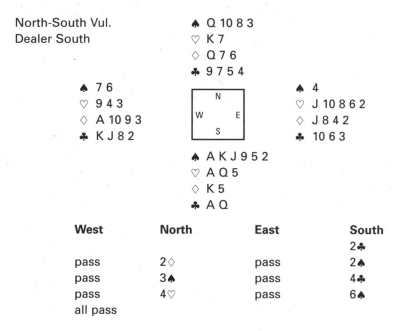

North-South Vul.
Dealer South

North:
♠ Q 10 8 3
♡ K 7
◇ Q 7 6
♣ 9 7 5 4

West:
♠ 7 6
♡ 9 4 3
◇ A 10 9 3
♣ K J 8 2

East:
♠ 4
♡ J 10 8 6 2
◇ J 8 4 2
♣ 10 6 3

South:
♠ A K J 9 5 2
♡ A Q 5
◇ K 5
♣ A Q

West	North	East	South
			2♣
pass	2◇	pass	2♠
pass	3♠	pass	4♣
pass	4♡	pass	6♠
all pass			

How will you play the slam when West leads the ♠6?

You win the trump lead and play a second round of trumps, East throwing a low heart. When you lead the ◇5 towards dummy, West cannot afford to play his ◇A on air or you will discard your ♣Q on the third round of diamonds. He plays low, therefore, and you win with dummy's ◇Q. You continue with three rounds of hearts, throwing one of dummy's two remaining diamonds. These cards are left:

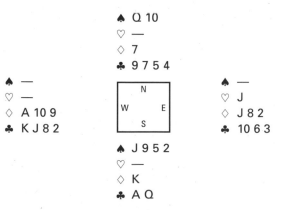

North:
♠ Q 10
♡ —
◇ 7
♣ 9 7 5 4

West:
♠ —
♡ —
◇ A 10 9
♣ K J 8 2

East:
♠ —
♡ J
◇ J 8 2
♣ 10 6 3

South:
♠ J 9 5 2
♡ —
◇ K
♣ A Q

You now put West on lead with the ◇K. He is endplayed and must lead into your ♣A-Q or give you a ruff-and-sluff.

Leading a low diamond towards dummy's queen was an example of the technique known as Morton's Fork. Whether West played the ace or a low card, you would make the contract. Do you see why it was right to lead towards dummy's queen rather than towards your king?

The answer is that it would be useless to endplay East on the second round of diamonds because he could then lead a club through your tenace. West was the only defender worth endplaying, so you needed to find him with the ◇A.

The stars come out to play:
avoidance play to set up an endplay ———————————— ☆

Few bridge stars have more luster than Omar Sharif. He played the deal below in the third round of the 1972 Spring Foursomes.

Neither Vul.
Dealer East

	♠ Q 8 7 3	
	♡ A 9 6 2	
	◇ A 6	
	♣ K 9 2	

♠ J		♠ 5
♡ J 7 3	N	♡ K Q 10 5 4
◇ J 9 7 5 4	W E	◇ K Q 10 2
♣ Q 10 5 3	S	♣ A J 8

	♠ A K 10 9 6 4 2	
	♡ 8	
	◇ 8 3	
	♣ 7 6 4	

West	North	East	South
	Schapiro		Sharif
		1♡	3♠
pass	4♠	all pass	

West led the ♡3 against Sharif's game in spades. How would you have played the contract?

The ♣A was likely to be with East, so Sharif planned to endplay him with the fourth round of hearts. If West was allowed to gain the lead when the diamond suit was eliminated, he could give the defenders three club tricks by switching to the ♣Q or the ♣10. To prevent this, Sharif ducked the heart lead into the safe East hand. He won the ◇K return with the ace and played the ♠Q, all following.

As a result of the avoidance play at Trick 1, declarer was able to cash the ♡A, throwing a diamond from his hand. A diamond ruff then eliminated that suit. Declarer crossed to the ♠8 and ruffed dummy's penultimate heart. A spade to the seven left this end position:

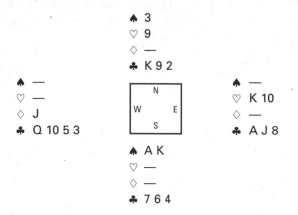

Sharif led the ♡9, covered by East's ♡10, and threw a club from his hand (a loser-on-loser play). East then had to play a club, giving a trick to dummy's ♣K, or concede a ruff-and-sluff.

Our next real-life example sees Indonesia's Franky Karwur as the declarer, playing in the 1st NEC Bridge Festival in 1995.

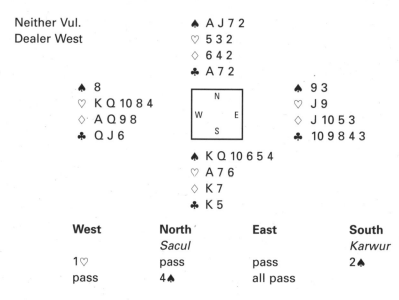

West	North	East	South
	Sacul		*Karwur*
1♡	pass	pass	2♠
pass	4♠	all pass	

West led the ♡K. How would you have played the spade game?

The opening bid and East's lack of response made West a strong favorite to hold the ◇A. Karwur aimed to endplay West with a heart. Suppose he had won the opening lead, drawn trumps in two rounds and eliminated clubs. When he played a second round of hearts, there would be an unfavorable development. East would win the trick and send a diamond through the king. One down!

Karwur saw that when hearts were 5-2, which was the most likely break, he could make the contract by ducking the ♡K opening lead. He would have to lose two heart tricks eventually, and he wanted to lose these to West, the safe hand who could not lead through his ◇K. He might look silly if he held up the ♡A when hearts broke 6-1 and East ruffed the second round, but it was roughly four times more likely that hearts would be 5-2.

Karwur duly ducked the opening lead and the game could not then be defeated. He could win any continuation, draw trumps, eliminate clubs and put West on lead with the third round of hearts.

NOW TRY THESE...

A.

    ♠ K Q 6 2
    ♡ 8 6 5 2
    ◇ 7 5 3
    ♣ K 7

```
        N
    W       E
        S
```

♠4 led

    ♠ A J 10 9 7
    ♡ A 10
    ◇ K 8 2
    ♣ A 4 2

West	North	East	South
1♡	pass	pass	1♠
pass	2♠	pass	4♠
all pass			

How will you play on a trump lead? (You will find that the trumps break 2-2.)

B.

    ♠ A K Q J
    ♡ Q 7 3
    ◇ 7 5 3 2
    ♣ K 10

```
        N
    W       E
        S
```

♡2 led

    ♠ 6 4 3
    ♡ K 6
    ◇ A K 8 6
    ♣ 8 7 6 3

West	North	East	South
		1♡	pass
pass	dbl	pass	1NT
pass	2NT	pass	3NT
all pass			

West leads the ♡2, covered by the ♡3 and East's ♡9. How will you play?

C.

♠ 10 9 4 2
♡ Q J 9 5
◇ 7 2
♣ Q J 10

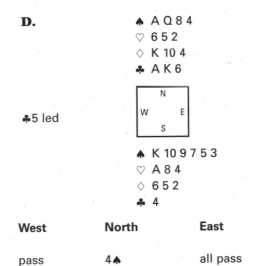

♠5 led

♠ A K Q J 8 6 3
♡ K 3
◇ A Q 3
♣ A

West	North	East	South
			2♣
pass	2◇	pass	2♠
pass	4♠	pass	6♠
all pass			

If you rate South's 6♠ as an overbid, I can only agree with you. Those who overbid need to overplay. How will you tackle the spade slam when West leads a low trump?

D.

♠ A Q 8 4
♡ 6 5 2
◇ K 10 4
♣ A K 6

♣5 led

♠ K 10 9 7 5 3
♡ A 8 4
◇ 6 5 2
♣ 4

West	North	East	South
			2♠
pass	4♠	all pass	

West leads the ♣5 against your spade game. How will you play the contract?

Answers ✏

A.

	♠ K Q 6 2	
	♡ 8 6 5 2	
	◇ 7 5 3	
	♣ K 7	

♠ 8 4		♠ 5 3
♡ K J 9 4 3	N	♡ Q 7
◇ A Q 6	W E	◇ J 10 9 4
♣ Q J 5	S	♣ 10 9 8 6 3

	♠ A J 10 9 7	
	♡ A 10	
	◇ K 8 2	
	♣ A 4 2	

West	North	East	South
1♡	pass	pass	1♠
pass	2♠	pass	4♠
all pass			

West leads the ♠4 against your spade game. How will you play the contract?

West is likely to hold the ◇A. If trumps break 2-2, however, you can end-play him with the fourth round of hearts. You win the trump lead in your hand and cross to the ♠K, encouraged by the 2-2 break. When you lead a heart, East follows with the seven and you cover with the ten, ducking into the safe West hand. It would do East no good to rise with the ♡Q, of course, since you would win and concede the second round of hearts to West.

You win West's ♣Q exit with the ace, cash the ♡A and cross to the ♣K. You ruff dummy's penultimate heart and ruff a club in dummy. These cards remain:

	♠ Q	
	♡ 8	
	◇ 7 5 3	
	♣ —	

♠ —		♠ —
♡ K 9	N	♡ —
◇ A Q 6	W E	◇ J 10 9 4
♣ —	S	♣ 9

	♠ J 10	
	♡ —	
	◇ K 8 2	
	♣ —	

It is time to enjoy the fruits of your labor. You lead the ♡8, throwing the ◇2. West wins and has no safe return.

B.

```
                    ♠ A K Q J
                    ♡ Q 7 3
                    ◇ 7 5 3 2
                    ♣ K 10

   ♠ 10 8 7 5          N          ♠ 9 2
   ♡ 8 5 2                        ♡ A J 10 9 4
   ◇ J 10 4      W        E       ◇ Q 9
   ♣ J 9 2            S           ♣ A Q 5 4

                    ♠ 6 4 3
                    ♡ K 6
                    ◇ A K 8 6
                    ♣ 8 7 6 3
```

West	North	East	South
		1♡	pass
pass	dbl	pass	1NT
pass	2NT	pass	3NT
all pass			

West leads the ♡2 against 3NT. You play low from dummy and East contributes the ♡9. How will you play?

You have seven top tricks after winning the first trick with the ♡K. You should aim to set up an eighth trick in diamonds and then endplay East to score a ninth trick in hearts or clubs. Since you cannot allow West to gain the lead, you may need an avoidance play in the diamond suit. Playing ace, king and another diamond will not be good enough as the cards lie, since West will win the third round and lead a heart through dummy's queen.

You cross to the ♠A at Trick 2 and lead a diamond towards your hand. If East plays the ◇9, you will win and cross to dummy with another spade to lead a second round of diamonds. When East plays the ◇Q, you allow it to win — he will now have to give you a ninth trick in one of the round suits. To avoid this fate, East will probably play the ◇Q on the first round. You must duck, leaving the safe hand on lead.

You win East's diamond return and cash the remaining spades, followed by the rest of the diamond suit. East will have to reduce to four cards. Unless you judge that he has reduced to the bare ♡A and three clubs, you will exit with a club to the ten. After cashing one or two clubs, East will then have to give dummy a trick with the ♡Q.

If East chooses to throw the ♡4, the ♡10 and the ♡J, you will exit with a heart to the bare ace instead. East will then have to concede a trick to dummy's ♣K.

C.

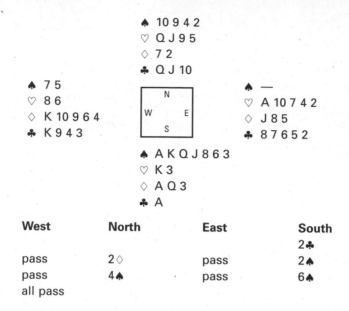

West	North	East	South
			2♣
pass	2♢	pass	2♠
pass	4♠	pass	6♠
all pass			

West leads the ♠5 and you win with the ♠A, continuing with the ♠6 to dummy's ♠9. West holds two more trumps than his partner, so East is a slight favorite to hold the ♡A. You lead a low heart from dummy and East cannot rise with the ace, since you would have two discards for your potential diamond losers.

You win with the ♡K, cash the ♣A and overtake the ♠8 with the ♠10. You then lead the ♣Q. If East produced the ♣K, you would ruff high and lead a heart to the queen, setting up a second discard for your diamond losers. Here East will play a low club. You throw your remaining heart and West wins, leaving this position:

West has no safe return. A diamond will be into your tenace and a heart will allow you to set up a heart trick while you still have the ♠4 as an entry. West's only other option is to play a club to dummy's jack. You will then take the ruffing heart finesse yourself, returning to dummy with the ♠4 to enjoy the spoils.

D.

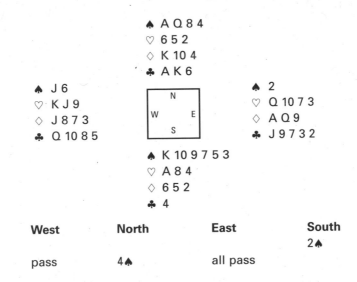

West	North	East	South
			2♠
pass	4♠	all pass	

West leads the ♣5 against your spade game. What is your plan?

The problem suit is diamonds. If you can eliminate the other three suits, you will be able to lead a diamond to the ten, endplaying East. However, the elimination must be done without allowing West to gain the lead. Otherwise, he will disrupt your diamond position by leading the suit while East has a safe exit.

To make sure that West does not gain the lead when you attempt to eliminate hearts, you must duck the ♣5 opening lead. East wins the trick with the ♣J and let's say he switches to a low heart. You rise with the ♡A, draw trumps in two rounds and cash the ♣A-K, throwing your two heart losers. You can then ruff a heart in your hand, return to dummy with a third round of trumps and ruff dummy's last heart. These cards remain:

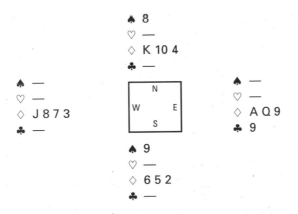

You lead a low diamond from your hand and have a guaranteed endplay on East, whether or not West opts to play the ◇J in the second seat.

Did anything strike you about the deal? West led the only card of his thirteen (the ♣5) that would give you a chance of making the contract!

Endplays to Gain an Entry

In this chapter we see some endplays — both throw-ins and ruff-and-sluff elimination plays — where one of your victim's options (sometimes the only option) is to give you an extra entry to the dummy.

Elimination play to force an entry

When you have a winner in a seemingly isolated dummy, it maybe be possible to force a defender to give you an entry. The deal below is unusual because the trump suit is one of the suits that the defender cannot play without assisting you.

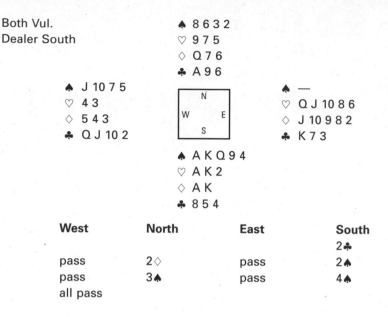

Both Vul.
Dealer South

North
♠ 8 6 3 2
♡ 9 7 5
◇ Q 7 6
♣ A 9 6

West
♠ J 10 7 5
♡ 4 3
◇ 5 4 3
♣ Q J 10 2

East
♠ —
♡ Q J 10 8 6
◇ J 10 9 8 2
♣ K 7 3

South
♠ A K Q 9 4
♡ A K 2
◇ A K
♣ 8 5 4

West	North	East	South
			2♣
pass	2◇	pass	2♠
pass	3♠	pass	4♠
all pass			

South declined to cuebid, indicating the minimum nature of his 2♣ opening. Since North had already shown a useful hand with his raise to 3♠ (rather than a weaker jump to the spade game), he took a good view to let the bidding die at the game level. How would you play 4♠ when West leads the ♣Q?

Since all will be easy unless there is a hostile trump break, you win the first club. When you play a trump to the ace, East discards a diamond. You are in danger of being cut off from the ◇Q, which would otherwise give you a discard for your losing heart. How can you rectify the situation?

You must aim to put West on lead at a time when he will have to give you an entry to dummy. The first step is to remove the losing cards in clubs. When you play a club, East wins with the ♣K and switches to the ♡Q. You win with the ace and play another club. West takes the trick and returns another heart to your king. You cash the ace and king of diamonds to leave this position:

North
♠ 8 6 3
♡ 9
◇ Q
♣ —

West
♠ J 10 7
♡ —
◇ 5
♣ J

East
♠ —
♡ J 8 6
◇ J 10
♣ —

South
♠ K Q 9 4
♡ 2
◇ —
♣ —

Hoping that West has no more hearts left, you exit with the ♠9. West wins with the ♠10 and (yes!) begins to look worried. Playing a club will give you a ruff-and-sluff. If instead he plays a trump or a diamond, he will give you access to dummy's ◊Q and you will be able to discard your losing heart.

If the defenders had not played two rounds of hearts, you would have had to cash the top two hearts yourself before putting West on lead.

Throw-in play to force an entry

Even when the threat of a ruff-and-sluff is not present, it may be possible to force a defender to give you an extra entry. On the next deal, this situation arises despite the fact that both defenders have a high card left in your exit suit.

```
Neither Vul.              ♠ K Q
Dealer West               ♡ —
                          ◊ A J 9 4 3
                          ♣ A K Q J 10 6

        ♠ 10 9              N          ♠ J 7 6 5 2
        ♡ Q J 9 8 7 5 2                ♡ 6 3
        ◊ K 7 2        W       E       ◊ Q 8
        ♣ 4                S           ♣ 9 8 7 3

                          ♠ A 8 4 3
                          ♡ A K 10 4
                          ◊ 10 6 5
                          ♣ 5 2
```

West	North	East	South
3♡	6♣	pass	6NT
all pass			

Your present partner is an adventurous bidder, to put it politely, and you give no thought to a grand slam. How will you play 6NT when West leads the ♠10?

One option is to overtake the first round of spades and hope that a single lead of diamonds from the South hand will bring in that suit. You would succeed when West held a doubleton (or singleton) diamond honor or a somewhat unlikely pair of honors in diamonds. A better idea is to hope you can end-play a defender who holds a doubleton diamond honor.

Dummy's ♠K wins the first trick and you play six rounds of clubs, throwing one spade, two hearts and a diamond from your hand. You then cash dummy's remaining spade honor, seemingly cutting yourself off from the three winners in the South hand. These cards remain:

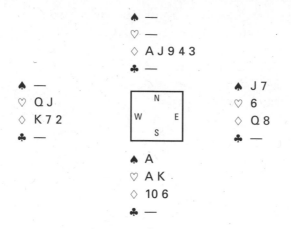

You cash the ◇A and the defenders are not happy bunnies. Let's suppose first that East retains the ◇Q. When you lead a second round of diamonds, East will have to win with the ◇Q and give you an entry to the three winners in the South hand.

East may prefer to unblock the diamond queen under the ace. A diamond to the ten and king will then allow West to choose which three tricks you will claim for the contract.

Defender must give a trick or an entry

Sometimes you can put a defender on lead and force him to choose between two alternatives: he can give you a trick by leading into a tenace, or he can give you an extra entry to dummy. You must play carefully on the next deal, but a high-level bid from East will help you to read the cards.

North-South Vul.
Dealer South

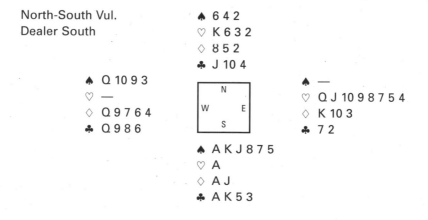

West	North	East	South
			2♣
pass	2◇	4♡	4♠
all pass			

West leads the ◇6 against your spade game. You win East's king with the ace and play the ace of trumps, sinking back in your chair when East shows out. How will you attempt to recover the position?

If you can eliminate the diamond suit, you will have a chance to put West on lead with a trump. West would have led a heart if he held one, so you can assume the hearts are breaking 8-0. Cashing the ♡A at this stage would serve no purpose and you should exit with the ◇J immediately.

West wins with the ◇Q and cannot safely play either black suit. He returns another diamond and you ruff in the South hand. With diamonds eliminated, the time has come to cash the ♡A. If West ruffs this card, he will be forced to assist you with his return. Let's say that he delays the painful moment, discarding a diamond. These cards remain:

```
                        ♠ 6 4
                        ♡ K 6 3
                        ◇ —
                        ♣ J 10 4
        ♠ Q 10 9                          ♠ —
        ♡ —             ┌─────────┐       ♡ Q J 10 8 7 5
        ◇ 9             │   N     │       ◇ —
        ♣ Q 9 8 6       │ W     E │       ♣ 7 2
                        │   S     │
                        └─────────┘
                        ♠ K J 8 7
                        ♡ —
                        ◇
                        ♣ A K 5 3
```

You put West on lead with the ♠7 and he has no safe return. A low club will allow you win with the ♣J and throw your other club loser on the ♡K. Alternatively, after a trump return, you will draw trumps and concede a club. West's final option is the ◇9, giving a ruff-and-sluff. You throw a club from dummy and ruff in your hand. You continue with the ♣A-K, ruff a club, and throw your last club on the ♡K.

The winner-on-loser unblock

A position much loved by problem setters is where you perform a throw-in while at the same time discarding a blocking high card from the opposite hand. The defender may then have to give an entry to an honor promoted by the unblock.

North-South Vul.
Dealer South

```
                    ♠ Q J 6
                    ♡ 7 6
                    ◇ J 8 5 2
                    ♣ K Q 8 5
  ♠ 10 8 5 4                      ♠ 9 7 2
  ♡ 10 9          ┌─────────┐     ♡ 8 5 4
  ◇ 4            │   N     │     ◇ Q 10 9 7
  ♣ A J 9 7 4 2  │ W     E │     ♣ 10 6 3
                 │   S     │
                 └─────────┘
                    ♠ A K 3
                    ♡ A K Q J 3 2
                    ◇ A K 6 3
                    ♣ —
```

West	North	East	South
			2♣
pass	2NT	pass	3♡
pass	3NT	pass	4◇
pass	5♣	pass	5NT
pass	6◇	pass	6♡
all pass			

North shows a diamond fit with his 5♣ cuebid and then denies any of the top three diamond honors. How will you play 6♡ when West leads the ♡10?

The contract is at risk only when East holds four or five diamonds to the queen. If he also holds the ♣A, you can succeed by cashing the ◇A and ducking a diamond. You could then win the spade return in your hand and run the trumps, followed by the spades (ending in dummy). East would be squeezed in the minor suits.

However, when East holds at least a 4-1 majority of the diamonds, he is likely to be shorter than West in clubs. This leaves West as the favorite to hold the ♣A. What can be done in that case?

You win the trump lead and draw trumps in two further rounds, throwing a club from dummy. You then test the diamond suit by cashing the ace and king. Is it bad news when West shows out on the second round? Yes and no. The slam may go down, it is true, but you will have the opportunity to attempt a very flashy play indeed! You cash the ♠A and play a low spade to dummy's ♠Q. These cards remain:

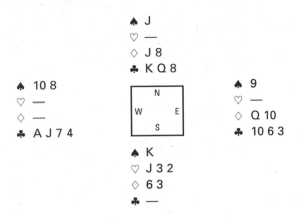

```
              ♠ J
              ♡ —
              ◇ J 8
              ♣ K Q 8
♠ 10 8                        ♠ 9
♡ —          ┌─────────┐      ♡ —
◇ —          │    N    │      ◇ Q 10
♣ A J 7 4    │ W     E │      ♣ 10 6 3
             │    S    │
             └─────────┘
              ♠ K
              ♡ J 3 2
              ◇ 6 3
              ♣ —
```

You lead dummy's ♣K, throwing the ♠K from your hand. West wins with the
♣A and has to return one of the black suits, reviving the dummy. You can then
discard your two diamond losers on the ♠J and the ♣Q. (West cannot duck the
♣K, of course, or you will simply cash the ♠J.)

Using the entry when a defender has to duck

When you are attempting to strip a defender of his cards in a particular suit,
you may have to manage your entries carefully. On the following deal, you take
advantage of the fact that a defender has to duck a couple of times when you
play on a different side suit.

```
East-West Vul.          ♠ 7 5
Dealer South            ♡ K 9
                        ◇ Q 8 6 3 2
                        ♣ K J 10 9
    ♠ 10 6          ┌─────────┐      ♠ 9 2
    ♡ Q 10 5 3 2    │    N    │      ♡ A J 7 6
    ◇ J 10 9 5      │ W     E │      ◇ A K 7
    ♣ 8 3           │    S    │      ♣ A 6 5 2
                   └─────────┘
                        ♠ A K Q J 8 4 3
                        ♡ 8 4
                        ◇ 4
                        ♣ Q 7 4
```

West	North	East	South
			1♠
pass	1NT	pass	4♠
all pass			

How will you play the spade game when West leads the ◇J?

The first move is to cover with dummy's ◇Q. Otherwise, West will be left on lead and may kill you with a heart switch. Let's say that East wins with the ◇K and refuses to assist you in eliminating his diamond holding, switching to a trump. What then?

You win the trump switch and draw trumps in one more round. All will be well if the ♡A is onside. Meanwhile, you have nothing to lose by playing on clubs. When you lead a club to the nine, East has to hold off the ace to prevent you from scoring three club tricks. You must take advantage of this entry to dummy by ruffing a diamond in your hand. You continue with a club to the ten. East, who noted his partner's high-low count signal in clubs, has to hold up the ace one more time. Again, you take advantage by ruffing a diamond in your hand. These cards remain:

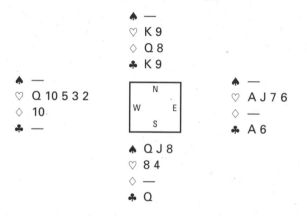

```
              ♠ —
              ♡ K 9
              ◇ Q 8
              ♣ K 9
♠ —                            ♠ —
♡ Q 10 5 3 2        N          ♡ A J 7 6
◇ 10          W         E      ◇ —
♣ —                S           ♣ A 6
              ♠ Q J 8
              ♡ 8 4
              ◇ —
              ♣ Q
```

When the ♣Q is led, East has to win with the ♣A. Since all of his diamonds have been stripped, he has to lead the ♣6 (giving dummy an entry and a trick) or play on hearts with the same effect. The spade game is yours.

Sacrificing a trick for the throw-in

When reaching the dummy will be worth more than one trick, sacrificing a trick to perform a throw-in can be good business. This happens most often in the trump suit, as on this deal:

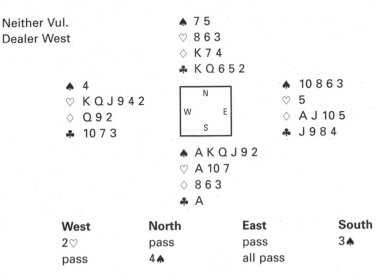

Neither Vul.
Dealer West

```
              ♠ 7 5
              ♡ 8 6 3
              ◇ K 7 4
              ♣ K Q 6 5 2
♠ 4                          ♠ 10 8 6 3
♡ K Q J 9 4 2                ♡ 5
◇ Q 9 2          N           ◇ A J 10 5
♣ 10 7 3      W     E        ♣ J 9 8 4
                 S
              ♠ A K Q J 9 2
              ♡ A 10 7
              ◇ 8 6 3
              ♣ A
```

West	North	East	South
2♡	pass	pass	3♠
pass	4♠	all pass	

How will you play the spade game when West leads the ♡K?

East surely holds the ◇A after West's weak two-bid, so there is no apparent entry to the dummy. You win with the ♡A and play two rounds of trumps, discovering the 4-1 trump break. After playing another top trump, you unblock the ♣A.

East has no more hearts left and will not be able to play a club or a diamond without giving you access to the two winners in dummy. It is therefore worthwhile to sacrifice a trump trick in order to put him on lead. You lead the ♠2 on the fourth round, giving East an unexpected trump trick. If he plays a diamond now, he will give you three tricks and the contract. The best he can do is to exit with a club. You discard two hearts on the ♣K-Q and then put East on lead again with a fourth round of clubs! Like it or not, he is forced to play on diamonds, giving you a trick with dummy's ◇K. Ten tricks are before you.

The stepping-stone squeeze

Suppose you have a suit where a blockage is preventing you from scoring the maximum number of tricks in the suit: for example, ◇A-Q opposite ◇K-J-6-2. You have no side entry to the hand containing the four-card diamond holding and if you overtake on the second round, you will score only three tricks from the suit. What can be done?

One defender will have to retain four diamonds to guard the suit. Perhaps you can squeeze him down to those four diamonds and a side winner. With five tricks to go, you can then unblock the diamond ace and queen and throw him in with his side winner. He will have to surrender the last two tricks to the stranded ◇ K-J. This, in a nutshell, is the 'stepping-stone squeeze'. Let's look at an example:

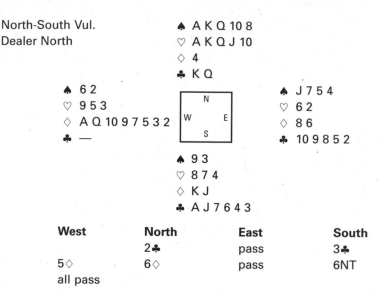

North-South Vul.
Dealer North

♠ A K Q 10 8
♡ A K Q J 10
◇ 4
♣ K Q

♠ 6 2
♡ 9 5 3
◇ A Q 10 9 7 5 3 2
♣ —

♠ J 7 5 4
♡ 6 2
◇ 8 6
♣ 10 9 8 5 2

♠ 9 3
♡ 8 7 4
◇ K J
♣ A J 7 6 4 3

West	North	East	South
	2♣	pass	3♣
5◇	6◇	pass	6NT
all pass			

How will you play 6NT when West leads the ♡5?

All will be easy if clubs break 3-2 because you will be able to overtake on the second round and run the whole suit. The ♠J may fall in three rounds too. (It might at the table, that is. Not in this book!)

You win the heart lead and play the top three spades, leaving East with the master ♠J. Next, you play the remaining four winners in hearts. This is the position with one heart still to be played:

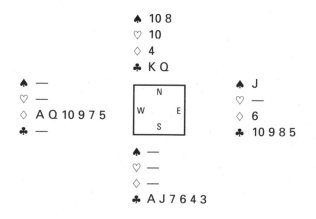

♠ 10 8
♡ 10
◇ 4
♣ K Q

♠ —
♡ —
◇ A Q 10 9 7 5
♣ —

♠ J
♡ —
◇ 6
♣ 10 9 8 5

♠ —
♡ —
◇ —
♣ A J 7 6 4 3

You lead dummy's ♡10 and East cannot afford to throw a black card. (If he threw a club, you could overtake on the second round.) He must therefore throw the ◊6, his link with partner's hand. You play the ♣K, West showing out, and continue with the ♣Q, playing low from your hand. East is down to the ♠J and two clubs. You put him on lead with a spade and he has to give the last two tricks to your ♣A-J.

The stars come out to play:
endplays to gain an entry

Teams from Ireland and the Netherlands met in the 2005 World Transnational Teams in Estoril, Portugal. Ireland's Hugh McGann played strongly on this deal:

North-South Vul.	♠ J 9 4 3 2		
Dealer East	♡ Q 10 6 2		
	◊ 9 6 3		
	♣ 10		

♠ Q 7 5		♠ A K 10 6
♡ A 8 7 5 4 3		♡ K J
◊ 7 4	N W E S	◊ J 8 5 2
♣ J 5		♣ 6 3 2

♠ 8
♡ 9
◊ A K Q 10
♣ A K Q 9 8 7 4

West	North	East	South
Jansma	Hanlon	Verhees	McGann
		1♣	pass
2◊	pass	2♡	5♣
all pass			

West's 2◊ response showed the values for a weak two-bid in one of the major suits. East's 2♡ meant that he was happy to play at that level if West's suit was hearts. McGann leapt to 5♣, ending the auction, and West led ace and another heart. Declarer ruffed the second round of hearts, noting the fall of the jack and king from East. How would you have continued the play?

McGann drew trumps in three rounds, pleased to see that East did not hold a trump trick. East had clearly opened 1♣ on a hand of weak notrump type. Since he was marked with two hearts and three clubs, his shape was likely to be 4-2-4-3. In that case, the odds favored him to hold the ◊J. McGann saw that

East would have discarding problems if the trump suit was run. Trumps were continued and West threw the ◇7, a count signal to alert East to the diamond position. With one trump still to be played, McGann cashed two diamonds to confirm the position in that suit. West duly showed out on the second diamond and these cards remained:

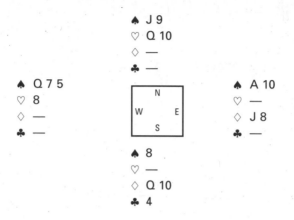

```
                          ♠ J 9
                          ♡ Q 10
                          ◇ —
                          ♣ —
   ♠ Q 7 5                              ♠ A 10
   ♡ 8              ┌─────────┐          ♡ —
   ◇ —             │ N       │          ◇ J 8
   ♣ —             │ W     E │          ♣ —
                    │    S    │
                    └─────────┘
                          ♠ 8
                          ♡ —
                          ◇ Q 10
                          ♣ 4
```

McGann led his last club, West and the dummy pitching hearts. What could poor Louk Verhees discard in the East seat? If he threw a diamond, declarer would score an extra trick in that suit. If instead he threw the ♠10, he would be endplayed with a spade to give declarer two diamond tricks. The only other possibility was to throw the ♠A. Declarer would then lead the ♠8, forcing West to win and concede the last two tricks to dummy's ♠J and ♡Q. Well played! To beat the contract, West needed to switch to a spade (or the ♣J) at Trick 2.

In the same year, 2005, Philip Silverstein played the following spade game at the NABC Spring Championships in Pittsburgh.

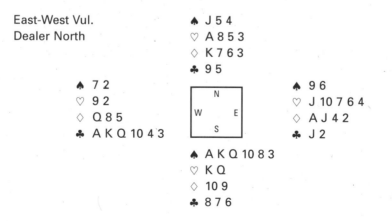

```
East-West Vul.            ♠ J 5 4
Dealer North              ♡ A 8 5 3
                          ◇ K 7 6 3
                          ♣ 9 5
   ♠ 7 2                                ♠ 9 6
   ♡ 9 2           ┌─────────┐          ♡ J 10 7 6 4
   ◇ Q 8 5         │ N       │          ◇ A J 4 2
   ♣ A K Q 10 4 3  │ W     E │          ♣ J 2
                    │    S    │
                    └─────────┘
                          ♠ A K Q 10 8 3
                          ♡ K Q
                          ◇ 10 9
                          ♣ 8 7 6
```

West	North	East	South
			Silverstein
	pass	pass	1♠
3♣	3♠	pass	4♠
all pass			

West's 3♣ was explained as a 'weak jump overcall', although it presumably contained good playing strength when vulnerable against not. West cashed the ace and king of clubs, East somewhat unwisely encouraging with the jack and two. How would you play the contract after West continues with the ♣Q at Trick 3?

Silverstein ruffed with dummy's ♠J to avoid an overruff. He then drew trumps, which left him in the South hand. The description given of West's overcall made it likely that East would hold the ◇A. How could the contract be made in that case?

Silverstein continued to play trumps, arriving at this end position:

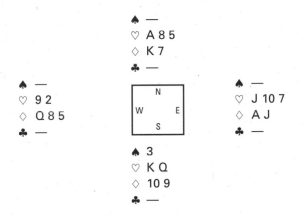

On the last trump, declarer threw the ◇7 from dummy. East was caught in a stepping-stone squeeze. If he threw another heart, declarer would be able to overtake the second round of hearts with the ♡A and score dummy's ♡8. East in fact chose to throw the ◇J. Silverstein then cashed the king and queen of hearts and put East on lead with the ◇A. At Trick 13, East had to lead a heart to dummy's stranded ♡A and the game was made.

NOW TRY THESE...

A.

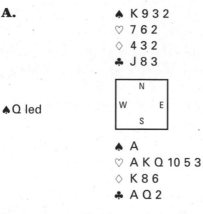

<pre>
                       ♠ K 9 3 2
                       ♡ 7 6 2
                       ◇ 4 3 2
                       ♣ J 8 3

  ♠ Q led   ┌─────────┐
                  │   N   │
                  │ W   E │
                  │   S   │
                  └─────────┘

                       ♠ A
                       ♡ A K Q 10 5 3
                       ◇ K 8 6
                       ♣ A Q 2
</pre>

West	North	East	South
1♠	pass	pass	dbl
pass	2♣	pass	4♡
all pass			

West leads the ♠Q against your heart game. How will you play the contract? (You will find that East holds three trumps to the jack.)

B.

<pre>
                       ♠ 8 5 3
                       ♡ 5 4 2
                       ◇ Q J
                       ♣ K Q 8 7 3

  ♠ K led   ┌─────────┐
                  │   N   │
                  │ W   E │
                  │   S   │
                  └─────────┘

                       ♠ A 10 4
                       ♡ A K J 10 9 7 6
                       ◇ A K
                       ♣ A
</pre>

West	North	East	South
2♠	pass	pass	dbl
pass	3♣	pass	3♡
pass	4♡	pass	6♡
all pass			

North's 3♣ response shows around 8-10 points, when the Lebensohl convention is in use. How will you play the heart slam after West leads the ♠K?

C.

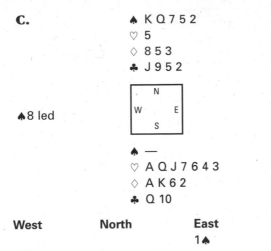

♠ K Q 7 5 2
♡ 5
◇ 8 5 3
♣ J 9 5 2

♠8 led

♠ —
♡ A Q J 7 6 4 3
◇ A K 6 2
♣ Q 10

West	North	East	South
		1♠	4♡
all pass			

How will you play your game in hearts when West leads the ♠8, covered by the ♠Q and the ♠A?

D.

♠ 6 5 3
♡ Q 8 7 6 3
◇ J 10 4
♣ K 4

♣2 led

♠ A K Q 10 9 7
♡ A K
◇ A 5 3
♣ 7 6

West	North	East	South
		1♣	dbl
pass	1♡	pass	2♠
pass	3♠	pass	4♠
all pass			

West leads the ♣2 against your spade game. How will you tackle the play? (You will find that trumps break 2-2.)

Answers

A.

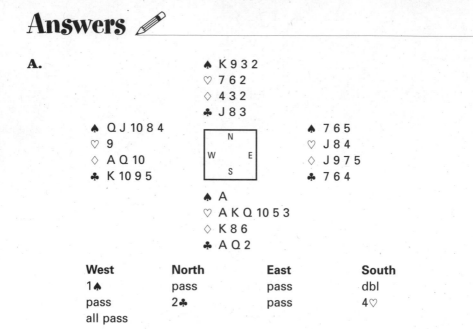

West	North	East	South
1♠	pass	pass	dbl
pass	2♣	pass	4♡
all pass			

West leads the ♠Q, won with the singleton ace. How will you play the contract?

Only 14 points are out, so you can place the missing big cards with West. After drawing trumps in three rounds, you should continue with the ace and queen of clubs. If West wins with the ♣K, he cannot attack diamonds successfully from his side of the table. On a black-suit exit, you will be able to throw one of your diamond losers on dummy's ♠K.

West does no better by ducking the second round of clubs, since he has to win the third round of the suit. These cards will then remain:

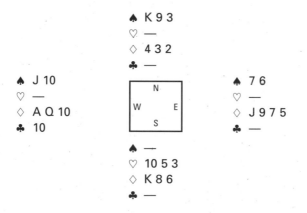

West can delay matters by cashing the ♣10, but you will counter by throwing a diamond loser. Now West will have to lead a diamond, giving you a trick with the ◇K, or play a spade, giving you access to dummy's ♠K. Ten tricks either way.

B.

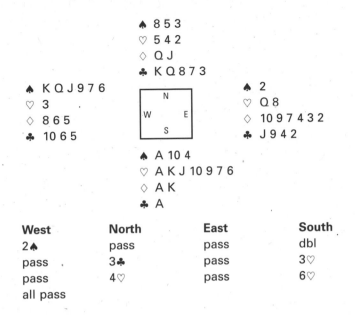

♠ 8 5 3
♥ 5 4 2
♦ Q J
♣ K Q 8 7 3

♠ K Q J 9 7 6
♥ 3
♦ 8 6 5
♣ 10 6 5

♠ 2
♥ Q 8
♦ 10 9 7 4 3 2
♣ J 9 4 2

♠ A 10 4
♥ A K J 10 9 7 6
♦ A K
♣ A

West	North	East	South
2♠	pass	pass	dbl
pass	3♣	pass	3♥
pass	4♥	pass	6♥
all pass			

North would respond 2NT (the Lebensohl convention) on most hands containing 0-7 points. His actual 3♣ response suggests 8-10 points, after which South's change of suit is forcing. How will you play the heart slam when West leads the ♠K?

Dummy's three tiny spot cards in the trump suit offer you no prospect of an entry, so it is not easy to see how you might reach the ♣K-Q. You must aim to endplay East on the second round of trumps. You win the spade lead and cash the ♥A, both defenders following. You then cash your three winners in the minor suits and exit with a low trump. By good fortune, it is East who holds the ♥Q. He has no spade to return, as you expected after West's weak-two opening. A club will give you access to dummy's winners in the suit, allowing you to discard the two spade losers. A diamond will concede a ruff-and-sluff, allowing you to throw one spade and ruff in the dummy. You can then discard your remaining spade loser on the ♣K.

Exactly the same play would succeed if dummy's clubs were slightly weaker, just ♣K-J-8-7-3. A club return would be into the king-jack tenace and a ruff-and-sluff would again concede the contract because you would then need only one further discard on the ♣K.

C.

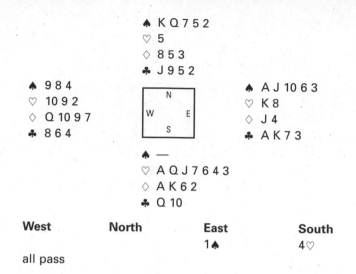

♠ K Q 7 5 2
♡ 5
◇ 8 5 3
♣ J 9 5 2

♠ 9 8 4
♡ 10 9 2
◇ Q 10 9 7
♣ 8 6 4

♠ A J 10 6 3
♡ K 8
◇ J 4
♣ A K 7 3

♠ —
♡ A Q J 7 6 4 3
◇ A K 6 2
♣ Q 10

West	North	East	South
		1♠	4♡
all pass			

How will you play 4♡ when West leads the ♠8, covered by the ♠Q and the ♠A?

Dummy is a distant island. The only serious chance is to find East with at most two diamonds, in which case a throw-in may be possible. You play the ♡A and continue with the ◇A-K. When you play the ♡Q, two wishes are granted — East wins with the bare king and he has no diamond to play. These cards remain:

♠ K 7 5
♡ —
◇ 8
♣ J 9 5 2

♠ 9 4
♡ 10
◇ Q 10
♣ 8 6 4

♠ J 10 6 3
♡ —
◇ —
♣ A K 7 3

♠ —
♡ J 7 6 4
◇ 6 2
♣ Q 10

If East plays ace, king and another club, you will discard both of your diamond losers — one on the ♣9 and one on the ♠K. You can then ruff a diamond and draw West's last trump. What will you do if East exits with the ♠J instead?

If you discard, you will go down. When you draw the last trump and exit in clubs, East will cash two clubs and exit safely in spades. So, ruff the ♠J, draw the last trump and lead the ♣Q. East must now give you two black-suit tricks.

One final point — when East takes his ♡K and cashes one top club, you must ditch the ♣Q! Otherwise, he can exit with a low club to the bare queen; you would lose only one club trick, yes, but would be left with two diamond losers.

D.

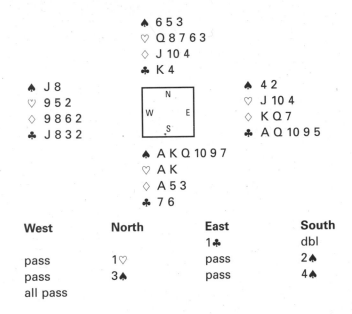

West	North	East	South
		1♣	dbl
pass	1♡	pass	2♠
pass	3♠	pass	4♠
all pass			

West leads the ♣2 against your spade game. How will you tackle the play?

At Trick 1, you must play the ♣4 from dummy. (Otherwise, East will be able to cross to the West hand with a club on the next trick and a diamond switch will break up your intended end position.) East takes two club tricks and switches to a trump. You win with the ace and play another top trump, pleased to find a 2-2 break. What now?

If East has the king and queen of diamonds, he is ripe for an endplay. You cash the ace and king of hearts to leave this end position:

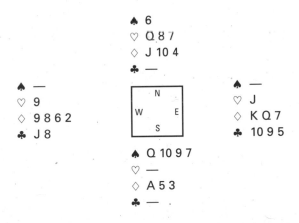

With the preliminary spadework over, you play a diamond to the jack. East wins with one of the honors — he can try a deceptive king if he wishes — but is then endplayed. Either he will have to give you an entry to dummy, leading a heart, or he will have to lead into your split tenace in diamonds.

CHAPTER 11

The Trump Coup

Suppose you have a trump holding of ♠A-Q-J-10-8-3, with ♠6-2 in the dummy, and cannot afford a trump loser. If the king is on your right and guarded no more than twice, a repeated finesse will do the business. What will happen if your right-hand-opponent holds ♠K-9-7-4? Life then becomes more difficult, but you may still be able to trap the king with a play known as a 'trump coup'.

Shortening your trumps to match the defender's

The general idea of a trump coup is that you take sufficient ruffs in the long trump holding to reduce your trumps to the same length as those of the key defender. In the situation described in the introduction above, you take two finesses and then aim for an end position where you hold the ♠A-10 over East's remaining ♠K-9. By leading a plain card towards this holding, or arranging for your left-hand-opponent to do this, you will avoid losing a trump trick.

A sample deal would make it clearer, you say? Your wish is my command.

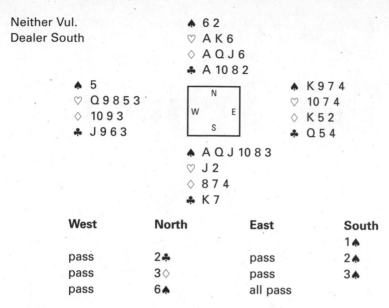

Neither Vul.
Dealer South

```
               ♠ 6 2
               ♡ A K 6
               ◇ A Q J 6
               ♣ A 10 8 2
♠ 5                              ♠ K 9 7 4
♡ Q 9 8 5 3                      ♡ 10 7 4
◇ 10 9 3                         ◇ K 5 2
♣ J 9 6 3                        ♣ Q 5 4
               ♠ A Q J 10 8 3
               ♡ J 2
               ◇ 8 7 4
               ♣ K 7
```

West	North	East	South
			1♠
pass	2♣	pass	2♠
pass	3◇	pass	3♠
pass	6♠	all pass	

How will you play the spade slam when West leads the ◇ 10?

Finessing the ◇Q is worth the risk. If the ◇10 is a singleton and you suffer a ruff when the ♠K is onside, so be it. The diamond finesse loses to the king and East returns a diamond, won in the dummy. You finesse the ♠Q successfully, return to dummy with a heart and repeat the spade finesse. This time, the news is less favorable, West discarding a heart. How can you prevent East's ♠K-9 from taking a trick?

You must shorten your trumps to the same length as East's, planning to return to dummy one more time for the actual trump coup. You play the king and ace of clubs and ruff a club, East following all the while. You then return to dummy with a third round of diamonds and ruff another club, East discarding a heart. A heart to dummy's king leaves these cards still out:

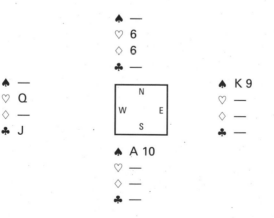

```
               ♠ —
               ♡ 6
               ◇ 6
               ♣ —
♠ —                              ♠ K 9
♡ Q                              ♡ —
◇ —                              ◇ —
♣ J                              ♣ —
               ♠ A 10
               ♡ —
               ◇ —
               ♣ —
```

When a red card is led from dummy, this has the same effect as taking a finesse of the ♠10. You score the last two tricks.

Suppose South had not reduced his trumps to the same length as East's. Let's give him an extra trump and add a side-suit card to the other three hands:

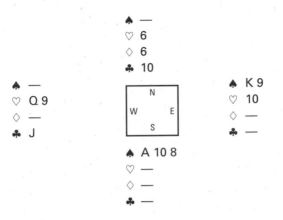

No good, is it? When you lead any card from dummy, East playing the ♡10, you will have to ruff. With the lead in the South hand at Trick 12, you will not be able to perform the trump coup. This is why reducing your trump length is such a vital part of a trump coup. Indeed, the play is sometimes called a 'trump reduction'.

Exiting to force a trump lead at the end

We have just seen the most familiar form of the trump coup, where you lead a plain card from dummy towards a trump tenace in your hand. It can be just as effective to exit to the defenders at Trick 11, which allows you to score two tricks with your trump tenace on any return. Let's see a straightforward example of that technique:

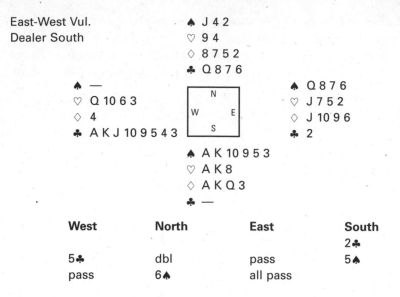

East-West Vul.
Dealer South

```
              ♠ J 4 2
              ♡ 9 4
              ◇ 8 7 5 2
              ♣ Q 8 7 6
♠ —                              ♠ Q 8 7 6
♡ Q 10 6 3        N              ♡ J 7 5 2
◇ 4           W       E          ◇ J 10 9 6
♣ A K J 10 9 5 4 3    S          ♣ 2
              ♠ A K 10 9 5 3
              ♡ A K 8
              ◇ A K Q 3
              ♣ —
```

West	North	East	South
			2♣
5♣	dbl	pass	5♠
pass	6♠	all pass	

North's initial double shows a weak hand, warning you not to expect much assistance in any contract that you might have in mind. When you nevertheless bid 5♠, North takes a rosy view of his three trumps and the doubleton heart and raises to 6♠. You ruff the ♣K lead and play the ace of trumps, West showing out. How will you continue?

You can enter dummy with a heart ruff, but only one trump finesse will be possible. You cannot therefore pick up East's ♠Q by direct means. All will still be fine if the diamonds break 3-2. You play the ace and king of the suit and are not happy to see West show out on the second round. What now?

You must aim to score the five top cards in the red suits, a heart ruff in dummy and all six trumps in your hand. You cash a third diamond winner and enter dummy by playing the top two hearts and ruffing your last heart. These cards remain:

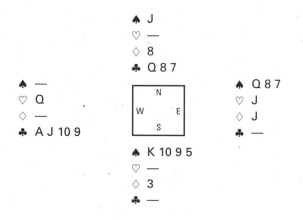

```
              ♠ J
              ♡ —
              ◇ 8
              ♣ Q 8 7
♠ —                    ♠ Q 8 7
♡ Q            N        ♡ J
◇ —        W       E    ◇ J
♣ A J 10 9     S        ♣ —
              ♠ K 10 9 5
              ♡ —
              ◇ 3
              ♣ —
```

You lead the ♠J and East cannot afford to cover or you will draw all of his trumps, losing just a diamond trick. Conveniently still in the dummy, you ruff a club with the ♠9. You don't mind at all which red jack East chooses to throw on this trick. You will simply exit with your diamond loser, certain to score the last two tricks with your ♠K-10.

Crossruff leading to a trump coup

Sometimes you could have picked up your right-hand opponent's trump holding of Q-x-x-x or J-x-x-x with a straightforward finesse, but the need to take several ruffs in dummy prevents this in practice. Provided you can shorten the trumps in your hand by ruffing one of dummy's suits, you may be able to reach a satisfactory trump promotion ending. That is what happens on this grand slam:

```
Neither Vul.              ♠ A 4
Dealer South              ♡ K Q 8 4
                          ◇ J 7 6 5 4 2
                          ♣ 2

        ♠ J 9 3              N          ♠ 10 8 7 5
        ♡ —                             ♡ J 9 6 2
        ◇ K Q 10 9 3   W         E      ◇ 8
        ♣ K Q J 10 9        S          ♣ 8 6 5 3

                          ♠ K Q 6 2
                          ♡ A 10 7 5 3
                          ◇ A
                          ♣ A 7 4
```

West	North	East	South
			1♡
2NT	4♣	pass	4NT
pass	5♠	pass	7♡
all pass			

A splinter bid and Roman Keycard Blackwood carry you to 7♡. You win the ♣K lead with the ace and play a trump to the king, West showing out. What now?

You could pick up East's ♡J-x-x-x with a straightforward finesse, but that would leave you with a bundle of losers in the South hand. West's Unusual Notrump overcall has told you that you cannot establish the diamond suit, so you will have to ruff your black-suit losers in dummy.

You cash the top three spades, unblock the ◇A and lead a fourth round of spades. West shows out and you ruff with the ♡4. At the moment, you hold four trumps to East's three. You are planning a two-card ending where you will hold ♡A-10 over East's ♡J-9, so you will need to shorten your trumps twice. You lead a diamond from dummy and East cannot gain by ruffing. He discards a club and you ruff low. A club ruff with dummy's ♡8 leaves these cards still to be played:

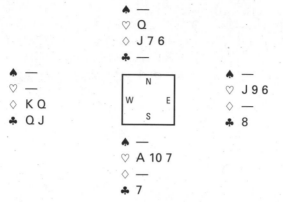

♠ —
♡ Q
◇ J 7 6
♣ —

♠ —
♡ —
◇ K Q
♣ Q J

♠ —
♡ J 9 6
◇ —
♣ 8

♠ —
♡ A 10 7
◇ —
♣ 7

'Diamond, please,' you say.

Four trump tricks are coming your way and East can do nothing about it. Let's say that he discards his last club. You ruff with the ♡7 and ruff your last club with the ♡Q. In the resultant two-card trump-coup position, you lead a diamond from dummy and score your ♡A-10 poised over East's ♡J-9.

The defender has to split touching cards

In the trump coups that we have seen so far, the key defender held only one trump honor that you needed to trap. When he has two trump honors, in a holding such as J-10-x-x, a trump coup may still be possible. You will need to force the defender to split his top cards on an early round of the trump suit. That is what happens here:

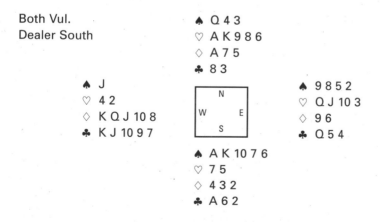

Both Vul.
Dealer South

♠ Q 4 3
♡ A K 9 8 6
◇ A 7 5
♣ 8 3

♠ J
♡ 4 2
◇ K Q J 10 8
♣ K J 10 9 7

♠ 9 8 5 2
♡ Q J 10 3
◇ 9 6
♣ Q 5 4

♠ A K 10 7 6
♡ 7 5
◇ 4 3 2
♣ A 6 2

West	North	East	South
			1♠
2NT	3♡	pass	3♠
pass	4♠	all pass	

West leads the ◇K, which you win in the dummy. How will you plan the play?

Five trump tricks, four side-suit winners and a club ruff in dummy will bring your total to ten. When you surrender a club trick, preparing for the ruff, West will be able to cash two diamond tricks, allowing East to discard a club. You will then have to ruff the third round of clubs with the ♠Q to prevent an overruff.

This glimpse into your crystal ball is enough to convince you that you should draw the first round of trumps with the ace rather than the queen. When you do so, West follows with the jack. What now?

You should play a low club, preserving the ♣A as an entry to your hand. East wins with the ♣Q and returns his remaining diamond. West scores two diamond tricks and East discards a club, as you foresaw. You win the heart switch with the ace and lead a trump towards your hand (leaving the bare ♠Q in dummy). Suspecting that you will take West's ♠J at face value, East does best to split his ♠9-8. You win with the ♠10, cash the ♣A and must consider your next move carefully.

It would be premature to ruff a club at this stage. You need to shorten your trumps to match East's and should therefore cross to the ♡K and ruff a heart. These cards remain:

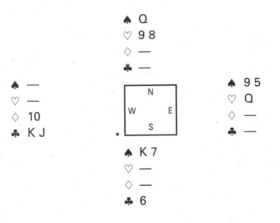

Only now do you ruff your club loser with the ♠Q. You can then lead a heart to perform the trump coup. Since East had to split his ♠9-8 earlier, your ♠K-7 is an effective tenace over East's last two trumps.

Ducking a round of trumps to set up the coup

Suppose, after one round of trumps has been played, that you hold K-10-6 of trumps over RHO's Q-J-9. You lead a low trump from dummy and East inserts the jack. You will have to lose one trump trick eventually, of course, and it may well be beneficial for you to duck this round, leaving yourself with a solid tenace over East's remaining honor. That may be true even when you will need a trump coup to take advantage of this trump tenace. Look at the following deal:

Both Vul.
Dealer North

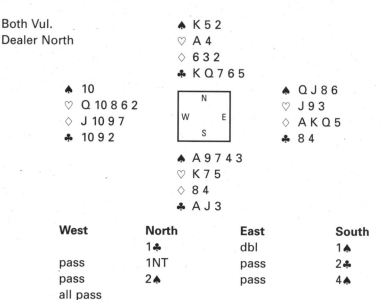

♠ K 5 2
♡ A 4
◇ 6 3 2
♣ K Q 7 6 5

♠ 10
♡ Q 10 8 6 2
◇ J 10 9 7
♣ 10 9 2

♠ Q J 8 6
♡ J 9 3
◇ A K Q 5
♣ 8 4

♠ A 9 7 4 3
♡ K 7 5
◇ 8 4
♣ A J 3

West	North	East	South
	1♣	dbl	1♠
pass	1NT	pass	2♣
pass	2♠	pass	4♠
all pass			

A Checkback 2♣ uncovers the 5-3 spade fit and West leads the ◇J against your game contract. The defenders persist with the suit and you ruff the third round. A trump to the king brings the ♠10 from West and you lead a second round of trumps from dummy. If East follows with the ♠8, you have a straightforward safety play available. You will cover with the ♠9 and make the contract easily whether or not this wins the trick. Let's suppose that East inserts the ♠Q instead. How will you play then?

If you win with the ♠A, you will go down. You will be left with ♠9-7 over East's ♠J-8. Leading towards the ♠9 will not rescue you because East will rise with the ♠J and force your last trump with another diamond. Nor can a trump coup succeed because East will ruff the third club with the ♠8 and score the ♠J as the setting trick.

Instead, you must duck the ♠J, leaving yourself with ♠A-9 over East's ♠J-8. To prevent you from simply drawing trumps with a finesse, East has to return a fourth round of diamonds, deliberately giving you a ruff-and-sluff. You ruff with dummy's last trump and throw a club from your hand. You must now catch East's remaining trumps in a coup. These cards remain:

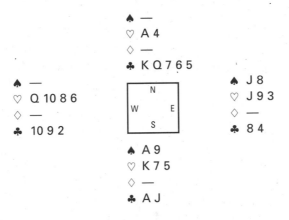

                ♠ —
                ♡ A 4
                ◇ —
                ♣ K Q 7 6 5

♠ —   ♠ J 8
♡ Q 10 8 6   ♡ J 9 3
◇ —   ◇ —
♣ 10 9 2   ♣ 8 4

                ♠ A 9
                ♡ K 7 5
                ◇ —
                ♣ A J

You cash the ♣A and overtake the ♣J with the ♣Q. You then lead good clubs through East. If he ruffs at any stage, you will overruff and draw his last trump, claiming the remainder. If instead East refuses to ruff, you will discard all of your hearts and lead a heart from dummy at Trick 12, catching East's trumps in a coup.

Avoiding a damaging discard

When you are taking ruffs in your hand to shorten your trumps in preparation for a trump coup, you sometimes have to be careful which suit you ruff. If you are not, the key defender may be able to spoil your communications with a damaging discard. Test yourself in this heart slam:

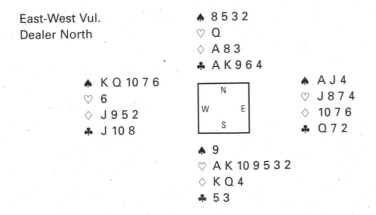

East-West Vul.   ♠ 8 5 3 2
Dealer North   ♡ Q
                        ◇ A 8 3
                        ♣ A K 9 6 4

♠ K Q 10 7 6   ♠ A J 4
♡ 6   ♡ J 8 7 4
◇ J 9 5 2   ◇ 10 7 6
♣ J 10 8   ♣ Q 7 2

                        ♠ 9
                        ♡ A K 10 9 5 3 2
                        ◇ K Q 4
                        ♣ 5 3

West	North	East	South
	1♣	pass	2♡
pass	3♣	pass	4♡
pass	6♡	all pass	

It is unconvincing bidding, you're right, but there is nothing wrong with the final contract. The defenders play two rounds of spades and you ruff the second round. A trump to the queen is followed by a diamond to the king and the ace of trumps. Oh dear! West shows out, discarding a spade. A trump coup will be needed to pick up East's remaining ♡J-8. How will you continue the play?

You need to take two more ruffs in your hand to shorten your trumps to match East's trump length. You will then need one further entry to dummy to lead a plain card towards your eventual ♡K-10. You cross to the ♣A and ruff a spade. A club to the king leaves you in dummy, with these cards still out:

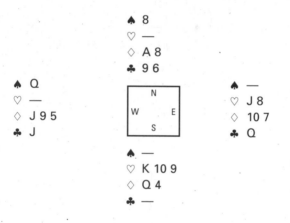

What now? If you ruff another spade at this stage, you will regret it. East will discard one of his diamonds. When you continue with the queen and ace of diamonds, East will strike with a ruff and you will be one down.

Instead, you should lead a club from dummy. As the cards lie, East will follow suit. You will ruff, cash the queen and ace of diamonds and lead one of dummy's two black cards towards your trump tenace. Slam made.

Suppose that East's last three minor-suit cards had been three diamonds instead. No damage would be done. He could discard one diamond as you ruffed the third round of clubs, but the queen and ace of diamonds would still stand up.

The stars come out to play:
the trump coup

You will not be surprised to hear that the world's top players are well versed in trump coup technique. We still start at the 1991 Venice Cup in Yokohama, where Austria faces China in the semifinals. Sitting South for Austria is the great Maria Erhart. Let's see how she handles a potential trump coup situation:

Neither Vul.
Dealer South

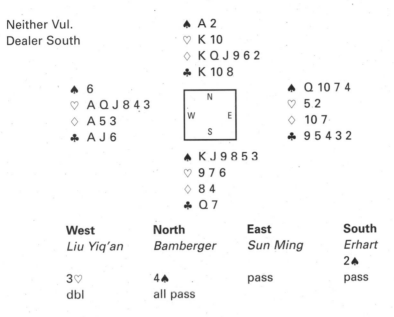

```
                    ♠ A 2
                    ♡ K 10
                    ◇ K Q J 9 6 2
                    ♣ K 10 8
  ♠ 6                              ♠ Q 10 7 4
  ♡ A Q J 8 4 3        N           ♡ 5 2
  ◇ A 5 3          W       E       ◇ 10 7
  ♣ A J 6              S           ♣ 9 5 4 3 2
                    ♠ K J 9 8 5 3
                    ♡ 9 7 6
                    ◇ 8 4
                    ♣ Q 7
```

West	North	East	South
Liu Yiq'an	Bamberger	Sun Ming	Erhart
			2♠
3♡	4♠	pass	pass
dbl	all pass		

The Chinese West began the defense by cashing her three aces. A club continuation would then have removed a key entry to dummy. This was difficult to judge and she played a diamond next. How would you play from this point?

Erhart placed East with the long trumps after this auction. After winning the second round of diamonds in dummy, she led the ♠2, finessing the ♠9. The appearance of West's ♠6 on this trick confirmed that declarer had read the cards correctly. She returned to dummy with the ♡K and called for the ◇Q.

Do you see Erhart's plan? She will discard the heart loser on a top diamond, ruff a good diamond, return to the ♣K and ruff another good diamond, thereby shortening her trumps to the same length as East's. She can then return to dummy with the ♠A (that's why she could not afford to lead that card at Trick 5) to lead a plain card towards her last two cards — the ♠K-J. Since the play involves ruffing two diamonds that are winners, it is classified as a Grand Coup.

It is entirely clear from the early play that this was the line that Erhart had in mind. The Chinese East in fact decided to ruff the third round of diamonds, which made the play a good deal easier. Erhart was able to overruff, draw trumps and discard her heart loser.

Round 15 of the 2001 Bermuda Bowl, contested in Paris, saw Poland facing Italy. Both sides reached 4♡ on this deal:

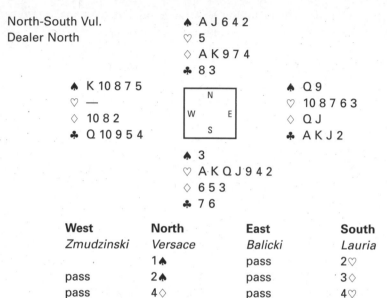

North-South Vul.
Dealer North

♠ A J 6 4 2
♡ 5
♢ A K 9 7 4
♣ 8 3

♠ K 10 8 7 5
♡ —
♢ 10 8 2
♣ Q 10 9 5 4

♠ Q 9
♡ 10 8 7 6 3
♢ Q J
♣ A K J 2

♠ 3
♡ A K Q J 9 4 2
♢ 6 5 3
♣ 7 6

West	North	East	South
Zmudzinski	*Versace*	*Balicki*	*Lauria*
	1♠	pass	2♡
pass	2♠	pass	3♢
pass	4♢	pass	4♡
all pass			

The Polish defenders claimed their two club tricks, East then switching to the ♢Q. Lorenzo Lauria won with dummy's ♢A and crossed to the ace of trumps, West showing out. How would you have continued?

Lauria could see three winners in the side suits. If he could add seven trump tricks, that would give him the heart game. The general idea was to ruff two spades in the South hand and then exit, forcing the defenders to give him a trick with the ♡9.

A spade to the ace was followed by a spade ruff, a diamond to the king and another spade ruff. These cards remained:

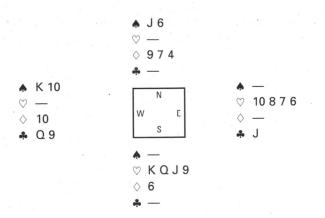

          ♠ J 6
          ♡ —
          ♦ 9 7 4
          ♣ —

♠ K 10   ♠ —
♡ —   N   ♡ 10 8 7 6
♦ 10   W   E   ♦ —
♣ Q 9   S   ♣ J

          ♠ —
          ♡ K Q J 9
          ♦ 6
          ♣ —

Lauria exited with the ◊6 and had to score a trick with his ♡9. Game made. At this level, it was a flat board. Lesniewski followed the same line at the other table.

Australia's Tim Seres performed much of his magic at the rubber bridge table. He played this splendid trump coup in 2007 at Sydney's Double Bay Bridge Centre:

North-South Vul.   ♠ Q J
Dealer North   ♡ A Q 4
                          ◊ A K Q 3
                          ♣ A Q 10 6

♠ —   ♠ A 9 7 6 3
♡ K 8 7 5   N   ♡ 9 6 2
◊ J 10 9 5 4 W   E   ◊ 7 6 2
♣ K 8 7 2   S   ♣ 9 5

                          ♠ K 10 8 5 4 2
                          ♡ J 10 3
                          ◊ 8
                          ♣ J 4 3

West	North	East	South
	Courtney		*Seres*
	2♣	pass	2◊
pass	2NT	pass	3♠
pass	3NT	pass	4♠
pass	6♠	all pass	

The 'rubber bridge style' bidding may not impress you, but take a look at the play! Seres won the ◊J lead in the dummy and led the ♠Q, East playing low and West showing out. Suppose you had been the declarer. How would you have continued?

Seres played the ♠J, East ducking once again, and continued with dummy's ◇K-Q. Since there was a greater chance of East following to three rounds of hearts than to three rounds of clubs, Seres chose to discard two clubs. He cashed the ♣A and reached his hand with a club ruff. Three rounds of hearts, finessing against West's king, left the lead in dummy with these cards still to be played:

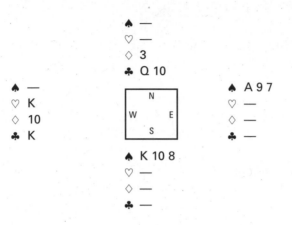

```
              ♠ —
              ♡ —
              ◇ 3
              ♣ Q 10
♠ —                        ♠ A 9 7
♡ K        ┌─────────┐     ♡ —
◇ 10       │    N    │     ◇ —
♣ K        │ W     E │     ♣ —
           │    S    │
           └─────────┘
              ♠ K 10 8
              ♡ —
              ◇ —
              ♣ —
```

When one of dummy's plain cards was led from dummy, East could not prevent declarer from scoring two of the last three tricks.

NOW TRY THESE...

A.

    ♠ A 8 5
    ♡ A 9 6 4 3
    ◇ 7
    ♣ K 7 4 2

♡K led

```
      N
  W       E
      S
```

    ♠ K 7 4
    ♡ 2
    ◇ A K Q 9 4 3 2
    ♣ A 5

West	North	East	South
	1♡	pass	3◇
pass	3♡	pass	4◇
pass	4♠	pass	5♣
pass	5◇	pass	6◇
all pass			

How will you play the diamond slam when West leads the ♡K?

B.

    ♠ A K 7 5
    ♡ K 8 5 2
    ◇ A K 2
    ♣ K 10

♡J led

```
      N
  W       E
      S
```

    ♠ J 6
    ♡ A Q 6
    ◇ 4
    ♣ A Q 8 7 5 4 2

West	North	East	South
			1♣
pass	1♡	pass	3♣
pass	4NT	pass	5♠
pass	7♣	all pass	

You win the ♡J lead with the ♡A and lead a trump. West alarms you by discarding a diamond. Life can be unfair, yes, but perhaps you can triumph over adversity.

C.

                              ♠ A 9 6 4
                              ♡ 4 2
                              ◇ A K 10
                              ♣ 8 6 5 3

♠ Q led
                        ┌─────────────┐
                        │   N   │
                        │ W   E │
                        │   S   │
                        └─────────────┘

                              ♠ 2
                              ♡ A Q J 10 6 5
                              ◇ Q 6 4
                              ♣ A K 2

West	North	East	South
			1♡
pass	1♠	pass	4♡
pass	6♡	all pass	

West leads the ♠Q and you win with dummy's ♠A. When you play a trump to the queen, West discards a spade. How will you counter this hostile break?

D.

                              ♠ J 7
                              ♡ A Q 6
                              ◇ A Q 7 3
                              ♣ K Q 8 3

♡ 10 led
                        ┌─────────────┐
                        │   N   │
                        │ W   E │
                        │   S   │
                        └─────────────┘

                              ♠ A Q 10 9 5 4
                              ♡ K J 4
                              ◇ K 8
                              ♣ 6 4

West	North	East	South
	1♣	pass	1♠
pass	2NT	pass	3♠
pass	4◇	pass	6♠
all pass			

How will you play 6♠ when West leads the ♡10? (Remember, the problem is in a chapter on trump coups, so it is just possible that East will hold ♠K-x-x-x.)

Answers ✐

A.

```
                    ♠ A 8 5
                    ♡ A 9 6 4 3
                    ◇ 7
                    ♣ K 7 4 2
♠ J 6 3 2                              ♠ Q 10 9
♡ K Q J 7          N                   ♡ 10 8 5
◇ 10          W         E              ◇ J 8 6 5
♣ Q 10 9 3         S                   ♣ J 8 6
                    ♠ K 7 4
                    ♡ 2
                    ◇ A K Q 9 4 3 2
                    ♣ A 5
```

West	North	East	South
	1♡	pass	3◇
pass	3♡	pass	4♠
pass	4♠	pass	5♣
pass	5◇	pass	6◇
all pass			

How will you play the diamond slam when West leads the ♡K?

There is no prospect of setting up and reaching a long heart, so you are likely to lose a spade trick. In that case, you will need a 3-2 trump break so that you can pick up the trump suit without loss. If your analysis dries up at this point and your next play is a trump to the ace, you will go down! There is an extra chance available in the trump suit — namely that West will hold a singleton jack or ten. A trump coup may be possible in that case and you must begin to shorten your trumps immediately as a precaution.

You ruff a heart and play a top trump, noting with interest the fall of the ◇10 on your left. Are you disappointed when West shows out on the next trump? No, because your early preparation might now bear fruit. You play the king and ace of spades and ruff another heart in your hand. You still have one more trump than East, so you continue with the ace and king of clubs and lead another heart from dummy. East discards (it would not assist him to ruff, of course) and you ruff once more in the South hand. Your last three cards are the ◇Q-9 and a spade loser. You exit with the spade, won by one of the defenders, and claim the last two tricks with your trump tenace.

Had you made any play other than a heart ruff at Trick 2, you would not have been able to shorten your trumps in time. One down would have been your fate.

B.

```
              ♠ A K 7 5
              ♡ K 8 5 2
              ◇ A K 2
              ♣ K 10
♠ Q 10 3                      ♠ 9 8 4 2
♡ J 10 9 3      ┌─────┐       ♡ 7 4
◇ J 9 8 6 5 3   │ N   │       ◇ Q 10 7
♣ —             │W   E│       ♣ J 9 6 3
                │   S │
                └─────┘
              ♠ J 6
              ♡ A Q 6
              ◇ 4
              ♣ A Q 8 7 5 4 2
```

West	North	East	South
			1♣
pass	1♡	pass	3♣
pass	4NT	pass	5♠
pass	7♣	all pass	

You win the ♡J lead with the ♡A and lead a trump. West discards a diamond! When your heartbeat has slowed down again, how will you continue?

You win the first round of trumps with the king and lead the ten of trumps, covered by the jack and queen. You must now aim for a trump coup to catch East's remaining ♣9-6. To shorten your trumps to the same length as East's, you will need to take three ruffs in your hand.

You cross to the ◇A and cash the ◇K, throwing the ♡6. A diamond ruff is followed by the queen of hearts to the king and a heart ruff, East showing out. You cross to the ♠A and ruff another heart, reducing your trump length to the same as East's. A spade to dummy's king leaves these cards to be played:

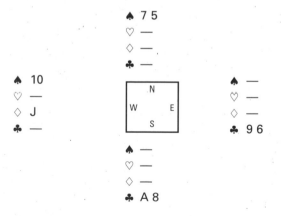

'Spade, please,' you say and East (with a respectful nod in your direction) has to surrender.

C.

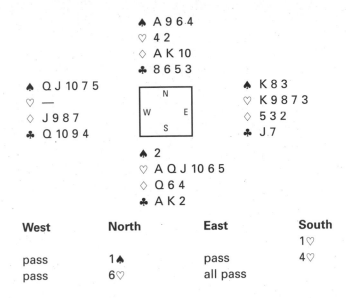

West	North	East	South
			1♡
pass	1♠	pass	4♡
pass	6♡	all pass	

'Even at our club they don't bid as badly as that!' you will be saying. Yes, yes, but look at the play for a moment. West leads the ♠Q and you win with dummy's ♠A. A trump to the queen brings good news and bad news. The finesse wins but West shows out, discarding a spade. How can you counter this hostile break?

Your general plan is to finesse the jack of trumps and to score the six and five of trumps by ruffing spades. You will then exit at Trick 11 so that you can make the last two tricks with your A-10 of trumps. Since this requires three entries to dummy (one to take a second trump finesse, two to ruff spades), you must steel yourself to finesse dummy's ◊10 next. Fortune favors the brave on this occasion and the diamond finesse wins. You continue with a second round of trumps to East's seven and your jack.

You then cash your top two club winners and re-enter dummy twice more in diamonds to ruff two spades with low trumps. Your last three cards are the two of clubs and the A-10 of trumps. There is no need to lead a plain card from dummy towards your trump tenace, as happens in many trump coups; you simply exit with a club. East has to ruff his partner's club winner and lead a trump from the king. The slam is yours.

D.

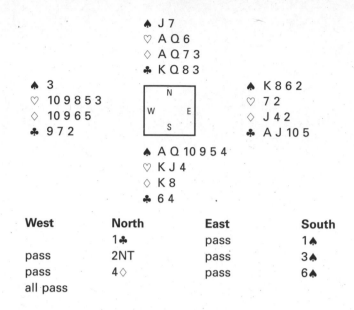

West	North	East	South
	1♣	pass	1♠
pass	2NT	pass	3♠
pass	4◇	pass	6♠
all pass			

South should have used Roman Keycard Blackwood, of course, but once again I ask you to ignore the back-street bidding. See if you can make the slam when West leads the ♡10.

You win in the dummy and run the ♠J successfully. When you continue with a spade to the ten, West shows out. What now?

It may look absolutely obvious to play a club to the king next, but appearances can be deceptive. If you do that, East can defeat you by winning with the ace and returning a second round of hearts. With hearts breaking 5-2, you will then be short of entries to achieve a trump coup. Instead, you should play the king and ace of diamonds. You ruff the ◇7, shortening your trumps, and only then play a club to the king and ace.

You win East's ♣J return with the ♣Q and ruff a club, matching your trump length to East's. You cross to dummy with a heart, leaving this end position:

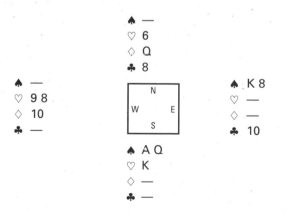

East has no answer to the ◇Q and twelve tricks are yours.

CHAPTER 1 2

Trump Elopement

What on earth does 'trump elopement' mean? It is a fancy term for scoring a trump that does not merit a trick by its rank alone. In other words, you promote it into a trick by leading a plain card towards it, hoping to score a ruff. That's enough of me struggling to explain the play with mere words. Let's see some examples of the technique.

Condensing two losers into one

One of the most spectacular plays in bridge can arise when you have a certain trump loser and an apparently certain loser in a side suit. It is sometimes possible to condense two losers into one. Here is the play in its most familiar form:

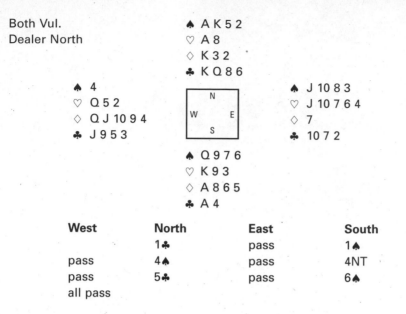

Both Vul.
Dealer North

North
♠ A K 5 2
♡ A 8
◇ K 3 2
♣ K Q 8 6

West
♠ 4
♡ Q 5 2
◇ Q J 10 9 4
♣ J 9 5 3

East
♠ J 10 8 3
♡ J 10 7 6 4
◇ 7
♣ 10 7 2

South
♠ Q 9 7 6
♡ K 9 3
◇ A 8 6 5
♣ A 4

West	North	East	South
	1♣	pass	1♠
pass	4♠	pass	4NT
pass	5♣	pass	6♠
all pass			

You win the ◇Q lead with the ◇K, since if anyone holds a singleton diamond, it is likely to be East. (It may suit you later to lead through East's diamond void towards your remaining honor). When you play the ace and king of trumps, West throws a diamond on the second round. How will you continue?

It would be premature to lead a diamond towards your ace immediately because East would discard one of his three clubs. Instead, you should bank your three club winners, throwing a diamond from your hand. Now is the time to lead a second round of diamonds. It will not help East to ruff a loser from a natural trump trick. He discards a heart and you win with the ◇A. You continue with the ♡K and a heart ruff, leaving the lead in dummy in this end position:

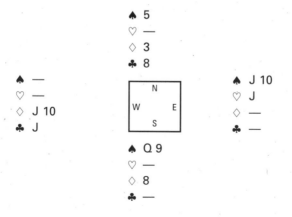

North
♠ 5
♡ —
◇ 3
♣ 8

West
♠ —
♡ —
◇ J 10
♣ J

East
♠ J 10
♡ J
◇ —
♣ —

South
♠ Q 9
♡ —
◇ 8
♣ —

At this stage, it might seem to a casual onlooker that you had certain losers in both diamonds and trumps. Anyone with such thoughts is about to witness a magical illusion! You lead dummy's last club and East has no good move to make. If he discards his heart, you will elope with the ♠9. If instead East ruffs with one of his trumps, you will discard the ◇8 and score the last two tricks. (The ending would have been similar if you had cashed the ♠Q at an earlier stage.)

Here is another example of the Vanishing Trick illusion, where a crossruff leads to the required end position:

North-South Vul.
Dealer North

```
                    ♠ A K 6 3
                    ♡ 8 5
                    ◇ 8 6 3
                    ♣ A 10 7 2
  ♠ Q 10 5                            ♠ J
  ♡ 10 4          ┌─────────┐        ♡ Q J 9 7 2
  ◇ J 10 9 5      │    N    │        ◇ Q 7 2
  ♣ K 9 6 5       │ W     E │        ♣ Q J 8 3
                  │    S    │
                  └─────────┘
                    ♠ 9 8 7 4 2
                    ♡ A K 6 3
                    ◇ A K 4
                    ♣ 4
```

West	North	East	South
	1♣	pass	1♠
pass	2♠	pass	3♡
pass	4♠	pass	4NT
pass	5♡	pass	6♠
all pass			

No one can be accused of underbidding and you arrived in a low point-count spade slam. How will you play it when West leads the ◇J?

All will be easy if trumps are 2-2. When they break 3-1, it may seem that you have an inescapable loser in both trumps and diamonds. Not when Houdini is declarer! You have five top winners in the side suits. If you can add seven trump tricks by crossruffing clubs and hearts, you may yet claim the slam bonus.

You win the diamond lead and begin the process of ruffing clubs in your hand straight away, in case trumps break 3-1. You cannot afford to test the trumps first because the ace and king of trumps will be needed as entries. After the ace of clubs and a club ruff, you cross to the ace of trumps and ruff another club. A trump to the king reveals the feared 3-1 break. Still, at least you have a plan to deal with it.

You ruff another club in your hand, West following suit again. You have scored three ruffs in your hand and must now aim to score the two remaining trumps in the dummy. You cash the ace and king of hearts to leave this end position, with the lead in the South hand:

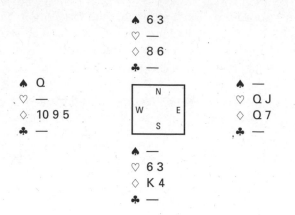

```
              ♠ 6 3
              ♡ —
              ◇ 8 6
              ♣ —
♠ Q                        ♠ —
♡ —           N            ♡ Q J
◇ 10 9 5   W     E         ◇ Q 7
♣ —           S            ♣ —
              ♠ —
              ♡ 6 3
              ◇ K 4
              ♣ —
```

Again, you seem to have two certain losers, but take a closer look. What can West do when you lead a heart? If he ruffs with the ♠Q, you will discard a diamond from dummy and easily make the remaining tricks. Let us say that West throws a diamond instead. You ruff with the ♠3, return to your hand with the ◇K and lead the last heart. This is the moment of the trump elopement. Dummy's ♠6 sits over the ♠Q and will score a trick whether or not West chooses to ruff with the queen on this trick. The slam is yours.

If West is an old adversary of yours, you can point out to him that the 'obvious trump lead' would have defeated the slam by removing a key entry to dummy!

Scoring low trumps when fourth seat has to follow

There is another way to condense a trump loser and a side-suit loser into just one trick — by scoring your low trumps when the key defender has to follow suit. You can follow West's predicament on this deal:

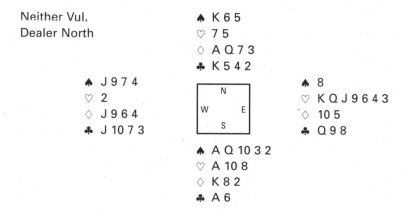

Neither Vul.
Dealer North

```
                    ♠ K 6 5
                    ♡ 7 5
                    ◇ A Q 7 3
                    ♣ K 5 4 2
♠ J 9 7 4                            ♠ 8
♡ 2               N                  ♡ K Q J 9 6 4 3
◇ J 9 6 4      W     E               ◇ 10 5
♣ J 10 7 3        S                  ♣ Q 9 8
                    ♠ A Q 10 3 2
                    ♡ A 10 8
                    ◇ K 8 2
                    ♣ A 6
```

West	North	East	South
	1◇	3♡	3♠
pass	4♠	pass	4NT
pass	5♡	pass	6♠
all pass			

How would you play the spade slam when West leads the ♡2?

You capture East's ♡J with the ♡A. With this trump holding it is normal to begin with the ace and king, allowing you to pick up ♠J-x-x-x with East. However, after East's preemptive overcall there is very little chance that he has such a trump holding. It is better to play the ace and queen of trumps instead. When West shows up with a sure trump trick, you might think that there is an unavoidable second loser in hearts. Not necessarily!

You have six side-suit winners and therefore need six trump tricks for the slam. If West's shape is 4-1-4-4, you can score all three of the trump spot cards in your hand. Dummy's ♠K will then bring the total to twelve. You cash the ace and king of clubs and ruff a club in the South hand. Returning to dummy with the ◇Q, you ruff dummy's last club. Finally, you cash the king and ace of diamonds and ruff a diamond.

Mission accomplished! The king of trumps will score the twelfth trick and at Trick 13, West will have the dubious pleasure of ruffing his partner's heart winner. You were able to elope with the small trumps in your hand because West had to follow suit all the way.

See if you can employ a similar technique on the next deal, which is also a slam contract:

Both Vul.
Dealer North

```
                 ♠ 7 6 2
                 ♡ A 8 7
                 ◇ A 10 3
                 ♣ A 9 8 4
♠ J 10 5 3                      ♠ —
♡ 10 6          ┌─────────┐     ♡ Q J 9 4 3
◇ J 6 2         │    N    │     ◇ 9 8 7 4
♣ K Q J 3       │ W     E │     ♣ 10 6 5 2
                │    S    │
                └─────────┘
                 ♠ A K Q 9 8 4
                 ♡ K 5 2
                 ◇ K Q 5
                 ♣ 7
```

West	North	East	South
	1♣	pass	2♠
pass	2NT	pass	3♠
pass	4♣	pass	4NT
pass	5♣	pass	6♠
all pass			

West leads the ♣K, won in the dummy. How will you play the slam?

Everything will be easy unless trumps break 4-0. If East holds four trumps, you can catch them with a straightforward repeated finesse. So, the only awkward case is when West holds four trumps. In that case, you will have potential losers in both spades and hearts. To make the slam, despite the certain trump loser, you would need to add six trump tricks to your six top winners in the side suits.

Just in case West does hold all four trumps, you should take advantage of being in the dummy by ruffing a club at Trick 2. When you cash the ♠A, East does indeed show out. You play three rounds of diamonds, ending in the dummy, and ruff another club. West follows to the king and ace of hearts, leaving this position:

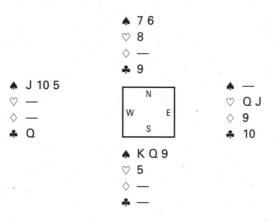

```
                    ♠ 7 6
                    ♡ 8
                    ◇ —
                    ♣ 9
   ♠ J 10 5                        ♠ —
   ♡ —              N              ♡ Q J
   ◇ —          W       E          ◇ 9
   ♣ Q              S              ♣ 10
                    ♠ K Q 9
                    ♡ 5
                    ◇ —
                    ♣ —
```

You lead dummy's ♣9, ruffing with the ♠9, and poor West has to follow suit! The king and queen of trumps then bring your total to twelve tricks.

Scoring the last trump *en passant*

The most clean-cut example of an elopement is when you have one trump in your hand and your right-hand opponent has a higher trump. By leading a plain-suit card towards it, you promote your lesser trump.

Neither Vul.
Dealer East

```
              ♠ Q 9 6 3
              ♡ J 7 5 2
              ◇ —
              ♣ 10 8 6 4 3
♠ K J 10 7                      ♠ —
♡ 10 8 6                        ♡ K Q 9 4 3
◇ Q 6 5 3                       ◇ K 10 7 4
♣ J 7                           ♣ A Q 9 2
              ♠ A 8 5 4 2
              ♡ A
              ◇ A J 9 8 2
              ♣ K 5
```

West	North	East	South
		1♡	1♠
2♡	3♠	4♡	4♠
dbl	all pass		

West leads the ♡6 to your singleton ace. How will you continue?

    You cash the ◇A, throwing a club from dummy, and ruff a diamond. When you lead a club from dummy, East rises with the ♣A and returns a club to your king. A four-trick crossruff in the red suits leaves these cards still out:

```
              ♠ Q
              ♡ J
              ◇ —
              ♣ 10 8
♠ K J 10 7                      ♠ —
♡ —                             ♡ K 9
◇ —                             ◇ —
♣ —                             ♣ Q 9
              ♠ A 8 5
              ♡ —
              ◇ J
              ♣ —
```

With eight tricks already taken, you lead the ◇J. West cannot prevent you from scoring dummy's ♠Q *en passant* and the doubled spade game is made.

Eloping with two trump tricks

Sometimes you can promote your last two trumps, even though two higher trumps lie in front of them. South scored a surprising triumph on this deal:

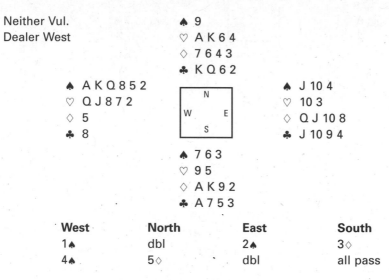

Neither Vul.
Dealer West

♠ 9
♡ A K 6 4
♢ 7 6 4 3
♣ K Q 6 2

♠ A K Q 8 5 2
♡ Q J 8 7 2
♢ 5
♣ 8

♠ J 10 4
♡ 10 3
♢ Q J 10 8
♣ J 10 9 4

♠ 7 6 3
♡ 9 5
♢ A K 9 2
♣ A 7 5 3

West	North	East	South
1♠	dbl	2♠	3♢
4♠	5♢	dbl	all pass

West cashed a high spade and switched to his singleton club, hoping to find East with the ace. How would you play the contract from this point?

The original declarer won with dummy's ♣K and led a trump. Thinking that he might well have tipped the trump position with his penalty double, East played the ♢10 in second seat. Declarer won with the ♢A. He then crossed to dummy with a spade ruff and led another trump towards his hand. East played the ♢J and declarer won with the ♢K, West discarding a heart. A spade ruff with dummy's last trump was followed by the ace and king of hearts. These cards were still in play:

♠ —
♡ 6 4
♢ —
♣ Q 6 2

♠ A 5 2
♡ Q J
♢ —
♣ —

♠ —
♡ .
♢ Q 8
♣ J 10 9

♠ —
♡ —
♢ 9 2
♣ A 7 5

Declarer, who has already lost one trick, appears to have one club loser and two possible trump losers. A heart is led from dummy and East has no constructive move. Suppose he throws a club. Declarer will ruff with the ◇2, cash the ♣A and ♣Q and lead another heart to score his ◇9 *en passant*.

The situation will be similar if East ruffs with the ◇8. South will overruff with the ◇9, cash two clubs and promote his ◇2 with a further heart lead. Nor will East fare any better by ruffing with the ◇Q. Declarer will simply discard the club loser and draw East's last trump when he regains the lead.

Elopement followed by throw-in

An exotic variation of the Vanishing Trick illusion can arise when the same defender holds both potential winners. You may then be able to throw him in with the side-suit winner, forcing him to surrender his trump trick.

North-South Vul.
Dealer South

```
                    ♠ K 9 8 3
                    ♡ 10 6 5
                    ◇ A K Q J
                    ♣ A 3
        ♠ —                         ♠ J 10 7 5
        ♡ 8 4 3          N          ♡ K J 9 2
        ◇ 10 6 3     W       E      ◇ 9 8 5 4
        ♣ K Q J 10 9 7 6    S       ♣ 2
                    ♠ A Q 6 4 2
                    ♡ A Q 7
                    ◇ 7 2
                    ♣ 8 5 1
```

West	North	East	South
			1♠
4♣	4NT	pass	5♠
pass	6♠	all pass	

West's four-level overcall, made at favorable vulnerability, aims to make life difficult for you. Unperturbed, your partner reaches for the RKCB card and a small slam is reached. How will you play this when West leads the ♣K?

You win with dummy's ace and play the ♠K, West showing out. Even if the heart finesse succeeds, you will still face potential losers in both trumps and hearts. Your next move is to lead the nine of trumps, forcing a cover from East. You win with the queen of trumps, cross to a diamond and take a successful heart finesse. The ace of hearts is followed by three more rounds of diamonds and you discard two clubs. These cards remain:

```
                    ♠ 8 3
                    ♡ 10
                    ◇ —
                    ♣ 3
  ♠ —                              ♠ J 7
  ♡ 8          ┌─────────┐         ♡ K 9
  ◇ —          │ N       │         ◇ —
  ♣ Q J 10     │ W     E │         ♣ —
               │    S    │
               └─────────┘
                    ♠ A 6 4
                    ♡ 7
                    ◇ —
                    ♣ —
```

'Club, please,' you say.

East is caught in an elopement position. If he ruffs with the ♠7, you will discard your heart loser and claim the remainder. When East discards the ♡9 instead, you ruff with the ♠4. You then exit with your last heart, putting East on lead. He is forced to lead from his ♠J-7 and you score the ♠8 and the ♠A as your last two tricks.

Look back at the play, which contained three elements. The lead of the ♠9 forced East to split his touching honors, rendering him liable to a later endplay. Ruffing dummy's last club reduced East to a master heart and his guarded trump honor. Finally, a throw-in compelled East to lead away from his trump combination. You deserve your slam bonus.

The stars come out to play!

the trump elopement ──────────────────────────── ☆

This first deal, from the 2005 Summer NABC in Atlanta, proved to be a test both in the bidding and the play. Sitting North-South were Richard and Mary Oshlag.

```
North-South Vul.        ♠ 6
Dealer South            ♡ J 7 4
                        ◇ K J 9 7 6 5
                        ♣ A 10 3
  ♠ A 10 9 7 5 3   ┌─────────┐      ♠ K Q J
  ♡ 10            │ N       │       ♡ Q 8 6 5 3
  ◇ Q 10 3        │ W     E │       ◇ 8 2
  ♣ 9 7 6         │    S    │       ♣ 8 4 2
                  └─────────┘
                        ♠ 8 4 2
                        ♡ A K 9 2
                        ◇ A 4
                        ♣ K Q J 5
```

West	North	East	South
	R. Oshlag		M. Oshlag
			1NT
2♣	3♠	pass	4♡
all pass			

West's 2♣ showed an unspecified one-suiter and North's 3♠ showed a singleton or void in spades. A contract of 5◇ would have been more comfortable, but Mary Oshlag was faced with the task of making 4♡. How would you have played this contract when West finds the best lead of the ♡10?

The opening lead was covered by the jack, queen and ace. To ensure one spade ruff in the dummy, Oshlag then led a spade. East won and returned a trump to declarer's king, West showing out. What now?

If declarer could score three top clubs and two top diamonds, she would need five trump tricks to bring the total to ten. She would need to take one spade ruff in dummy and score her ♡2 with an elopement.

Oshlag ruffed a spade and cashed three rounds of clubs successfully. She then played the ace and king of diamonds to leave this position:

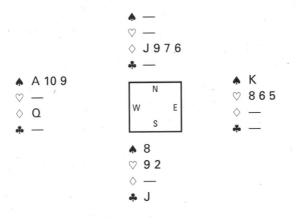

When a diamond was led from dummy, East had no counter. If he discarded, declarer would score her ♡2 immediately and the ♡9 would then be the tenth trick. East decided to ruff with the ♡5 and declarer discarded the ♠8. What could East do now? If he played the ♠K, Oshlag would score the ♡2 with a ruff. When he played one of his remaining trumps instead, declarer won with the ♡9 and forced East's last trump by playing the master club. The lowly ♡2 scored at Trick 13.

Here is a heart game played by Sævar Thorbjornsson in the 1998 NEC championship in Yokohama City. It illustrates the technique of scoring the low trumps in declarer's hand.

Both Vul.
Dealer East

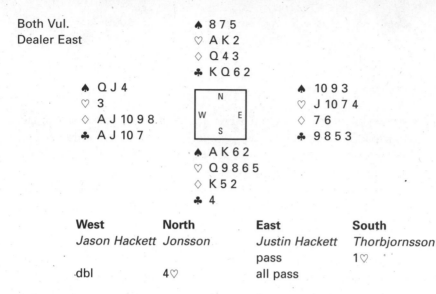

♠ 8 7 5
♡ A K 2
◇ Q 4 3
♣ K Q 6 2

♠ Q J 4
♡ 3
◇ A J 10 9 8
♣ A J 10 7

♠ 10 9 3
♡ J 10 7 4
◇ 7 6
♣ 9 8 5 3

♠ A K 6 2
♡ Q 9 8 6 5
◇ K 5 2
♣ 4

West	North	East	South
Jason Hackett	Jonsson	Justin Hackett	Thorbjornsson
		pass	1♡
dbl	4♡	all pass	

West led the ♠Q, his partner signaling with the ♠10, and Thorbjornsson won with the ♠A. When the ♣4 appeared at Trick 2, Jason Hackett rose with the ♣A and continued with the ♠J. Declarer won with the ♠K, played the ace, queen and king of trumps and discarded his remaining spades on the ♣K-Q. A club ruff with his penultimate trump left these cards still to be played:

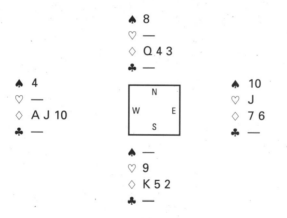

♠ 8
♡ —
◇ Q 4 3
♣ —

♠ 4
♡ —
◇ A J 10
♣ —

♠ 10
♡ J
◇ 7 6
♣ —

♠ —
♡ 9
◇ K 5 2
♣ —

Thorbjornsson led a low diamond from his hand and West had no answer. If he rose with the ◇A and returned the ◇J, the second of declarer's established diamond winners would force East's last trump, setting up the ♡9. When West instead played low on the first round of diamonds, declarer won with dummy's ◇Q and led the ♠8 to score his ♡9.

We end this section with a fine deal played by Alfredo Versace in the Life Master Pairs at the 2002 Fall Nationals in Phoenix.

North-South Vul.
Dealer West

♠	A K 8 6
♡	K Q 9 5 2
◇	K 7 4
♣	7

West
♠ 10 5 3
♡ 7 3
◇ A 10 8 6
♣ J 6 4 3

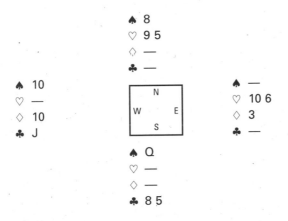

East
♠ J 9
♡ A J 10 6
◇ J 5 3 2
♣ K 10 9

South
♠ Q 7 4 2
♡ 8 4
◇ Q 9
♣ A Q 8 5 2

West	North	East	South
	Jacobs		Versace
pass	1♡	pass	1♠
pass	3♠	pass	4♠
all pass			

West led the ♡7, covered by dummy's queen and East's ace. Versace won the ♡J return with the king. How would you play the contract from this point?

Versace called for the ◇K. West won with the ace and returned a diamond to South's queen. A trump to the king allowed Versace to finesse the ♣Q. He cashed the ♣A, throwing a heart from dummy, and led a trump to the ace. He ruffed a diamond in his hand and ruffed a club in dummy. Two more tricks were needed and these cards remained:

North
♠ 8
♡ 9 5
◇ —
♣ —

West
♠ 10
♡ —
◇ 10
♣ J

East
♠ —
♡ 10 6
◇ 3
♣ —

South
♠ Q
♡ —
◇ —
♣ 8 5

Versace ruffed a heart with the ♠Q, West discarding the ♣J. He could then lead a club towards dummy's singleton ♠8, scoring that card *en passant*. If only we could all play so well!

NOW TRY THESE...

A.

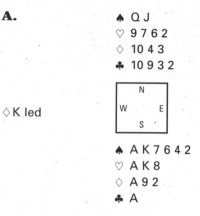

♠ Q J
♡ 9 7 6 2
◇ 10 4 3
♣ 10 9 3 2

◇ K led

♠ A K 7 6 4 2
♡ A K 8
◇ A 9 2
♣ A

West	North	East	South
			2♣
pass	2◇	pass	2♠
pass	2NT	pass	3♠
pass	4♠	all pass	

How will you play the spade game when West leads the ◇K?

B.

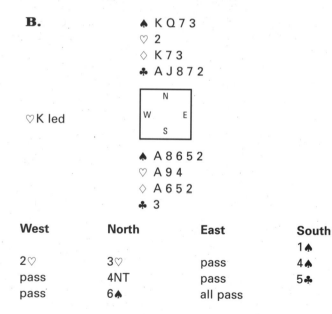

♠ K Q 7 3
♡ 2
◇ K 7 3
♣ A J 8 7 2

♡ K led

♠ A 8 6 5 2
♡ A 9 4
◇ A 6 5 2
♣ 3

West	North	East	South
			1♠
2♡	3♡	pass	4♠
pass	4NT	pass	5♣
pass	6♠	all pass	

You win the ♡K lead with the ♡A and lead a low trump towards dummy, West discarding a heart. How will you continue the play?

C.

      ♠ 7 6 4
      ♡ 10 7 5 2
      ◇ A 4
      ♣ 10 8 6 3

◇ Q led

```
    N
W       E
    S
```

      ♠ A K 8 5 3
      ♡ A 6 4
      ◇ K 6 5
      ♣ A K

West	North	East	South
			2NT
pass	3♣	pass	3♠
pass	4♠	all pass	

Puppet Stayman unearths the 5-3 spade fit and West leads the ◇Q against your eventual game in that suit. How will you play the contract?

D.

      ♠ A 4 3 2
      ♡ Q 8
      ◇ A K 6 5
      ♣ A 7 3

◇ Q led

```
    N
W       E
    S
```

      ♠ K 9 6 5
      ♡ K 5 4 2
      ◇ 4
      ♣ 10 5 4 2

West	North	East	South
	1◇	pass	1♠
pass	3♠	pass	4♠
all pass			

How will you attempt to make the moderate contract of 4♠ when West spares you a club lead, placing the ◇Q on the table?

Answers ✎

A.

```
                    ♠ Q J
                    ♡ 9 7 6 2
                    ◇ 10 4 3
                    ♣ 10 9 3 2
   ♠ —                              ♠ 10 9 8 5 3
   ♡ Q 10 4 3          N            ♡ J 5
   ◇ K Q 7        W         E       ◇ J 8 6 5
   ♣ K J 8 6 5 4        S           ♣ Q 7
                    ♠ A K 7 6 4 2
                    ♡ A K 8
                    ◇ A 9 2
                    ♣ A
```

West	North	East	South
			2♣
pass	2◇	pass	2♠
pass	2NT	pass	3♠
pass	4♠	all pass	

How will you tackle the spade game when West leads the ◇K?

Six trump tricks and four side-suit winners add up to ten. What can possibly go wrong? Ah yes, the trumps might break 5-0. What can be done in that case?

There is no need to abandon the winning formula: six trump tricks + four side-suit winners = 10. When trumps are 5-0, however, you can achieve these six trump tricks only by ruffing two clubs in the South hand. You win the diamond lead with the ace and cash the ♣A, just in case two club ruffs should prove necessary. You continue with a trump to dummy's jack and West does indeed show out. You ruff a club in your hand. What is your next move?

If you have followed the correct line so far and now return to dummy with the queen of trumps to ruff another club, you may award yourself nine marks out of ten. Unfortunately, East has two hearts and two clubs. When you take your second club ruff, he will discard one of his hearts and you will not live to enjoy your two heart winners. The game will go one down.

To score full marks on this problem, you must cash the ace and king of hearts before returning to dummy for the last time with the ♠Q. East is then powerless as you lead your last club. If he chooses to ruff with the ten, nine or eight, you will simply discard a red-suit loser and later score all of the remaining trumps in the South hand.

B.

                          ♠ K Q 7 3
                          ♡ 2
                          ◇ K 7 3
                          ♣ A J 8 7 2

    ♠ —   ♠ J 10 9 4
    ♡ K Q J 10 7 3   ♡ 8 6 5
    ◇ Q J 9 8   ◇ 10 4
    ♣ K 10 5   ♣ Q 9 6 4

                          ♠ A 8 6 5 2
                          ♡ A 9 4
                          ◇ A 6 5 2
                          ♣ 3

West	North	East	South
			1♠
2♡	3♡	pass	4♠
pass	4NT	pass	5♣
pass	6♠	all pass	

You win the ♡K lead with the ♡A and lead a low trump towards dummy. How will you continue when West rudely discards on this trick?

As is normal on this type of hand, you plan the play by counting winners rather than losers. You have four side-suit winners and will therefore need eight trump tricks. Assuming you can score four trump tricks in the dummy (two with the ♠K-Q and two heart ruffs), you will need to score four club ruffs in the South hand.

You continue with the ♣A and a club ruff, followed by a heart ruff in dummy and another club ruff. A second heart ruff allows you to ruff another club and you continue with the ace and king of diamonds. These cards remain:

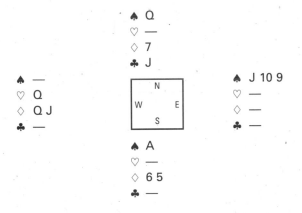

You lead dummy's last club, overruffing East's ♠9 with the ♠A. East ruffs his partner's diamond winner on the next trick and dummy's ♠Q gives you the slam. With a dashing wave of your wand, you have condensed two 'certain' losers into one.

C.

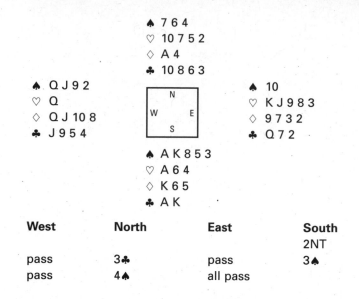

♠ 7 6 4
♡ 10 7 5 2
◇ A 4
♣ 10 8 6 3

♠ Q J 9 2
♡ Q
◇ Q J 10 8
♣ J 9 5 4

♠ 10
♡ K J 9 8 3
◇ 9 7 3 2
♣ Q 7 2

♠ A K 8 5 3
♡ A 6 4
◇ K 6 5
♣ A K

West	North	East	South
			2NT
pass	3♣	pass	3♠
pass	4♠	all pass	

West leads the ◇Q against your spade game. How will you play the contract?

If you win the opening lead with dummy's ace, you will go down! With trumps 4-1, you will lose two trumps and two hearts. You should win with the ◇K. You continue with the ace and king of trumps. If the suit breaks 3-2, you can proceed with your diamond ruff, losing just one trump and two hearts. When trumps break 4-1, the presence of the ◇A in dummy will allow you to launch the rescue boat.

You must aim to score two low trumps in your hand by ruffing clubs. You cash the ace and king of clubs and cross to the precious ◇A. You then ruff a club and return to dummy with a diamond ruff. These cards remain:

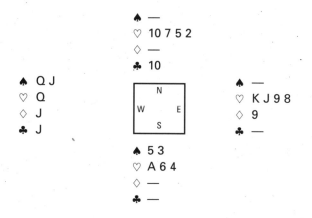

♠ —
♡ 10 7 5 2
◇ —
♣ 10

♠ Q J
♡ Q
◇ J
♣ J

♠ —
♡ K J 9 8
◇ 9
♣ —

♠ 5 3
♡ A 6 4
◇ —
♣ —

You lead dummy's last club and East shows out. Yes! You ruff again with a low trump and West has to follow suit. When the ♡A stands up, the game is yours. You have scored five side-suit winners, two top trumps, one ruff in dummy and two ruffs in your hand.

D.

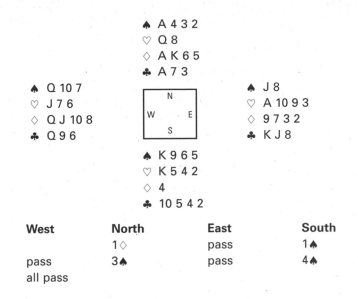

♠ A 4 3 2
♡ Q 8
◇ A K 6 5
♣ A 7 3

♠ Q 10 7   ♠ J 8
♡ J 7 6   ♡ A 10 9 3
◇ Q J 10 8   ◇ 9 7 3 2
♣ Q 9 6   ♣ K J 8

♠ K 9 6 5
♡ K 5 4 2
◇ 4
♣ 10 5 4 2

West	North	East	South
	1◇	pass	1♠
pass	3♠	pass	4♠
all pass			

It is not a particularly good contract and it goes without saying that you or I would find some way to keep low. Still, how will you play 4♠ when West leads the ◇Q?

You have some chance of scoring two heart tricks and throwing one of dummy's club losers. (You would need to find West with the ♡A guarded no more than twice.) After winning the diamond lead in dummy, you cross to the ♠K and lead a heart to the queen. Visions of two heart tricks disappear when East wins with the ♡A. You win the ♠J return with dummy's ace. What now?

You must aim to score all four remaining small trumps separately. You play a heart to the king and ruff a heart with the ♠3. The ◇K is followed by a diamond ruff with the ♠6. A club to the ace allows you to ruff dummy's last diamond with your ♠9. These cards remain:

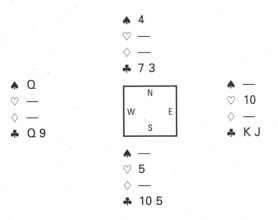

♠ 4
♡ —
◇ —
♣ 7 3

♠ Q   ♠ —
♡ —   ♡ 10
◇ —   ◇ —
♣ Q 9   ♣ K J

♠ —
♡ 5
◇ —
♣ 10 5

Nine tricks are before you and you lead the ♡5 from your hand. You will score a trick with dummy's ♠4 unless East is out of hearts and also holds the ♠Q.

The Trump Endplay

The time has come to survey (and admire) a somewhat rare play, where you reduce a defender to nothing but trumps. You then throw him in with a trump — either directly or by forcing him to ruff — after which he will have to surrender a trump trick.

Exiting with a trump to force a trump return

When a defender holds a strong trump holding such as Q-J-8-2 under your own good trumps, you can sometimes reduce its power with a trump coup, as we have already seen. When such a holding lies over the ace-king, a different sort of magic may be required. Look at this deal:

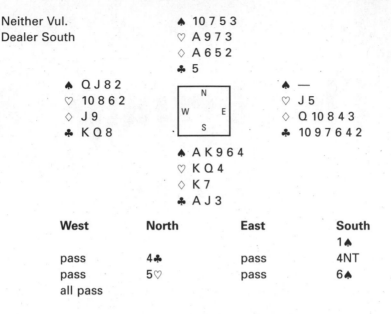

Neither Vul.
Dealer South

```
                          ♠ 10 7 5 3
                          ♡ A 9 7 3
                          ♢ A 6 5 2
                          ♣ 5
        ♠ Q J 8 2                          ♠ —
        ♡ 10 8 6 2                         ♡ J 5
        ♢ J 9                              ♢ Q 10 8 4 3
        ♣ K Q 8                            ♣ 10 9 7 6 4 2
                          ♠ A K 9 6 4
                          ♡ K Q 4
                          ♢ K 7
                          ♣ A J 3
```

West	North	East	South
			1♠
pass	4♣	pass	4NT
pass	5♡	pass	6♠
all pass			

There was little chance of missing a game if partner could not respond to a simple 1♠ opening, so South saw no reason to open 2NT. North's 4♣ was a splinter bid, showing a game raise in spades and at most one card in the club suit. South won the ♣K lead against his spade slam and cashed the ♠A, East throwing a club. How would you have reacted to this setback?

You must aim for a three-card ending where West holds just his ♠Q-J-8. You can then endplay him with one honor, forcing him to lead away from the other honor. Reaching the required end position will not be possible unless West holds three or four hearts, so your next move is to cash (or at least attempt to cash!) your top three honors in that suit. Yes, that works all right. East shows out on the third round.

To reduce West to his three trumps, you will need to score the first ten tricks. You have already scored the ace of trumps and you have six top winners in the side suits. You will need to add one red-suit ruff in your hand and two club ruffs in dummy. You ruff a club, cash the king and ace of diamonds and ruff a heart in your hand. (If West had shown up earlier with three hearts instead of four, you would have ruffed a diamond instead at this point.) A second club ruff in dummy leaves these cards still to be played:

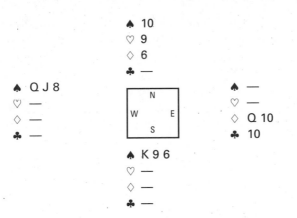

```
                    ♠ 10
                    ♡ 9
                    ◇ 6
                    ♣ —
    ♠ Q J 8                        ♠ —
    ♡ —          ┌─────────┐       ♡ —
    ◇ —          │    N    │       ◇ Q 10
    ♣ —          │  W   E  │       ♣ 10
                 │    S    │
                 └─────────┘
                    ♠ K 9 6
                    ♡ —
                    ◇ —
                    ♣ —
```

The time has come for the trump endplay. You lead dummy's ♠10, passing it to West's ♠J. He has to lead back a trump into your ♠K-9 tenace and the slam is yours.

Underruffing to set up the endplay

Suppose you reach a three-card end position where your right-hand opponent holds J-10-8 of trumps and you sit over him with Q-9-6. You lead a plain card from dummy and he ruffs with the jack. To score two of the last three tricks, you will have to underruff, forcing him to lead away from his remaining trump honor. Let's see an example of this impressive technique:

```
Both Vul.                ♠ 7 4
Dealer North             ♡ A K Q 7
                         ◇ A 8 6 4 2
                         ♣ A 9
    ♠ —                                  ♠ Q J 10 8
    ♡ J 10 4 3        ┌─────────┐        ♡ 9 6 2
    ◇ K Q J 5         │    N    │        ◇ 10 9 3
    ♣ Q J 7 6 2       │  W   E  │        ♣ 10 8 4
                      │    S    │
                      └─────────┘
                         ♠ A K 9 6 5 3 2
                         ♡ 8 5
                         ◇ 7
                         ♣ K 5 3
```

West	North	East	South
	1◇	pass	1♠
pass	2♡	pass	3♠
pass	4♣	pass	4NT
pass	5♣	pass	6♠
all pass			

West leads the ♢K against your spade slam. You win in the dummy and lead a low trump. If West follows with the ♠8, you will have the chance to cover with the ♠9 (a safety play that will more or less guarantee the contract). Let's say that East decides to insert the ♠10, expecting to score two trump tricks thereafter. You win with the ♠A and West discards a club. How will you continue?

The next stage of the play is to ruff some diamonds in your hand. Scoring tricks with low trumps will be one benefit of this; you will also reduce your trump length to match East's. You cross to the ♡A and ruff a diamond low. Returning to dummy with the ♡K, you ruff another diamond with a low trump. A club to dummy's ace is followed by a heart ruff in your hand. These cards remain:

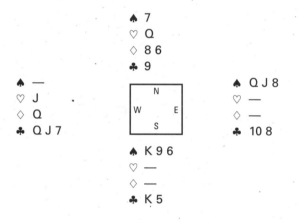

```
              ♠ 7
              ♡ Q
              ♢ 8 6
              ♣ 9
  ♠ —                        ♠ Q J 8
  ♡ J          N             ♡ —
  ♢ Q      W       E         ♢ —
  ♣ Q J 7       S            ♣ 10 8
              ♠ K 9 6
              ♡ —
              ♢ —
              ♣ K 5
```

You press onwards with the ♣K and a club ruff. In the three-card ending, you lead a red card from dummy and East ruffs with the ♠J. If you overruff, you will have to give East the last two tricks. Instead, you underruff with the ♠6. East is left on play and has to lead from his ♠Q-8 into your ♠K-9. You score the last two tricks and mark up your slam.

Defender has to ruff and return a trump

Another method of forcing a trump return into a tenace is to leave the defender with so many trumps that he has to ruff a side-suit card, perhaps even a loser. Look at West's predicament on this deal:

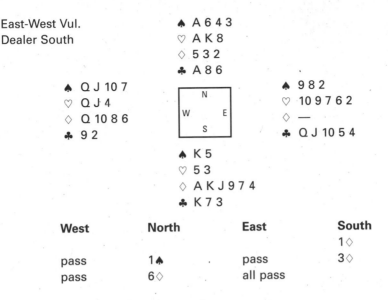

East-West Vul.
Dealer South

```
                 ♠ A 6 4 3
                 ♡ A K 8
                 ◇ 5 3 2
                 ♣ A 8 6
♠ Q J 10 7              N          ♠ 9 8 2
♡ Q J 4          W         E      ♡ 10 9 7 6 2
◇ Q 10 8 6             S          ◇ —
♣ 9 2                            ♣ Q J 10 5 4
                 ♠ K 5
                 ♡ 5 3
                 ◇ A K J 9 7 4
                 ♣ K 7 3
```

West	North	East	South
			1◇
pass	1♠	pass	3◇
pass	6◇	all pass	

West leads the ♣Q against your diamond slam. You win with the ♠K and draw a round of trumps with the ace, sucking in breath as East discards a low heart. Can you see any prospect of a recovery?

If West holds four spades and three hearts, you will be able to ruff those suits three times in your hand. You can then play ace, king and another club, forcing West to ruff and then lead back into the ◇K-J.

You cross to the ace of spades and ruff a spade in your hand. You then return to dummy with the ♡A and lead another spade. East shows out, which is what you wanted to see, and you ruff in your hand. A heart to the king is followed by a heart ruff and you continue with the king and ace of clubs. These cards remain:

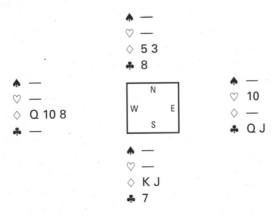

```
                 ♠ —
                 ♡ —
                 ◇ 5 3
                 ♣ 8
♠ —                   N          ♠ —
♡ —              W         E      ♡ 10
◇ Q 10 8              S          ◇ —
♣ —                              ♣ Q J
                 ♠ —
                 ♡ —
                 ◇ K J
                 ♣ 7
```

When you lead the ♣8, West will wish that he had one trump fewer. He is forced to ruff the trick and then lead a trump into your ◇K-J. Slam made!

Endplay after establishing a trump tenace

To set up a trump endplay, some preparation may be required. When a defender holds four trumps to two touching honors, he may need to split his honors on an early round (as we saw in the chapter on trump coups). West is your intended victim on this deal:

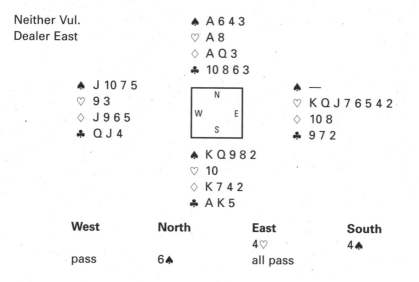

Neither Vul.
Dealer East

♠ A 6 4 3
♡ A 8
♢ A Q 3
♣ 10 8 6 3

♠ J 10 7 5
♡ 9 3
♢ J 9 6 5
♣ Q J 4

♠ —
♡ K Q J 7 6 5 4 2
♢ 10 8
♣ 9 7 2

♠ K Q 9 8 2
♡ 10
♢ K 7 4 2
♣ A K 5

West	North	East	South
		4♡	4♠
pass	6♠	all pass	

How will you play 6♠ when West leads the ♡9?

You win with dummy's ♡A, noting that the only possible problem is a 4-0 trump break. Looking at the trumps in isolation, you would normally cash the ♠A first. That is because you can successfully finesse against a defender's ♠J-10-7-5 only if it lies with East. That is hardly possible here, with East holding such long hearts. You play a trump to the king at Trick 2, East showing out. What now?

You must aim to put West on lead with the third round of clubs, forcing him to lead away from his remaining trumps. This will not help you if West still has his ♠J-10-7 intact. With dummy's trumps reduced to ♠A-6 after you have ruffed your fourth diamond, West could then exit safely with the ♠J .

Needing to weaken West's trumps, you should lead the ♠9 from your hand. West has to cover (with the ♠10, let's say) or he would surrender his trump trick. You win the trick with dummy's ♠A and continue with three top diamonds, followed by a diamond ruff.

You ruff a heart in your hand, removing West's last card in the suit, and cash the ace and king of clubs. These cards remain:

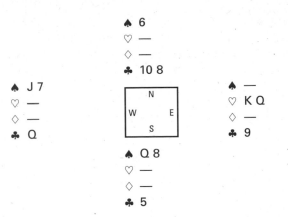

```
                    ♠ 6
                    ♡ —
                    ◇ —
                    ♣ 10 8
    ♠ J 7          ┌─────────┐        ♠ —
    ♡ —            │    N    │        ♡ K Q
    ◇ —            │ W     E │        ◇ —
    ♣ Q            │    S    │        ♣ 9
                   └─────────┘
                    ♠ Q 8
                    ♡ —
                    ◇ —
                    ♣ 5
```

The hard work is over and you are about to receive the payoff. You exit with the ♣5, pleased to see that West wins the trick. He has to lead from his weakened trump holding into your tenace and the contract is yours.

The stars come out to play:

the trump endplay ☆

One of the brightest stars in the game's firmament was Helen Sobel, a long-time partner of Charles Goren. Let's see how she made a seemingly impossible spade game during the 1944 Summer Nationals.

North-South Vul.
Dealer East

```
                    ♠ A 10 9 5
                    ♡ A 10 6 4 3
                    ◇ 9 8 6
                    ♣ 6
    ♠ 6                               ♠ K Q J 2
    ♡ K            ┌─────────┐        ♡ Q 9 8 7 5
    ◇ K Q J 5 4 3 2│    N    │        ◇ 7
    ♣ 10 8 4 2     │ W     E │        ♣ 9 7 5
                   │    S    │
                   └─────────┘
                    ♠ 8 7 4 3
                    ♡ J 2
                    ◇ A 10
                    ♣ A K Q J 3
```

West	North	East	South
			Sobel
		pass	1♣
1◇	1♡	pass	1♠
2◇	2♠	pass	2NT
pass	4♠	dbl	all pass

Sobel, who had bid the South cards boldly, won the ◇K lead with the ◇A and played three rounds of clubs, throwing dummy's remaining diamonds. She then led a low heart to the ace, the king appearing from West. East won the next round of hearts with the queen, West throwing a diamond. Declarer had lost one trick already and had to avoid losing three more tricks to the ♠K-Q-J-2 sitting over dummy's ♠A.

When East returned a heart, Sobel ruffed with the ♠7, avoiding an overruff by West. A trump went to the six, nine and jack. Sobel won the heart return with dummy's ♡10, throwing the ♣3. She ruffed a heart in her hand, leaving this position:

```
                    ♠ A 9 5
                    ♡ —
                    ◇ —
                    ♣ —

   ♠ —                              ♠ K Q 2
   ♡ —          ┌─────────┐         ♡ —
   ◇ Q J        │    N    │         ◇ —
   ♣ 10         │ W     E │         ♣ —
                │    S    │
                └─────────┘
                    ♠ 8
                    ♡ —
                    ◇ 10
                    ♣ J
```

When Sobel ran the ♠8, East had to win and lead into dummy's ♠A-9.

Did you spot how the defenders might have beaten the contract? When East won the second round of hearts with the queen, West needed to ruff her partner's trick! A diamond or club return would then allow East to overruff the dummy and the timing would be gone for a subsequent trump endplay.

Next, Great Britain faces Finland in the 1979 European Championships. The declarer is Tony Priday, who recently celebrated his 85th birthday in London.

North-South Vul.
Dealer North

```
                    ♠ Q 6
                    ♡ A K 5 4
                    ◇ Q 10 9
                    ♣ 9 5 4 2

   ♠ J 10                            ♠ A K 7 5 4 3
   ♡ Q 9 8 7 3    ┌─────────┐        ♡ —
   ◇ 7 4 2        │    N    │        ◇ 8 6 5
   ♣ J 10 6       │ W     E │        ♣ Q 8 7 3
                  │    S    │
                  └─────────┘
                    ♠ 9 8 2
                    ♡ J 10 6 2
                    ◇ A K J 3
                    ♣ A K
```

West	North	East	South
Jarvinen	*Rodrigue*	*Laine*	*Priday*
	pass	2♡	dbl
pass	pass	2♠	pass
pass	3♠	pass	4♡
all pass			

I found this deal on a Chinese website, the automated English translation of which did not clearly specify the meaning of East's opening bid. Anyway, the Finnish West led the ♠J against the heart game and this was covered by the ♠Q and ♠K. East cashed a second spade winner and switched to a diamond. Priday won with the ace and led the ♡J, covered by the queen and ace. How would you have continued when East showed out, discarding a spade?

Priday cashed the two clubs in his hand and crossed to the ◇Q to ruff a club. He then cashed one more round of diamonds, all following, to leave this position:

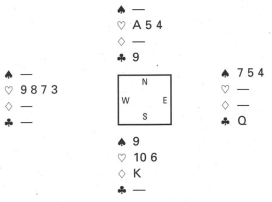

West had to ruff the ♠9 with the ♡7 to prevent declarer scoring a cheap ruff in dummy. Priday discarded the ♣9, won the ♡9 exit with the ♡10 and finessed the ♡6 at Trick 12. Excellent stuff!

To end this section, we will see Australia's Tim Bourke in action during the semifinals of the 2004 National Open Teams, where he faced an Indonesian team captained by Ferdy Waluyan.

North-South Vul.
Dealer North

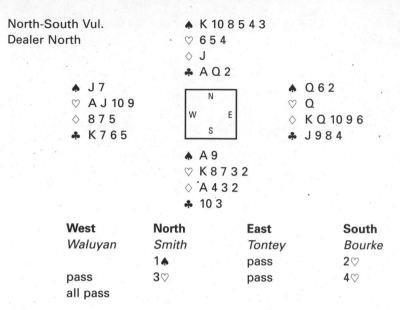

	♠ K 10 8 5 4 3
	♡ 6 5 4
	◇ J
	♣ A Q 2

♠ J 7		♠ Q 6 2
♡ A J 10 9		♡ Q
◇ 8 7 5		◇ K Q 10 9 6
♣ K 7 6 5		♣ J 9 8 4

	♠ A 9
	♡ K 8 7 3 2
	◇ A 4 3 2
	♣ 10 3

West	North	East	South
Waluyan	*Smith*	*Tontey*	*Bourke*
	1♠	pass	2♡
pass	3♡	pass	4♡
all pass			

West led the ♣5 and Bourke finessed dummy's ♣Q successfully. It seems that he is destined to lose four trump tricks, but watch the play develop. Bourke crossed to the ace of diamonds and ruffed a diamond. After a spade to the ace, he ruffed another diamond and cashed the ♠K. The ace of clubs and a club ruff to hand then allowed Bourke to lead his last diamond.

Waluyan could not allow declarer to score yet another diamond ruff in the dummy. He ruffed with the ♡9 to leave these cards still out:

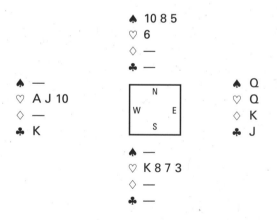

	♠ 10 8 5
	♡ 6
	◇ —
	♣ —

♠ —		♠ Q
♡ A J 10		♡ Q
◇ —		◇ K
♣ K		♣ J

	♠ —
	♡ K 8 7 3
	◇ —
	♣ —

Like it or not, Waluyan now had to lead the ♣K. If Bourke were to ruff this in his hand, he would have to lead away from the trump king. East would win with the queen and that would be one down. Instead, declarer ruffed with dummy's ♡6 and underruffed with the ♡3, leaving the lead in dummy.

When a spade was led, East had to follow suit. Bourke ruffed with the ♡7, overruffed with the ♡10 and West then had to concede the game-going trick to declarer's trump king. This was a fine piece of card play, particularly when you bear in mind that West had not tipped his hand by doubling the contract. You would have to ask the judges why the deal was placed only second in the 2004 'Best Played Hand of the Year'.

In the other semifinal of this event, the two West players did double the heart game. They had no reason to regret this decision either, since they both picked up 500 for two down!

NOW TRY THESE...

A.

- ♠ A 8
- ♡ A K 7 4
- ◇ K 7 3
- ♣ A 6 5 2

♠Q led

```
    N
  W   E
    S
```

- ♠ 9 7 2
- ♡ 10 6 5 3
- ◇ A Q 2
- ♣ K 9 7

West	North	East	South
	1♣	pass	1♡
pass	3♡	pass	4♡
all pass			

You win the ♠Q lead with the ♠A. When you play the ace of trumps, West shows out, discarding a spade. Your partner is looking worried, but perhaps you can bring a smile to his face.

B.

- ♠ 6 4 3
- ♡ 7
- ◇ A K Q 7
- ♣ Q 10 9 5 2

♡J led

```
    N
  W   E
    S
```

- ♠ A K J 8 5 2
- ♡ A 6 5 3
- ◇ 4
- ♣ J 6

West	North	East	South
			1♠
pass	2♣	pass	2♡
pass	4♠	pass	4NT
pass	5◇	pass	6♠
all pass			

West leads the ♡J against your slam with two top club losers. How will you play the contract?

C.

       ♠ 9 8 5 3
       ♡ K 10 2
       ◇ A 7 5 4
       ♣ 6 2

♣10 led

```
    N
 W     E
    S
```

       ♠ A K J 6 2
       ♡ A 4 3
       ◇ K 6
       ♣ A K 8

West	North	East	South
			2♣
pass	2◇	pass	2♠
pass	3♠	pass	4♠
pass	6♠	all pass	

West leads the ♣10. You win with the ♣A and play the ♠A, East discarding a heart. How will you continue?

D.

       ♠ 5
       ♡ A 10 9 3 2
       ◇ A 6 4
       ♣ K 8 4 2

◇ K led

```
    N
 W     E
    S
```

       ♠ A K Q 8 7 4 3
       ♡ 5
       ◇ 8 3 2
       ♣ A 5

West	North	East	South
	1♡	pass	2♠
pass	3♣	pass	4♠
all pass			

You win the ◇K lead and play a trump to the ace, West discarding a heart. How will you continue?

Answers ✎

A.

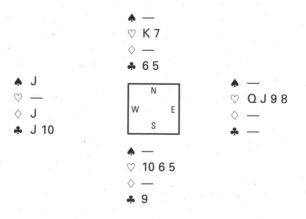

	♠ A 8	
	♡ A K 7 4	
	♢ K 7 3	
	♣ A 6 5 2	

♠ Q J 10 6 5		♠ K 4 3
♡ —		♡ Q J 9 8 2
♢ J 8 6 4		♢ 10 9 5
♣ J 10 8 4		♣ Q 3

	♠ 9 7 2	
	♡ 10 6 5 3	
	♢ A Q 2	
	♣ K 9 7	

West	North	East	South
	1♣	pass	1♡
pass	3♡	pass	4♡
all pass			

You win the ♠Q lead with the ♠A. When you play the ace of trumps, West shows out, discarding a spade. How will you continue?

You must aim to force East to ruff at Trick 10, after which he will have to lead away from this trump holding. If you cash three diamonds immediately, you will go down. East will let West win the ducked spade and a fourth diamond will kill you. You should give up a spade at Trick 3. East wins and switches to the ♢10. You win, cash your remaining minor-suit winners and ruff a spade. This will be the end position:

	♠ —	
	♡ K 7	
	♢ —	
	♣ 6 5	

♠ J		♠ —
♡ —		♡ Q J 9 8
♢ J		♢ —
♣ J 10		♣ —

	♠ —	
	♡ 10 6 5	
	♢ —	
	♣ 9	

When you lead a club, East finds he has one trump more than is good for him. He has to ruff his partner's club winner and surrender a trick by leading away from his ♡Q-J-9.

B.

```
                    ♠ 6 4 3
                    ♡ 7
                    ◇ A K Q 7
                    ♣ Q 10 9 5 2
♠ Q 10 9 7      ┌─────────┐      ♠ —
♡ J 10 9 8      │    N    │      ♡ K Q 4 2
◇ J 6 5         │ W     E │      ◇ 10 9 8 3 2
♣ K 3           │    S    │      ♣ A 8 7 4
                └─────────┘
                    ♠ A K J 8 5 2
                    ♡ A 6 5 3
                    ◇ 4
                    ♣ J 6
```

West	North	East	South
			1♠
pass	2♣	pass	2♡
pass	4♠	pass	4NT
pass	5◇	pass	6♠
all pass			

West leads the ♡J against your slam with two top club losers. How will you play the contract?

You win with the ♡A and ruff a heart in dummy. Three rounds of diamonds stand up and you discard your two club losers (the defenders exchange a glance). Club ruff, heart ruff, club ruff, heart ruff leaves this end position:

```
                    ♠ —
                    ♡ —
                    ◇ 7
                    ♣ Q 10 9
♠ Q 10 9 7      ┌─────────┐      ♠ —
♡ —            │    N    │      ♡ —
◇ —            │ W     E │      ◇ 10 9
♣ —            │    S    │      ♣ A 8
                └─────────┘
                    ♠ A K J 8
                    ♡ —
                    ◇ —
                    ♣ —
```

You lead a plain card from dummy and ruff with the ♠8. Even if West holds all four trumps, as he did at the table, the contract is yours. West overruffs with the ♠9, but he has to lead back into your tenace.

This amazing deal actually arose in a 2000 match between Iceland and Poland! A club lead or even a trump lead, both of which were unthinkable from West's hand, would have defeated the slam.

C.

	♠ 9 8 5 3	
	♡ K 10 2	
	◇ A 7 5 4	
	♣ 6 2	

♠ Q 10 7 4		♠ —
♡ Q 7		♡ J 9 8 6 5
◇ Q 9 3 2	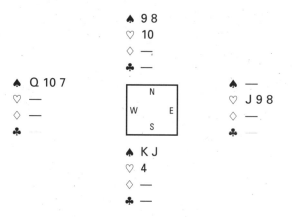	◇ J 10 8
♣ 10 9 4		♣ Q J 7 5 3

	♠ A K J 6 2	
	♡ A 4 3	
	◇ K 6	
	♣ A K 8	

West	North	East	South
			2♣
pass	2◇	pass	2♠
pass	3♠	pass	4♠
pass	6♠	all pass	

West leads the ♣10. You win with the ♣A and play the ♠A, East discarding a heart. How will you continue?

You must reduce West to ♠Q-10-7 and throw him in to return a trump into your ♠K-J. Since you have a heart loser, the only option is to exit at Trick 11 with a heart, which West must ruff. West's shape will have to be 4-2-4-3.

You play the king and ace of diamonds and ruff a diamond in your hand. The king of clubs is followed by a club ruff and you ruff another diamond in your hand. West follows to the ace and king of hearts and these cards remain:

	♠ 9 8	
	♡ 10	
	◇ —	
	♣ —	

♠ Q 10 7		♠ —
♡ —		♡ J 9 8
◇ —		◇ —
♣ —		♣ —

	♠ K J	
	♡ 4	
	◇ —	
	♣ —	

West has to ruff your heart exit and lead into the ♠K-J. The slam is yours.

D.

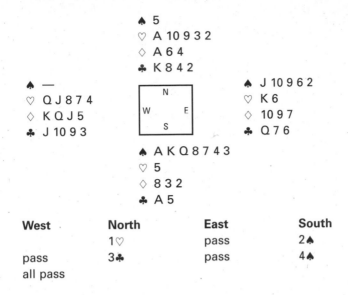

♠ 5
♡ A 10 9 3 2
◇ A 6 4
♣ K 8 4 2

♠ —
♡ Q J 8 7 4
◇ K Q J 5
♣ J 10 9 3

♠ J 10 9 6 2
♡ K 6
◇ 10 9 7
♣ Q 7 6

♠ A K Q 8 7 4 3
♡ 5
◇ 8 3 2
♣ A 5

West	North	East	South
	1♡	pass	2♠
pass	3♣	pass	4♠
all pass			

You win the ◇K lead and play a trump to the ace, the defenders trying not to look smug as West throws a diamond. How will you continue?

You have two losers in the diamond suit and must somehow restrict East to one trump trick. You cross to the ♡A and ruff a heart with a low trump. The ace and king of clubs are followed by a club ruff, again with a low trump. You exit with a diamond, allowing West to score two tricks in the suit and these cards remain:

♠ —
♡ 10 9 3
◇ —
♣ 8

♠ —
♡ Q J 8
◇ —
♣ J

♠ J 10 9 6
♡ —
◇ —
♣ —

♠ K Q 8 7
♡ —
◇ —
♣ —

Whatever card West leads, East will ruff with the ♠J. You overruff with the ♠Q and exit with the ♠7. East wins with the ♠10 and then has to lead away from his ♠9-6 into your ♠K-8 tenace. You score the last two tricks and make the spade game.

Endplay Exotica

The hard work is over. You can sit back now and enjoy some endplays that are rare creatures indeed — bridge's equivalent of the snow leopard, perhaps, or the Javan rhino. Despite keeping a good lookout at the table, it is possible that you may never spot an opportunity for such remarkable plays. The search will be good fun anyway.

The smother play

The first of these exotic plays arises when a defender has a guarded trump honor in front of a bare higher honor. For example, he may hold K-8 of trumps under the bare ace. He seems certain to score a trick with the king but... his partner is thrown in to lead and the defender's king is then trapped in a most unusual end position. Let's see an example of the play.

East-West Vul.
Dealer South

```
                    ♠ Q 2
                    ♡ A 9 4 2
                    ◇ A 9 6
                    ♣ J 7 6 3
   ♠ A K 8                         ♠ J 10 9 7 4
   ♡ K 8 6 3        ┌─────────┐    ♡ —
   ◇ Q 7 5          │    N    │    ◇ J 10 8 4 3
   ♣ 10 4 2         │  W   E  │    ♣ Q 9 8
                    │    S    │
                    └─────────┘
                    ♠ 6 5 3
                    ♡ Q J 10 7 5
                    ◇ K 2
                    ♣ A K 5
```

West	North	East	South
			1♡
pass	3♡	pass	4♡
all pass			

West leads the ♠A against your heart game. Observing that the ♡A lies over his ♡K, he decides to persevere with spades. By forcing dummy to ruff, he hopes to guarantee a trick for the trump king. West continues with the king and another spade and you ruff the third round in the dummy. When you cross to the ♣A and run the ♡Q, the finesse wins, but East discards a diamond. How will you continue?

You cannot catch West's ♡K by straightforward play and there is a potential further loser in the club suit. You lead a low trump to dummy's nine, followed by the king and ace of diamonds and a diamond ruff in the South hand. The ace and king of clubs fail to drop the queen and an ordinary mortal might now think that he had certain losers in clubs and trumps. However, this is the position:

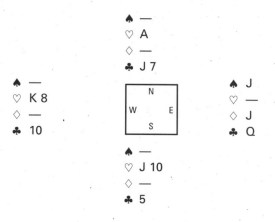

```
              ♠ —
              ♡ A
              ◇ —
              ♣ J 7
♠ —                        ♠ J
♡ K 8        ┌─────────┐   ♡ —
◇ —          │ N       │   ◇ J
♣ 10         │ W     E │   ♣ Q
             │    S    │
             └─────────┘
              ♠ —
              ♡ J 10
              ◇ —
              ♣ 5
```

When you exit with a club, it is East who has to win the trick. (If West had held the ♣Q, he could have played a low trump to set up his ♡K.) East has to play one of his jacks and you ruff in your hand with a third jack. Whether or not West decides to overruff, you will score the last two tricks and make the contract.

The sluff-and-sluff

This next rare creature, lurking on a dimly lit table in the far corner, is known as the sluff-and-sluff. Let's take a look at it (don't get too close).

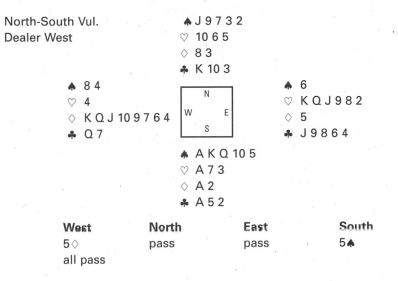

North-South Vul.
Dealer West

♠ J 9 7 3 2
♡ 10 6 5
◇ 8 3
♣ K 10 3

♠ 8 4
♡ 4
◇ K Q J 10 9 7 6 4
♣ Q 7

♠ 6
♡ K Q J 9 8 2
◇ 5
♣ J 9 8 6 4

♠ A K Q 10 5
♡ A 7 3
◇ A 2
♣ A 5 2

West	North	East	South
5◇	pass	pass	5♠
all pass			

How will you play this contract when West leads the ◇K?

You win the diamond lead with the ace and draw trumps, noting that it is West who shows up with two trumps. Four losers are staring you in the face. North is also staring you in the face and, if you go down, he will perhaps want to know why you didn't prefer to double 5◇. How can you possibly make this contract?

You will need West to hold one heart and two clubs, in which case you can strip him of his non-diamonds. You cash the ♡A and the ♣A-K, pleased to see West follow all the way. These cards remain:

♠ J 9 7
♡ 10 6
◇ 8
♣ 10

♠ —
♡ —
◇ Q J 10 9 7 6 4
♣ —

♠ —
♡ K Q J 9
◇ —
♣ J 9 8

♠ Q 10 5
♡ 7 3
◇ 2
♣ 5

You throw West in with a diamond and he has to return a third round of diamonds. On this trick, you throw the ♣10 from dummy and the ♡3 from your hand (a sluff-and-sluff). You have eradicated one loser and West is still on lead. When he leads yet another diamond, you ruff in the dummy and throw the ♡7 from your hand. You now have no hearts in your hand, while dummy has no clubs. You can crossruff the remainder and claim your contract of 5♠, losing only two diamond tricks.

What did you make of that? Did everyone do as well as possible on the deal? Look back at the end position. When you led the second round of diamonds, West could have beaten you by allowing the ◇8 to win! You could not then escape three subsequent losers in the rounded suits. So, to make the contract against a brilliant defender in the West seat, you would need to unblock dummy's ◇8 at Trick 1. With the ◇3 in dummy and the ◇2 in your hand, West would then be forced to win the second round of diamonds.

The Devil's Coup

One of the most famous examples of trump elopement is attributed to that most notorious of tricksters, the Devil himself. In its most common setting (a misnomer, really, since the play is a great rarity), the defenders start with Q-x-x of trumps opposite J-x, yet fail to take a trick against a grand slam. Impossible, you say? Watch closely.

Both Vul.
Dealer South

```
                    ♠ A 10 6
                    ♡ K Q J 3
                    ◇ K 6
                    ♣ A K Q 8
  ♠ Q 8 4                              ♠ J 7
  ♡ 9 8 5          N                   ♡ 7 6 4
  ◇ 8 3 2      W       E               ◇ Q 10 9 4
  ♣ J 7 5 3        S                   ♣ 10 9 4 2
                    ♠ K 9 5 3 2
                    ♡ A 10 2
                    ◇ A J 7 5
                    ♣ 6
```

West	North	East	South
			1♠
pass	4NT	pass	5♡
pass	5NT	pass	6◇
pass	7♠	all pass	

No, they weren't playing RKCB and North took a rosy view of the trump situation. How would you seek a miracle in the grand slam?

The probability of a defender holding ♠Q-J doubleton, with five cards missing, is one tenth of that for a 3-2 break, around 7%. This is reduced a bit by the fact that if East had that holding, West might have led a trump from 8-7-4. Anyway, the opportunity to achieve a Devil's Coup does not occur very often and it is tempting indeed to head in that direction.

We will see in a moment that you need East to have begun with 2-3-4-4 shape. You win the heart lead and play two more rounds of hearts, finding a 3-3 break. You cash the ♣A, ruff a club, cross to the ◇K and ruff another club (even though it is a winner). The ◇A is followed by a diamond ruff and a third club ruff in your hand. You have reached this end position:

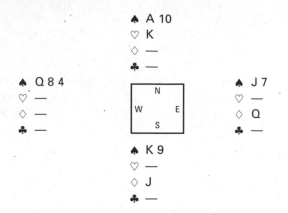

```
                        ♠ A 10
                        ♡ K
                        ◇ —
                        ♣ —
    ♠ Q 8 4          ┌─────────┐         ♠ J 7
    ♡ —              │    N    │         ♡ —
    ◇ —              │  W   E  │         ◇ Q
    ♣ —              │    S    │         ♣ —
                     └─────────┘
                        ♠ K 9
                        ♡ —
                        ◇ J
                        ♣ —
```

You lead the ◇J and West has to choose which trump to play. If he ruffs with the ♠Q, you can overruff with the ♠A and finesse against East's ♠J on the way back. If instead West ruffs with a lower trump, you will overruff with dummy's ♠10 and score the last two tricks with the ace and king of trumps.

The distribution had to be exactly so in order to reach the desired end position. Both players had to follow to three hearts and four clubs. The last diamond then had to lie with East.

One of the reasons why the Devil's Coup is rare in practical play is that you usually have a much simpler alternative line of play. That is the case on this deal:

```
Neither Vul.              ♠ K 8 5 2
Dealer North              ♡ A 10 9 2
                          ◇ 4
                          ♣ A 8 5 3
    ♠ 10 6             ┌─────────┐         ♠ A J 3
    ♡ Q 8 7 3          │    N    │         ♡ J 6 4
    ◇ J 8 5 2          │  W   E  │         ◇ Q 9 7 6
    ♣ J 10 9           │    S    │         ♣ 7 6 4
                       └─────────┘
                          ♠ Q 9 7 4
                          ♡ K 5
                          ◇ A K 10 3
                          ♣ K Q 2
```

West	North	East	South
	1♣	pass	1♠
pass	2♠	pass	4NT
pass	5♣	pass	6♠
all pass			

No bidding prizes will be handed out, obviously, and it is a poor contract. How would you tackle it when West leads the ♣J?

The original declarer won with the ♣K and cashed the top two diamonds, throwing a club from dummy. He then ruffed a diamond. A heart to the king allowed him to ruff his last diamond, the suit breaking 4-4. The ace of hearts and a heart ruff came next, followed by the queen and ace of clubs, everyone following. The side suits could not have been more favorably disposed and this was the end position he reached:

```
              ♠ K 8
              ♡ 10
              ◇ —
              ♣ —
  ♠ 10 6               ♠ A J 3
  ♡ Q         ┌─────┐  ♡ —
  ◇ —         │  N  │  ◇ —
  ♣ —         │W   E│  ♣ —
              │  S  │
              └─────┘
              ♠ Q 9 7
              ♡ —
              ◇ —
              ♣ —
```

When the ♡10 was led from dummy, East had no good defense. If he ruffed with the ♠3, declarer would score the ♠7 on this trick and the queen or king of trumps subsequently. Ruffing with the ♠A was no good, of course, and if East ruffed with the ♠J, declarer would be able to overruff with the ♠Q and finesse against West's ♠10 at Trick 12.

What did you make of that? There are two advantages of playing for a Devil's Coup on that deal. Firstly, it is the only way to make the contract as the cards lie. Secondly, you are guaranteed a mention in the bridge column of the local newspaper. It must be admitted, however, that if your sole aim is to make the contract, you should simply hope that a chosen defender holds a double-ton ace of trumps. You can then lead through the ace, ducking on the second round of trumps to bring down the ace. You can then ruff or discard your potential loser in the diamond suit.

The stars come out to play:

endplay exotica

At this stage of the book, you are not expecting some little-known performer to take his seat in the spotlight. The publisher and I will allow nothing but the very best in this final chapter. Here is Giorgio Belladonna, competing in Venice in 1976.

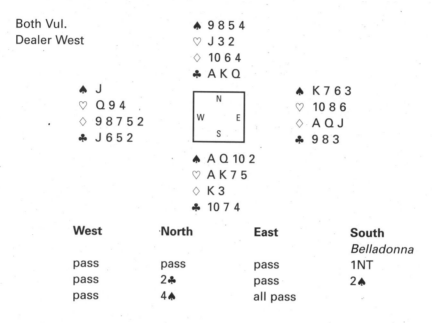

Both Vul.
Dealer West

```
                        ♠ 9 8 5 4
                        ♡ J 3 2
                        ◇ 10 6 4
                        ♣ A K Q
  ♠ J                                    ♠ K 7 6 3
  ♡ Q 9 4            N                   ♡ 10 8 6
  ◇ 9 8 7 5 2      W   E                 ◇ A Q J
  ♣ J 6 5 2          S                   ♣ 9 8 3
                        ♠ A Q 10 2
                        ♡ A K 7 5
                        ◇ K 3
                        ♣ 10 7 4
```

West	North	East	South
			Belladonna
pass	pass	pass	1NT
pass	2♣	pass	2♠
pass	4♠	all pass	

North might well have raised to 3NT on his 4-3-3-3 shape. With the diamond suit blocked, that contract would have been a fortunate make. Declarer could even afford to lose an early spade finesse to the jack. Anyway, Belladonna arrived in 4♠. West led a diamond, East winning with the ace and returning the diamond queen. How would you have played the contract?

After winning the diamond return, Belladonna crossed to dummy with a club and led a low spade (at the other table, in the same contract, declarer led the ♠9 at this stage and ended up regretting it.) A finesse of the ♠10 lost to the ♠J and West played a third round of diamonds. Belladonna ruffed with the ♠2 and returned to dummy with another club. A finesse of the ♠Q succeeded, but West showed out, throwing a diamond. What now?

If East held ♡Q-x-x, declarer could cash the ♠A and cross to dummy with a club to put East on lead with a trump. At Trick 11 he would have to lead away from the ♡Q, giving declarer the last three tricks. Belladonna was not attracted to this line. (East had already shown up with 10 points and would doubtless have opened the bidding if he held the ♡Q in addition). Instead, declarer cashed a third round of clubs and continued with ace, king and another heart, putting West on lead. These cards remained:

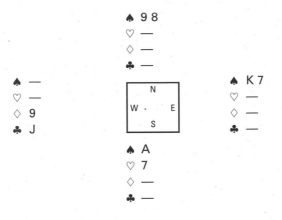

```
                          ♠ 9 8
                          ♡ —
                          ◇ —
                          ♣ —
    ♠ —                                    ♠ K 7
    ♡ —          ┌──────────────┐          ♡ —
    ◇ 9          │      N       │          ◇ —
    ♣ J          │  W   ·   E   │          ♣ —
                 │      S       │
                 └──────────────┘
                          ♠ A
                          ♡ 7
                          ◇ —
                          ♣ —
```

You don't see many two-card end positions, so make the most of it. When West exited with one or the other of the minor-suit cards, Belladonna ruffed with dummy's ♠9 and East's ♠K was caught in a smother play. Whether or not he played the trump monarch on this trick, he would fail to score another trick.

(Many thanks to maestro Pietro Forquet, who committed this deal to posterity in one of my favorite bridge books, *Bridge with the Blue Team*.)

Has the very rare Devil's Coup ever been achieved in championship play? Yes, indeed! Step forward Miklos Dumbovich, playing for Hungary against Great Britain in the 1979 European Championships in Lausanne.

```
Both Vul.                 ♠ A 10 6 4
Dealer East               ♡ Q J 3
                          ◇ 6
                          ♣ K Q 9 8 2
    ♠ Q 8 5                                 ♠ J 7
    ♡ K 9 5      ┌──────────────┐           ♡ 8 7 6 4
    ◇ 8 3 2      │      N       │           ◇ A Q J 10 9
    ♣ A 7 5 4    │  W        E  │           ♣ 10 3
                 │      S       │
                 └──────────────┘
                          ♠ K 9 3 2
                          ♡ A 10 2
                          ◇ K 7 5 4
                          ♣ J 6
```

West	North	East	South
Rodrigue	Linczmayer	Priday	Dumbovich
		pass	pass
pass	1♣	1◇	1♠
2◇	2♠	pass	3◇
pass	4♠	all pass	

At the other table, the British declarer had played in the same contract and lost the four seemingly obvious tricks, one in each suit. Dumbovich had other ideas. Tony Priday, sitting East, won the diamond lead with the ace and switched to a heart, West winning with the king. Claude Rodrigue cashed the ♣A and returned a heart, won in the dummy.

Dumbovich played the ♣K-Q, East throwing a heart and declarer ditching the ♡A. After ruffing a heart in his hand, Dumbovich cashed the ◇K. He then ruffed a diamond in dummy and a further club in his hand. He had reached this classic Devil's Coup position:

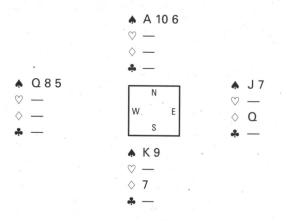

When the ◇7 was led, the defenders had no counter. If West ruffed with a spot card, declarer would overruff and score the last two tricks with the ace and king of trumps. If instead West ruffed with the ♠Q, declarer would overruff with the ♠A and finesse against East's ♠J-7.

When Priday wrote up the deal for the championship bulletin he described, very amusingly, how his impertinent younger teammates had blamed him for missing what they described as the 'standard defense against the Devil's Coup'! Had East discarded diamonds on the third and fourth round of clubs, he would have held a heart instead of a diamond in the three-card end position shown above. Not even Satan himself could then have scored the last three tricks.

NOW TRY THESE...

A.

    ♠ J 10 9 2
    ♡ K 6 5
    ◇ A K Q 4
    ♣ A Q

```
        N
    W       E
        S
```

♡Q led

    ♠ A Q 5 4
    ♡ A 3
    ◇ 9 6 5 3
    ♣ 8 4 3

West	North	East	South
	1◇	pass	1♠
2NT	4♠	pass	5♡
pass	6♠	all pass	

You reach 6♠ after West has shown hearts and clubs with an Unusual Notrump overcall. You win the ♡Q lead with the ♡K. When you run the ♠J, East plays the ♠3 and West the ♠7. How will you continue?

B.

    ♠ J 4
    ♡ Q J 10 9 3
    ◇ K 5 4
    ♣ K 7 2

```
        N
    W       E
        S
```

♠K led

    ♠ 9 7 6
    ♡ A 8 5
    ◇ A Q 3
    ♣ A J 5 3

West	North	East	South
			1NT
2♠	3◇	pass	3♡
pass	3♠	pass	4♡
all pass			

North begins with a transfer bid of 3◇ and West leads out the king, ace and queen of spades against your eventual game in hearts. You ruff the third round with the ♡9, East following suit, and run the ♡Q successfully. When you lead low to your ♡8, West shows out. How will you continue?

Answers ✏

A.

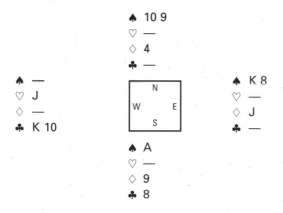

♠ J 10 9 2
♡ K 6 5
◇ A K Q 4
♣ A Q

♠ 7
♡ Q J 10 9 4
◇ 8
♣ K 10 9 7 5 2

♠ K 8 6 3
♡ 8 7 2
◇ J 10 7 2
♣ J 6

♠ A Q 5 4
♡ A 3
◇ 9 6 5 3
♣ 8 4 3

You reach 6♠ after West has shown hearts and clubs with an Unusual Notrump overcall. You win the ♡Q lead with the ♡K. When you run the ♠J, East plays the ♠3 and West the ♠7. How will you continue?

You must assume that the ♣K is onside. If both spades and the diamonds break 4-1, you will be a trick short after four rounds of trumps. To make the slam, you need to score a ruff—a heart ruff in your hand or a club ruff in dummy.

As the cards lie, it would be fatal to continue with the ♠10 at Trick 3. Instead, play a low trump to the queen, retaining a low trump in the South hand in case you need to ruff a heart there. West shows out on the second round of trumps. All will still be well if West's shape is 1-5-2-5. You finesse the ♣Q successfully and play the ◇A-K, West showing out on the second round. As your early play was so accurate, you will survive! You cash your remaining side-suit winners and ruff dummy's last heart with a low trump. These cards remain:

♠ 10 9
♡ —
◇ 4
♣ —

♠ —
♡ J
◇ —
♣ K 10

♠ K 8
♡ —
◇ J
♣ —

♠ A
♡ —
◇ 9
♣ 8

You lead the ♣8, dummy and East throwing diamonds. Whichever card West plays next, you ruff in the dummy. East's ♠K is smothered and the slam is yours.

B.

```
              ♠ J 4
              ♡ Q J 10 9 3
              ◇ K 5 4
              ♣ K 7 2

♠ A K Q 10 2         ┌─────────┐         ♠ 8 5 3
♡ 4                  │    N    │         ♡ K 7 6 2
◇ J 9 7 6            │ W     E │         ◇ 10 8 2
♣ Q 8 6              │    S    │         ♣ 10 9 4
                     └─────────┘
              ♠ 9 7 6
              ♡ A 8 5
              ◇ A Q 3
              ♣ A J 5 3
```

West	North	East	South
			1NT
2♠	3◇	pass	3♡
pass	3♠	pass	4♡
all pass			

North begins with a transfer bid of 3◇ and West leads out the top three spades against your game in hearts. You ruff the third round with the ♡9, East following suit, and run the ♡Q successfully. When you lead low to your ♡8, West shows out. How will you continue?

You have further potential losers in both trumps and clubs. You cash three rounds of diamonds successfully, followed by dummy's ♣K. These cards remain:

```
              ♠ —
              ♡ J 10
              ◇ —
              ♣ 7 2

♠ 10                 ┌─────────┐         ♠ —
♡ —                  │    N    │         ♡ K 7
◇ J                  │ W     E │         ◇ —
♣ Q 8                │    S    │         ♣ 10 9
                     └─────────┘
              ♠ —
              ♡ A
              ◇ —
              ♣ A J 5
```

You lead the ♣2 and must now guess who holds the ♣Q. If East has it, you can simply finesse the ♣J. West's overcall perhaps suggests that you should play him for the ♣Q. (Also, opportunities for a smother coup are few and far between!) You rise with the ♣A and exit with a third club to West queen. Whether he plays a spade or a diamond now, East's ♡K will be smothered into oblivion.

Marquis Book Printing Inc.

Québec, Canada
2008